Praise for
Seeing, Knowing, Being

"This book draws on the great mystical traditions and philosophies of the West and East and shows, in an extremely artful way, how spiritual realization can be lived in the fullest and most inclusive way possible. John Greer uses delightful metaphors to provide an accessible and deep introduction to the transcultural unitive dimension. I highly recommend it."

—Peter Fenner, Ph.D., author of *Radiant Mind: Awakening Unconditioned Awareness* and founder of Radiant Mind and Natural Awakening: Advanced Nondual Training

"Books often describe journeys. *Seeing, Knowing, Being* actually takes you on one. It moves the reader from a sense of isolation and loss of innocence to an intimate connection with Divine Reality. A profound expedition into the true nature of life."

—Matthew Flickstein, author and producer of the award-winning film *With One Voice*

"This book shows an author who has wrestled with the truly difficult questions of a spiritual life and who has emerged with grace and insight. Greer bases his work on the great spiritual systems, but he then leads the way to a significant understanding beyond tradition."

—Deng Ming-Dao, author of *365 Tao: Daily Meditations, The Living I Ching,* and *Chronicles of Tao: The Secret Life of a Taoist Master*

"A beautifully written and comprehensive guide to the best of the wisdom traditions. *Seeing, Knowing, Being* abounds with images, metaphors, and stories to help the reader perceive the unseen, grasp the ephemeral."

—Catherine Ingram, author of *Passionate Presence, In the Footsteps of Gandhi,* and *A Crack in Everything*

"The great psychiatrist Carl Jung described Gnostic Intermediaries as people who imbibe a wisdom tradition so deeply that they are able to translate and transmit its ideas to another culture. John Greer is a Gnostic Intermediary who has imbibed core ideas from the world's major spiritual traditions and transmits them beautifully for our culture and time."

—ROGER WALSH, M.D., Ph.D., author of
Essential Spirituality: The Seven Central Practices

"Weaving together wisdom from the world's great mystics, John Greer skillfully penetrates the core issues and endless possibilities that welcome us on our personal spiritual quest. *Seeing, Knowing, Being* is a beautiful and genuine work that touches both heart and spirit and gently helps us break through old ways of thinking to the wonder of what's real."

—PATRICIA SPADARO, author of *Honor Yourself:*
The Inner Art of Giving and Receiving

SEE*i*NG,
KNOW*i*NG,
BE*i*NG

SEE*i*NG, KNOW*i*NG, BE*i*NG

A Guide to Sacred Awakenings

JOHN GREER

TRUE COMPASS PRESS

For information, address:

True Compass Press
4728 Spottswood Ave.
No. 184
Memphis, TN 38117
E-mail: info@TrueCompassPress.com

For foreign and translation rights, contact Nigel J. Yorwerth
E-mail: nigel@PublishingCoaches.com

Library of Congress Control Number: 2011936082

ISBN: 978-0-615-52183-1

10 9 8 7 6 5 4 3 2 1

Cover design: Nita Ybarra
Interior design: Alan Barnett Design

The information and insights in this book are solely the opinion of
the author and should not be considered as a form of therapy, advice,
direction, diagnosis, and/or treatment of any kind. This information
is not a substitute for medical, psychological, or other professional
advice, counseling, or care. All matters pertaining to your individual
health should be supervised by a physician or appropriate health-
care practitioner. Neither the author nor the publisher assumes any
responsibility or liability whatsoever on behalf of any purchaser
or reader.

*To my teacher and friend of many years, Matt Flickstein,
who embodies the very truth I write about.*

*To my wife and children, Bonnie, Christopher, and Tiffany,
who have taught me so much about the wonder of living.*

*And to the readers who, now or later, feel the yearning
stir within them and have the courage to follow where it leads.*

CONTENTS

ACKNOWLEDGMENTS

Given the scope of what I have attempted to convey in this book, there is little in my life that has not had some influence on what you are about to read. I have been extraordinarily blessed over the years by the people I have known, in this country and abroad, who have touched my heart deeply—family and friends, teachers and students, fellow travelers in the journey of life with whom I have shared laughter and tears, skepticism and faith, confusion and clarity, and an unquenchable yearning for truth. They all have left their mark on my consciousness, and to them all, I bow deeply.

For her help during the crucial beginning stages of writing this book, I am deeply indebted to Carol Flickstein. She tirelessly assisted me in the daunting challenge of putting the unnamable into words. As I was pulling the material together and organizing it into chapters, Carol was an indispensable sounding board, helping me decide what content to add or delete, which metaphors or analogies were most effective for each chapter, and where unnecessary redundancy could be eliminated. Bringing her own spiritual insight, patient attention to detail, and devotion to the truth, she skillfully edited the material in each chapter as I wrote it. Throughout this endeavor, Carol's friendship, sense of humor, kindness, and timely encouragement were invaluable.

I was also fortunate to have the expert assistance of Nigel J. Yorwerth and Patricia Spadaro of PublishingCoaches.com. Drawing on their many years of experience in all aspects of the publishing industry as well as their wonderful creative vision and marketing savvy, Nigel and Patricia guided me step by step through the intricacies of the publishing process. I am grateful for all their hard work and care in helping me with every aspect of this work, from editing and design to marketing, distribution, and foreign rights. Anne Barthel, their editor who assisted with the final manuscript, displayed keen instincts for exactly what was needed to highlight key ideas and make subtle and counterintuitive subjects more understandable. Nigel, Patricia, and Anne are highly competent professionals whom I now also regard as personal friends. I couldn't have done it without them.

I would also like to acknowledge that many of the metaphors used in this book were drawn from the treasure of metaphors and analogies that can be found in the sacred texts of the wisdom traditions and the writings of countless teachers, ancient and modern.

INTRODUCTION

**And you? When will you begin
your long journey into yourself?**

—Rumi

We are all seekers. When the circumstances of life shake us out of our complacency and bring us face to face with the bare fact of our existence, we yearn for something we feel but cannot express. It is normal then to feel lost and alone, estranged from some essential source of meaning in our life.

Our longing to belong has left traces in even the earliest beginnings of our species: from cave paintings to sacred ruins, from burial grounds to the ageless songs of tribal shamans, human beings have always endeavored to find their place in the greater scheme of things. Gauguin was giving voice to the same ancient concern when he inscribed on one of his Tahiti paintings: "Where do we come from? What are we? Where are we going?"

If you have selected this book to read, it is likely you too are at a point in your life when these fundamental questions have grown too compelling to ignore. The quest for answers echoes in the hearts of many today more strongly than ever as it grows more difficult to see where we, as individuals, fit into the greater scheme of things. When meaning can sometimes prove elusive even in the shifting sands of our personal relationships, our place as individuals on a crowded planet is that much harder to discern. Buffeted by human conflict and natural calamities, our bonds with each other often seem as tenuous as those we share with the natural environment. Storms and droughts, floods and fires remind us constantly of our vulnerability and limits. And as the edges of the universe are pushed back further each year with new discoveries of its incomprehensible immensity, we can hardly help but wonder where we belong in this seemingly inhospitable world.

For generations, untold millions around the world turned to the traditional religions of their cultures for understanding and direction in times of uncertainty. The time-honored teachings provided a safe haven amidst the chaos and complexity of life. From them, believers could draw reassurance and comforting answers to life's most pressing questions. *What is life's purpose? How did it begin? Why is there suffering? What will happen when we die?* Traditional religion offers a divinely ordained view of life within which the faithful can find personal meaning and a promise of life after death. For countless believers in the throes of hardship and loss, such conventional spirituality was the lifeline to which they clung.

In contemporary society, this long-established relationship with orthodox religion is changing. Survey after survey reflects fundamental shifts in people's attitudes toward organized religion and their growing disillusionment with it. Our world is starkly different from that of our parents: we live in an extraordinarily diverse "global village," connected in limitless ways by the World Wide Web. Through such Internet phenomena as Google, YouTube, Facebook, and Twitter, we are exposed to other cultures and ideas in ways previous generations could never have imagined. While we may long for the security we drew from the religion of our youth, we often find even that refuge closed to us; for many of us, the dogma we were taught no longer resonates, and the old beliefs no longer satisfy our need for real understanding. Blind faith is losing its relevance for those schooled in a present-day world and conversant in scientific thinking, and more and more people are turning away from the standard answers that mainstream religions can offer. Though most people still consider themselves "spiritual," they struggle with feelings of emptiness and find themselves longing for fulfillment.

I was one of these people. I was born into a close and loving family. My parents shared a deep religious faith, and Sundays meant church. My father was an elder and my mother sang in the choir; my brother and I attended Sunday school and then church services together as soon as we were old enough. Many of my fondest memories come from those times of worshiping together, and my beliefs were thickly interwoven with those recollections. It was a time in my life when all seemed right in the world; every question found an answer and my faith felt strong.

When I went to college, that began to change. A flood of new and provocative ideas challenged many of my youthful assumptions about life, but it was the arguments about religion that had the greatest impact. For a growing list of concerns I could identify no apparent solutions. Though I had once considered going into the ministry, certainty was now giving way to confusion and doubt. This was a very difficult and troubling time for me, for everything I held dear in life seemed threatened.

I had opportunities to travel during this time, and I thought I might resolve my issues by doing so. I did volunteer work in church-related programs in the United States, spent time with missionaries in Ecuador and Peru, served two years in Nepal with the Peace Corps, and traveled through Africa afterwards. Ironically, these experiences only increased my misgivings about religion. My exposure to other peoples, cultures, and faiths put into context the happenstance of my own beliefs. The religion I believed to be superior to all others, the only true way, was merely the one into which I had by chance been born. Its doctrinal assurances of a monopoly on spiritual truth and its dogmatic criteria for a reward in the afterlife excluded vast segments of humankind in ways that now seemed both unjust and untenable.

My graduate studies further reinforced my skepticism. I pursued a Ph.D. at Pennsylvania State University in the Education of Exceptional Children, with a concentration on experimental analysis of behavior and operant conditioning. A strategy for shaping socially appropriate behavior by designing environments that prompted and/or contingently rewarded desired actions, this theory had many practical applications.

It was already enjoying considerable success in education programs for individuals with disabilities, and I enthusiastically embraced this exciting new paradigm. Inherent in its principles, however, was an implied disregard for matters of the spirit, as they did not lend themselves to systematic observation and reliable measurement—a stark contrast to the unquestioning faith so much a part of my spiritual upbringing. For thirty years I felt as if in exile, separated from the kind of meaning and peace of mind that I had once enjoyed as a childhood believer. Recognizing the chasm of doubt that now blocked the way back to the safe haven of my earlier faith, I experienced a very real sense of grief and resignation, and I shared a stoic sympathy with the existentialist thinking of Kierkegaard, Camus, and Sartre: the meaning I found in life was limited to what I made of it and the values by which I chose to live. I concentrated my attention and energies on family and career, but felt a growing undercurrent of emptiness.

In 1994, I picked up a book on Zen Buddhism that stirred something deep within me. I started reading more books on Buddhism and soon began meditating on my own. Though I had no teacher at the time, I gained the basics from my reading and soon discovered that sitting quietly and focusing on my breath yielded a dramatically different orientation to life that would prove to be an essential part of my spiritual journey. Daily meditation is still an important part of my day.

Two years later I was sitting in my backyard on a pleasant fall afternoon. I had been reading, but had put my book aside and was just resting in the peaceful beauty of that moment. There was a gentle breeze and leaves were beginning to fall. Without any expectation, in a single instant, outside of time, I realized that life was a seamless unity. It came out of silence with no apparent cause. Sitting there in my neighborhood populated with all the myriad things found in such a setting, from trees, birds, and squirrels to passing cars, the mailman, and the children next door, I knew intuitively that there were no divisions, no boundaries, no separation—only wholeness. It was an intuitive, gut-level certainty I did not doubt then and have never doubted since. It wasn't an idea or an object that I perceived; *it was what I was.* Afterwards, I sat in stunned silence, with feelings of deep reverence, peace, and humility.

Words are incapable of conveying this kind of experience. It wasn't like suddenly getting the answer to a problem I had been working on or coming up with a creative new idea for artistic expression. There was nothing cognitive about it. It was a glimpse of the way things are, the unconditioned, that which exists before thinking and memory. As the coming chapters will explain, without thought there is no time. Thoughts are founded on division, contrast, and comparison. They are linear, pieced together one by one to solve a problem, describe an event, or communicate an opinion on some subject. Almost everything we do is guided or preceded by thought. The experience I had was an all-at-once recognition of wholeness. Even the separation between subject and object was absent. Seeing, seer, and seen were united.

This unexpected breakthrough changed the course of my life, but it was more of a beginning than an end to my spiritual yearnings. From that moment, my spiritual practice and quest for meaning became the focus of my life. I knew this moment was pivotal—it instantly called into question all the assumptions and mental habits that created my dualistic worldview—but I lacked the background to effectively put it into context. There was no place in the framework of what I already knew for what I experienced that afternoon.

My reading list grew steadily more inclusive as I sought to find those core elements that had consistently appeared in the great wisdom traditions of the world, across thousands of years and many highly diverse cultures. This was an outgrowth of my time abroad and the recognition that what we hold in common as human beings far outweighs the more apparent but superficial cultural differences. I reasoned that if there were such spiritual universals, they would likely reveal what was closest to the truth. Three books provided the springboard for my quest: Joseph Campbell's *Hero with a Thousand Faces*, Aldous Huxley's *Perennial Philosophy*, and William James's *Varieties of Religious Experience*. The nonsectarian approach of these three groundbreaking authors has remained a central feature of my own work.

In 1998, I met Matthew Flickstein, an insight meditation teacher and founder of the Forest Way, and soon after became his student. I had been meditating on my own but had no teacher or instruction. Under Matt's guidance, I practiced Buddhist insight meditation over the ensuing years. Through a series of stunning insights, my identification with mind and body steadily loosened. There was a feeling of letting go, of release, of traveling light. My sense of joy, peace, and freedom grew, even when I had to face serious difficulties and challenges. Along with the transformation that I was experiencing came a keen desire to share this truth with others. While I have enjoyed teaching meditation over the last decade, it is into this book that I have poured most of my energy. It is the culmination of my own search for what was missing in my life.

I was reluctant to mention my personal story. Though it may be valuable to show how my interest and my inquiries evolved, it is contradictory to all that follows. While the self you now imagine yourself to be is the one who will begin your personal quest for spiritual understanding, the concept of a separate self also represents the biggest obstacle to completing that quest. As you will see in the coming chapters, there is no one who practices, no one who has experiences or realizations. There is no one who awakens spiritually, and there never was. There is no one, because in the light of full understanding, the illusion of an individual self dissolves. There is only life. As paradoxical and counterintuitive as this may sound, it is the truth that lies at the heart of all the wisdom traditions of the world. Mariana Caplan, author and teacher, expresses it this way: "One pays with oneself.... The one who signs up for the spiritual journey does not get to complete it, and one cannot *really* understand this until the moment that it has become true of them."[1]

The Myth of Duality

Most people give little thought to the reasons *why* they see the world as they do—why they see themselves as separate and alone. Our view of reality is something taken for granted, too obvious to be questioned.

But in fact it's not intrinsic, it is *learned*.

Today, as in ancient times, our spiritual malaise arises from the unreal nature of our perceptions. Though we are born into oneness, unselfconscious and unaware of any separation between ourselves and everything else, that soon begins to change. From the earliest stages of life, we learn to "see" the same reality as everyone else in our family and community. We are taught to label everything around us, to master the temporal framework of past, present, and future, and most importantly, to assume the name and separate identity we are told is ours. The conceptual worldview and collective beliefs of our society become so ingrained in us that we gradually lose the fresh, innocent vision of our beginnings. We find ourselves in a virtual, mind-created world we mistakenly believe to be real.

Owing to the vast complexity of modern life, the problems created by the unconscious nature of our conditioning are now more pronounced than ever. We find ourselves in an infinite and continually proliferating maze of arbitrary conceptual divisions, distinctions, boundaries, and polarities, and through it all we intuitively sense the wholeness that is missing. The feeling of safety, connection, and stability many once drew from a small-town setting, an extended family, or a close-knit neighborhood is now replaced by the anonymity of high-rise condos, numberless commuters home only on the weekends, and relationships maintained at a distance. Much of contemporary life is mental and abstract, replacing the living, breathing flesh and blood of each human moment. We constantly voice the need to be ourselves and seek what is authentic, yet never find lasting satisfaction in the countless substitutes we so desperately chase.

We become self-conscious as a separate and tiny fragment of what is—of the indivisible totality of life—and our sense of vulnerability and incompleteness is pronounced. This consciousness is reflected in virtually every bookstore, where countless self-help books are prominently displayed, promising to help people fit in, feel better, be more assertive, reduce stress, compete, find a mate, survive the workweek, and deal with a thousand other perceived inadequacies. As we learn to see life through the prism of me and mine versus you and yours, the greed, hatred, delusion, and suffering that have characterized the human experience for millennia grow steadily, until it seems impossible to bridge the gaping chasms that divide us from each other. Even our relationship with nature is often characterized by conquest, control, or callous disregard where harmony and balance prevailed in earlier times. Aimless and alone as *the self we think we are*, we become seekers for that which we intuit to be missing. Spurred by our yearning for wholeness, we set off on our quest to find what really is.

From meditation to mantras, from koans to the Kabbalah, the shared objective of all the great wisdom traditions is clear: *all* strive to penetrate the conditioning and habituation that blinds us to our true nature. Whether these paths are called mysticism, the way of nonduality, or esoteric spirituality, they find unity where conventional religions see only division and separation. Though separated by centuries, if not millennia, and embedded in cultures that have little in common on the surface, they declare with extraordinary consensus that the world is a seamless whole.

Many readers may doubt whether any such spiritual consensus can even exist. Religious intolerance and conflict not only capture the headlines today, they can be traced far back into history. But the cause of the conflict is not found in the living truth that all the great spiritual traditions share; it is found in the dogmatic forms of belief so fundamental to conventional expressions of religion. Spiritual traditions that put great emphasis on written doctrines are inherently divisive. They are known as exoteric religions, and the concepts they embody are dualistic, taking their meaning from the distinctions and comparisons they draw. Differences of interpretation concerning religious doctrine can quickly multiply. Estimates of the number of Protestant denominations in the United States, for example, are in the tens of thousands!

Mystical practices, in contrast to faiths codified in written creeds, are based on direct, unmediated experience: *knowing by being rather than by thinking and believing*. In every age and culture, these esoteric spiritual paths have consistently directed practitioners to go within to discover their true nature and their place in the world. They share the belief that language, through its omnipresent and often unconscious role in defining our everyday reality, lies at the heart of our melancholy and alienation. While the practical value of language is beyond question, we fall into delusion when we mistake the map for the territory. When we see life through the prism of thought and conceptualization, division replaces wholeness. The symbols we use to communicate with each other must not be confused with the essential reality they represent. Serious seekers come to realize that *it is our way of seeing the world that has caused our suffering, not the world itself.*

This realization is reflected in a theme that appears over and over again in the mythology and sacred writings of humanity. It appears in the regions producing major civilizations, as well as in areas supporting the world's indigenous populations. This theme, known as the Perennial Philosophy and popularized by Aldous Huxley's book of the same title, is found at the core of the mystical, nondual forms of Hinduism, Buddhism, Taoism, Sufism, Judaism, and Christianity. In one variation or another, it is also fundamental to the work of many great thinkers, such as Plotinus, Hegel, Teilhard de Chardin, and Sri Aurobindo, and is espoused by many others, from Plato, Spinoza, and Jung to William James, Alan Watts, and Ken Wilber.

The central thesis of the Perennial Philosophy claims that there is something hidden from us by the numberless names and forms of manifestation. The *ground of our being* is the formless elemental source of all things. It is not envisioned as the creator of the world, a deity to be worshipped, appeased, or obeyed; rather, it is *what we are*. While most belief systems are content to posit some form of *relationship* with the Divine, the Perennial Philosophy recognizes our *identity* with the divine source. Throughout the history of human spirituality, its message is unequivocal: we are That.

Inherent in this understanding is the belief that the preeminent purpose and desire of humankind is to find its way back to this fundamental origin of what is. In contrast to the external rewards—salvation, an afterlife—sought by believers in more traditional forms of religion, the Perennial Philosophy sees something within us that calls us back to our beginnings. It is not a return to something we left behind so much as a recognition of something that has always been. As it is impossible to attain that which we never lost, seekers must simply remember what is, and *be* the "suchness" that they are—in other words, experience directly the most basic fact of being alive in this very moment. This suchness, so often mentioned in the mystical wisdom traditions, is simply what always is, but often goes unnoticed in our busy days and thought-filled minds.

The Mystical Journey

Seen through the lens of the Perennial Philosophy, our spiritual journey is a path that connects the two essential but seemingly incompatible halves of our being. The half with which we are all familiar is defined by duality; opposition and contrast are everywhere in our ordinary surroundings. We are conditioned to see things dualistically, within an either/or framework. Our lives constantly swing between fortune and loss, pleasure and pain, good and evil, and all the other polarities that characterize everyday experience as we know it. This is the realm where we get snarled in traffic, win at tennis, watch our 401(k) go down, and grow old. The Eastern term for this state of being is *samsara*, the state of constant change in which the cycles of birth and death unfold.

The other half of this fundamental polarity is nonduality, that forgotten dimension where unity is found in multiplicity. All the world's sacred traditions and sages identify nonduality as our true nature. It is the source from which we came. Sometimes referred to as the absolute, the invisible, the Divine, or simply suchness, this aspect of our being has no boundaries, divisions, or oppositions. It is the state of being we yearn for and the goal of our journey home. In the East, the name for this state is *nirvana*, where the fires of greed, hatred, and delusion no longer burn and where joy, wholeness, and freedom are found.

The mythologies of the world offer us a model for this journey to self-realization in a theme that, like the Perennial Philosophy, is threaded through the whole history of our species, from Egyptian and Greek lore to the legends of the Orient and the timeless stories of indigenous peoples. This portrayal of the mystical journey has been central to the life work of Joseph Campbell, who is considered by many to be the preeminent authority on world mythology. From a multitude of diverse cultural images and descriptions, he distills what he calls the cosmogonic cycle, the prototypical spiritual epic of humanity. According to Campbell, this archetypal story is "the mythical image of the world's coming into manifestation and subsequent return into the nonmanifest condition."[2] He sees the general motif to be the dismemberment of a primordial Being into phenomenology, with the untold diversity of life unfolding from a single Source.

In this mythical rendering, the Divine is pictured in an undivided state, the nondual source of all worldly manifestation, and humankind's entrance into the scheme of things is portrayed as a separation from wholeness. We are plunged into a "fallen" world, a painful and meaningless reality of name and form, time and space, division and conflict. We remain in this "exile" from meaning and connection until we awaken to our true nature. In Campbell's view, our individual birth, life, and death are no more than a descent and return on this universal cycle.

The hero of Campbell's cosmic adventure is the one who, while still alive, unravels the paradox of creation. He symbolizes "that divine creative and redemptive image which is hidden within us all, only waiting to be known and rendered into life."[3] When self-consciousness gives humankind a unique vantage point from which the inequities, injustices, and sufferings in life are seen, questions about meaning and longing for wholeness arise. It is then that the hero is summoned by destiny and sets forth on what Campbell calls the Journey of the Hero.

The hero first has to overcome the resistance of conventional wisdom, as well as the self-annihilation demanded of all in crossing beyond duality. Initiation comes after a time when the hero encounters various trials, dangers, and demons. Entering into a mystical marriage of opposites, a fusion of subject and object, his identity with the All is consummated. While the Source has been unveiled, though, the journey is incomplete until the hero revisits the land of his birth, bringing the life-giving boon discovered in his quest. The secret knowledge he brings is that *both realms are one.* The yonder kingdom of the gods is a dimension of everyday reality long forgotten. Self and other are one and the same.

When the suffering and hardships of our lives awaken our longing for completion, the esoteric teachings begin to resonate and we are drawn back to the Source on a hero's journey of our own. The role of hero or heroine is filled by each of us, but as you will come to see, it is the Divine itself, masquerading within our body and mind, that plays this cosmic game of hide-and-seek. To paraphrase modern Zen master Alan Watts, what is dismembered in the beginning is remembered in the end. Through the continuous cycle of the mystical quest, the Unknowable endlessly rediscovers the glories of its own Being.

This cyclic model of the human spiritual journey echoes over and over in the timeless wisdom traditions of the world. We find variations on orbital or circular designs in many different cosmologies, from the wheel of samsara, or dharma wheel, so prominent in the Hindu and Buddhist traditions to the iconic yin/yang image of Taoism and the whirling swastika found in the symbolism of Native Americans. Campbell's cosmogonic cycle shares similarities with Ken Wilber's portrayals of the human life cycle in his *Atman Project,* as well as ideas from Mircea Eliade's *Myth of the Eternal Return.*

On the mystical journey, as also in the Perennial Philosophy, *what is* never changes; only our perception of it does. Think of the player lost in the virtual reality of the video game: life as we typically know it is an adventure that takes place primarily in the mind. As long as we view experience through the prism of conceptualization, we are blinded to what is. We forget what is real, suffer in its perceived absence, and eventually rediscover what was only hidden.

How to Read This Book

The human spiritual experience can be understood as a progression of exile from and return to the wholeness of our true nature, as depicted in figure 1. The right side of the figure shows the Exile: from a state of wholeness, or nonduality, our lives first unfold on an outward arc that carries us into the conventional world of duality, shown at the bottom of the circle. Through years of conditioning, we learn to see ourselves as separate and alone in a world of endless divisions, and this delusion of self brings the suffering and meaninglessness so characteristic of the human condition. The Return, shown on the left side of the figure, begins when our yearning for wholeness grows strong. The inward arc is a process of unlearning through mystical practice that serves to weaken the hold of conditioning and draw us homeward toward nonduality, shown at the top of the circle. Within the circle lies what is, the suchness that we have forgotten we are.

As the conceptual boundaries that imprison us grow increasingly transparent on our journey of Return, our awareness opens to the possibility of glimpsing what conditioning has concealed. We cannot, however, produce mystical insights through our own effort, for the very notion of "our own" anything reinforces that same delusion of self that perpetuates our blindness. Only when we let go of our fixed ideas of truth and yield to the innocence of unknowing can our vision clear. All mystical practice is designed to help us to prepare the way for this possibility.

The last vestige of dualistic thinking is the distinction between duality and nonduality themselves. When this too is transcended through insight, our eyes open to unmediated truth, the wholeness of our true nature. The mystical adventure is all in the seeing: from departure to arrival, nothing changes but our eyes. While suchness retains all the traits and features of creation—we still go to work, the earth still turns—we no longer mistake the concepts and descriptions used conventionally to objectify them for the actual reality they symbolize. Transcending all dualistic divisions of the conceptualized world, we awaken to the freedom inherent in selflessness, and life is imbued with wisdom, love, compassion, and wonder.

To correspond with this cyclic model of the spiritual journey, I have divided the book into two halves: "The Exile" and "The Return." The chapters in the first half explore how we come to forget what is real and experience life as if in exile from our true being. We begin with an examination of the nature of duality itself, followed by chapters on thought, time, knowledge, self, and attachment that detail how these aspects of our conditioning blind us to our true nature. The last three chapters explore karma, suffering, and the loss of meaning, universal characteristics of our experience in exile.

The second half of the book begins with a look at the yearning that arises from suffering and transforms us into seekers. The chapters on paths, alignment, practices, and the way of non-doing investigate

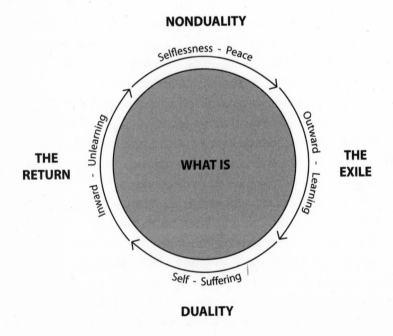

Figure 1: The Spiritual Cycle of Exile and Return

the nature of mystical practice. While it is not the intent of this book to suggest a path or identify a particular practice for you, these chapters examine the range of paths that numberless seekers of the past have followed, exploring how each is designed to facilitate our quest for spiritual truth. The final five chapters look into the universal aspects of spiritual transformation: insight, awakening, selflessness, freedom, and finally homecoming.

The Language of Wholeness

Mystical insight has always been difficult to convey to others. When Joseph Campbell's hero returns from his journey, the wisdom he brings is so counter to prevailing beliefs that he faces a fresh challenge in sharing it with his people. Our perceptual habits are deeply ingrained and often resistant to even small changes, much less total reversals of long-held assumptions or common sense. Considering how tenaciously we defend our everyday beliefs and opinions, how much more fiercely will we resist changes to a worldview ingested with our mothers' milk?

The assumptions we most need to examine are the last we think of questioning: our assumptions about the way we see the world. And no matter how we hunger for a more integrated vision of life, we cannot resolve the problems of conceptualization with yet more conceptualized thinking or reasoned debate. The challenge here is like trying to describe a melody in words. Clearly, the only way to truly grasp the melody is to hear it, to experience it. Words are only the proverbial finger pointing at the moon—they are not the moon itself. To taste the meaning and peace inherent in wholeness, the language of science, commerce, or law is of little use. An integral vision of reality cannot be unveiled logically with a linear presentation that systematically moves from one conclusion to the next. Something reminiscent of the quantum leap is called for. Just as the particle becomes the wave in a mysterious reversal of states that New Physics cannot explain, the insights that open the door to mystical truth happen suddenly and paradoxically, and our understanding of reality is irrevocably changed.

Ironically, any written exploration of mystical spirituality is by definition a conceptual presentation. Words represent the concepts that divide a unified reality into scattered bits; how is it possible to use words, dualistic by nature, to tell the secrets of nonduality? How can a book such as this one convey intuitive wisdom in a manner that might penetrate the conceptual version of reality we have all unconsciously absorbed and continuously reconfirm by collective belief and habit?

Throughout the history of religion, people have used metaphors, similes, and parables to suggest new and often dramatically different ways of seeing the world and our place in it. For example, when Jesus spoke of putting a lit lamp under a basket or building a house on sand rather than rock, he was offering comparisons that were not meant literally. Just as poetry and mythology can unite disparate facts into one verbal picture, metaphors and other such figures of speech can help us see relationships that are otherwise veiled in concepts. To paraphrase author and physician Leonard Shlain, metaphors can jump the gaps between thoughts, introducing multiple levels of meaning simultaneously. According to him, they give a "plasticity to language" without which language would be impoverished and, at times, impossible.[4] Shlain sees such figures of speech revealing a kind of synergy between the two lobes of the brain, essential in conveying emotional and feeling states, but also indispensable in decoding the meaning of poetry, myth, and religious parables.

We cannot always articulate what something *is*, but more often than not, it is possible to say *what it is like*. Analogies provide concrete comparisons: parallels found in other life experiences that shed light on the new and the strange. As an artist can paint in two dimensions on a flat canvas and quite effectively suggest three, we can use dualistic language to suggest a nondualistic reality. And like the image a painter renders in oils, metaphors and similes are pictures painted in words. So, in each of the following chapters, I have chosen analogies to capitalize on the well-known capacity of the right hemisphere of the brain to see in pictures and find unity where the left brain cannot. I hope you will be able to "see" the likeness I am presenting and view the topic in a different light. I hope that your imagination may be kindled and your intuition awakened to the possibility of seeing the world in a completely different way.

Words and concepts are circular, spinning like a wheel from the known to the known. The challenge is to use them to *suggest* the unknown. Consider, for example, Jesus's words to his disciples: "I am the light that is over all things. I am All: From me all has come forth, and to me all has reached. Split a piece of wood; I am there. Lift up the stone, and you will find me there."[5] For the uninitiated, such enigmatic expressions are unfathomable. How is one who is new to mystical ideas to grasp the meaning of these words? It might be possible by comparing them to something with which we are already familiar. In this case, metaphorically, saying that "I am All" would be like a wave realizing that water is its true nature. This insight would allow it to see that the distinctions and boundaries between it and other waves, and the ocean itself, are only apparent. There is nothing but wholeness. The shared identity of all names and forms is a mystical truth that remains deeply buried in the unconscious levels of our being. The fact remains, however, that all is one, and one is all.

Exploring a difficult and paradoxical idea should be like looking at a sculpture in a museum. When we observe it from different positions, it is the same sculpture, but we gain new appreciation for its beauty as we see its many details in differing lights. While a visitor could honestly say that he or she had "seen" the work after just one look, someone who was able to study it from many angles would surely come away with a deeper and more complete understanding of the artist's creation. In the same manner, when we examine an aspect of nondual spirituality through metaphor, I use several different comparisons to help you gain a deeper appreciation of the part that element plays in the journey toward wholeness—especially the more intractable and subtle truths encountered on the mystical path, topics such as selflessness, non-doing, and enlightenment, which have confounded even the most devoted seekers. Many of the metaphors I use have been gleaned from the sacred texts and teachings, ancient and modern, of all the mystical traditions. This kind of exploration will give you a hint of the freedom and joy that can be found on this path when insights occur and deeper understanding unfolds.

Books may function as maps for our spiritual journey. They can show us the possible routes to take and point out many of the landmarks and obstacles we are likely to encounter. Nevertheless, you cannot climb a mountain on a map, and you cannot experience life-changing insights by reading about them. Such aids are useful, if not indispensable, in the early stages of practice, but they eventually take a back seat to existence itself, the greatest teacher. Life's constantly changing mix of success and failure, health and sickness, happiness and grief, has been extraordinarily effective for thousands of years in preparing fertile ground wherein the seeds of wisdom can sprout. When a yearning within pulls you toward the light, and you choose a proven mystical path by which to make the timeless crossing to the far shore, your sacred quest for wholeness can begin in earnest.

PART ONE ~ THE EXILE

Everything has mind in the lead, has mind
in the forefront, is made by mind.

—*The Buddha*

Man behaves as if he were the maker and master of
language but language remains the master of man.

—*Martin Heidegger*

If we have not, before all else, apprehended the phenomenon
constructed by the mind, its nonexistence cannot be established.

—*Shantideva*

You become an outcast from the unity of Nature; though born of it,
your own hand has cut you from it. Yet here is the beautiful proviso:
it lies within your own power to join Nature once again. God has
not granted such a favor to any other part of creation: to return
again, after having been separated and left asunder.

—*Marcus Aurelius*

I

DUALITY

He who wants to have right without wrong, order without
disorder, does not understand the principles of heaven and earth.
He does not know how things hang together. Can a man cling
only to heaven and know nothing of earth? They are correlative: to
know one is to know the other. To refuse one is to refuse both.

—Chuang Tzu

The world's mystics have taught for millennia what modern
science is only now accepting: everything in life is a form of
vibration, a back-and-forth pulse that is as fundamental as the
beat of our hearts. In Hindu cosmology, the sacred mantra *Om* is considered the source of all manifestation. The Indian sage Paramahansa
Yogananda spoke of the Om as the "vibration of the Cosmic Motor"
and the "creative voice of God," whose deep, resonating single syllable
has been heard in Hindu and Buddhist temples for thousands of years.
Today, quantum physics postulates striking parallels to the ancient
teachings with research that shows the smallest units of our universe
to have the properties of a wave—like a cosmic motor vibrating at the
very source of life. According to superstring theory, the fundamental
elements are not particles but rather the vibrations of infinitely small
strings of energy. As University of Virginia astrophysicist Trinh Xuan
Thuan explains, these strings generate tones and harmonics like the

strings of a violin and can be measured in the laboratory as such elements as protons, neutrons, and electrons.[1]

It may be difficult to picture this phenomenon working at such a minute level of existence, but vibration is also the motor that drives the realms with which we are better acquainted. It is the ability of our senses to distinguish varying wavelengths that is the basis of the colors we see, the sounds we hear, and the sensations we feel. Vibration's characteristic pattern of back-and-forth is evident at a larger level, too: in the tides, the seasons, the harvest cycle, the rise and fall of civilizations, and even, as some visionary scientists suggest, the expansion and contraction of the universe. When the alternation is at a high frequency, we cannot discern any movement, but only what appears to be a single object—as with a wave that oscillates so fast we don't see the back-and-forth, only the ray of light that results. At the macro level, though, the alternating opposites shift slowly enough that we easily perceive the separate phases—low tide and high tide, sowing and reaping—and recognize "back" and "forth" by virtue of the contrast between them.

In the Gestalt theory of perception, contrast defines the relationship between figure and ground, or between an object and the backdrop against which it stands out, and that relationship effectively defines reality for us. This theory asserts that without opposition and contrast, the world as we know it would not appear, because it is impossible for us to identify a figure without its ground. It is only the *relationship* of the contrasting elements that we perceive at all: dark/light, sound/silence, movement/stillness, order/disorder, and so on.

A central feature of figure/ground perception is multistability: the fact that we cannot perceive both aspects of a pattern simultaneously. Rather, our focus shifts from object to background and back again, as first one jumps out at us and then the other, keeping us from recognizing the inherent unity of the pair. The classic example of this phenomenon is the famous face-and-vase illusion developed by Danish psychologist Edgar Rubin, a variation of which is shown in figure 2. When you look at it, you quickly notice that it is difficult, if not impossible, to see both images at the same time. You will see the vase, and then suddenly the faces will replace it. Each figure serves as the ground for the other and is indispensable to its existence, but they seem completely separate to our eyes.

In an illustration, this effect is fascinating and entertaining—but in our lives, the same perceptual dynamic produces a dualistic reality replete with divisions and dilemmas that tear us apart. Instead of seeing a single drawing divided by our perception into "this" and "that," we see life, which is essentially one unified whole, as if it were split up into parts. Throughout history, countless variations of "us versus them," often violent and destructive, stand witness to the unrecognized unity of opposites. We see objects, or events, or qualities, or even people, in pairs of opposites—rich and poor, success and failure, illness and

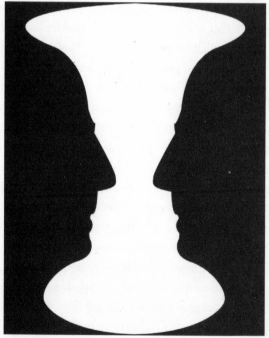

Christopher Greer

Figure 2: Rubin's Vase

health, you and I—and we accord substance to each, imagining it to have its own independent existence, when in fact it depends entirely on the other. Without the vase, there would be no faces; without the faces, there would be no vase. We suppose that each thing is real all on its own, when in fact the only thing that is real is *the relationship between them*. We do not see that they are one and the same.

In the human drama, the first and most fundamental pair of opposites, the duality that defines our lives and our world, is that of subject and object. Nothing is distinguished without the separation of these two: there is no seeing without a seer, no hearing without one who hears, no sensory input without someone to receive it. Subject and object rise and fall together, each serving as the ground for the other. In the absence of either, both cease to exist. It's like trying to look at something when we are too close to see it, too close for our eyes to focus. Life partitions itself in order to know itself, splitting that which was originally undivided into one state that knows and another state that is known. Neither science nor mystical wisdom has an explanation for *how* this happens. The experts who have studied this dilemma call it the "hard problem," and no viable explanation for it exists. As Alan Watts once put it, "No one ever found an 'I' apart from some present experience."[2] But separation is the *sine qua non* of consciousness. This is the beginning of our human story—the commencement of life as we know it, and the moment when our exile from wholeness begins.

As you read in the introduction, Joseph Campbell frames this event in mythological terms as the dismemberment of a primordial Being whose division results in the vast diversity of life. In the biblical version of this motif, God first creates an androgynous Adam in his own image, but it is in the removal of the feminine into a separate form—Eve made from Adam's rib—that Campbell finds the symbolic beginning of the fall into duality. Recognition of those primal opposites, good and evil, logically follow, and the original pair is banished from the Garden of Eden. Campbell interprets the wall that surrounds the garden in the Biblical story as symbolic of duality, cutting off Adam and Eve from the vision or even recollection of the face of God. That barrier is the cause of the yearning that impels his "hero" to venture forth on his journey of return. In the mythological garb of innumerable cultures and times, this figure must find his way back from exile in duality to his roots in wholeness.[3]

The mythological story unfolds in our existence through the uniquely human perception of otherness—from the apparent separation of subject and object. When we are taught to identify with our body/mind, our psychophysical makeup, we emerge from the timeless innocence of infancy, with its unselfconscious spontaneity, into the self-consciousness of our supposed individuality. From the contrast that this subject/object separation creates, we learn what we are, and we learn to define all other things in our world, and we perceive our difference from everything else. The boundaries we learn to see are the real wall of Paradise, and we are left feeling alone and vulnerable; inevitably, fear and suffering follow.

The mind acts like a prism, separating what is originally one into the manifold aspects of existence. Just as a single ray of sunlight passing through the prism is divided into the colors of the rainbow, the unity of life is divided by the mind into the multiplicity we call reality. And all humanity is caught in this dream, to a greater or lesser extent. Some cultures and belief systems, including many Eastern spiritual traditions, take a different view, teaching the integration of opposites and the unity of all things. In the West, though, we are imbued instead with the dualism of a Greek and Hebrew heritage, and only rarely exposed to Taoism's inseparable yin and yang or the Hindu deities that embody both good and evil. The Greeks esteemed reason over the senses in their quest for knowledge, while the Hebrew tradition split reality into the domains of spirit and flesh, impugning the natural realm of the body and wary of its temptations. Both ancient schools of thought halved existence in fundamental ways, replacing wholeness with separation at the very foundation of their worldview.

From early childhood, we are taught to see a fragmented reality that we can navigate only by making endless choices and decisions: that and not this, this but not that. By making distinctions and remembering those given social priority, we find our way through our dualistically envisioned world. The dos and don'ts, the "yours" and "mine," of childhood become the liberal and conservative, believer and infidel, friend and foe of adulthood. Oftentimes, the boundaries we superimpose on life resemble the proverbial lines drawn in the sand by a movie character distinguishing friend from foe. In reality, we forget their arbitrary nature and defend the edges of our perceived separation with deadly seriousness. We live in a maze of opposites within which we have lost our way. The eternal drama of good and evil is but the most pronounced of the numberless pairs of opposites between which we are torn.

∾

IMAGES OF DUALITY

CHINESE VILLAGER ∾ There is an ancient Taoist story about a man who succeeded in corralling a beautiful wild stallion. The entire village admired the steed and marveled at the man's good fortune. Before long, however, the horse broke free, and the neighbors extended deep sympathy. A few days later, the runaway stallion returned with a beautiful mare by its side. The villagers could hardly contain their amazement at this twist of fate; no one in the area had ever had such good luck. Later that day, the villager presented the stallion to his son for a gift, but not long after, the boy had a riding accident and broke his leg. All lamented this terrible event. The following week, the army arrived in the village and started drafting young men for war. The injured youth was spared, and his father's joyful friends were once again amazed at his good fortune. We can never know what life holds in store, and as good and bad fortune alternate in our vision like Rubin's vase and faces, today's curse may be tomorrow's blessing. Wisdom comes from knowing that this too shall pass.

OCEAN WAVES ∾ If you enjoy swimming in the ocean and catching waves to ride in to shore, you know their undulating pattern.

As you tread water and wait for a good wave to ride, you float up and down with the swells. Obviously, if there were no troughs between the waves, you would not be able to distinguish the swells at all. There are big waves because there are deep troughs. The circumstances of our lives unfold before us in a similar pattern, and like the swimmer, we are always trying to catch the biggest waves: the best deal, the nicest house, the most impressive promotion. But just as the swimmer must wait out the troughs and small waves to get to the bigger ones, we must navigate the lows of life as well as the highs. We cannot change the waves of our lives any more than the swimmer can control those of the ocean, but we can learn to float over them with grace and ease.

STEERING WHEEL ∿ As anyone who drives a car knows, when you turn the steering wheel, its top half moves one way and its bottom half moves the other. If you rotate the steering wheel 180 degrees, the top and bottom exchange positions. Now think of the innumerable relationships in everyday life that function in a similar way: when one team wins, another loses; when one person sells, another buys. This is the nature of the universe, and misunderstanding its reciprocity can only lead to suffering. While a person may enjoy triumphs in one area of life, failure may appear in another. A CEO of a large corporation achieves financial success and amasses enormous wealth only to lose all meaningful connection with his or her children. Just as it is impossible to steer a car by turning the wheel in only one direction, it is likewise futile to pursue success and avoid failure. None of us can avoid the inevitable ups and downs of life.

PENDULUM ∿ The pendulum of a clock swings back and forth incessantly, gaining strength at the top of one arc for its return swing in the opposite direction. It cannot work without both halves of the motion, each balancing the other. So it would make little sense to prefer one side over the other or get excited about each swing in that direction. Cheering on either of the alternating movements would seem absurd. Yet this is essentially what we do in modern society. When our jobs are going well and our children are happy, our moods reflect it and our attitudes toward life are positive. Sometimes we think that things are finally going our way, but then reversals overwhelm us. When life is experienced dualistically, our moods swing with each turn of events, with confidence following pessimism or discouragement replacing optimism. However, those who come to understand the nondual nature of life have a very different attitude. When we see that life is all one thing, and realize that opposites are inseparable aspects of a unified whole, we develop equanimity. With the perspective that comes with that recognition, we can view the vacillations of life from a higher vantage point.

MUSIC ∾ People make music in every corner of the globe, in astounding varieties and countless modes. Something all musical forms have in common, though, is the element of contrast. From classical masterpieces to indigenous melodies to contemporary rock and blues, all work by alternation, using sound and silence, high and low pitches, and loud or soft volume to produce a captivating experience. William James claimed that music was the form through which we best received mystical truth. The philosopher Arthur Schopenhauer asserted that the greatest music could pull sensitive listeners beyond themselves into unselfconscious awareness. Musicians often speak of getting lost in the mesmerizing filigrees of ascending and descending notes and the magical dance of rhythm and cadence. Music is dualistic in every aspect, but in its very midst listeners can briefly transcend the bounds of duality and lose themselves in the sheer rapture of sound. In a similar way, a mystic can find transcendence within the dualistic play of fortune and tragedy, fame and disgrace, life and death. This is what the Hindu tradition calls *lila*, or the play of the Divine—their term for life seen with eyes and heard with ears that no longer perceive division.

∾

There is a fundamental sense of insecurity in a world defined by opposition. We all ride the roller coaster of existence, climbing to unimagined highs and then suddenly plunging into chaos. Our lives ebb and flow across the shifting sands of overdue bills and unexpected promotions, the kindness of strangers and the betrayal of friends, coloring our days with alternating moods of happiness and angst, excitement and dismay. We are blessed with the convenience of modern transportation and confronted with the effects of global warming. The miracles of robotics and genetic engineering hold great promise, yet bring with them terrifying specters of society's dehumanization and the world's decline. The improvements we make in one area are inevitably counterbalanced by side effects in another, reflecting the interconnectedness of what is.

Those who have had glimpses of Eden, who have dared to challenge the fearsome pairs of symbolic monsters that traditionally guard the temple secrets in the East, give voice to a very different vision and call us home to a world reunited. The mystics and sages all direct us to the same understanding of existence, one that transcends the stark dualism of our contemporary world and the aggressive partition of humanity into good and evil, saved and lost, us and them. They speak of a time when the suffering and torment of life can be seen from a higher perspective, one that heals the divisions that tear us apart. In the Book of Isaiah, we read: "I form the light and create darkness. I bring prosperity and create disaster; I, the LORD, do all these things."[4] The *Tao Te Ching*, attributed to Lao Tzu and thought to have been written several centuries before the start of the Common Era, tells us that "heaven and earth . . . are impartial," and that the Tao—the underlying, eternal principle of the universe—gives rise to all things, good and evil alike.[5]

From the starkly different world of nineteenth-century America, the mystical writing of Walt Whitman resounds with the same inclusive vision. In the poem "Song of Myself," he sees unity where others would find opposites:

> A learner with the simplest,
>   a teacher of the thoughtfullest,
> A novice beginning, yet experient
>   of myriads of seasons,
> Of every hue and caste am I,
>   of every rank and religion,
> A farmer, mechanic, artist,
>   gentleman, sailor, quaker,
> Prisoner, fancy-man, rowdy,
>   lawyer, physician, priest.

Later he adds:

> I am not the poet of goodness only—I do not decline
>   to be the poet of wickedness also...
> My gait is no fault-finder's or rejecter's gait;
> I moisten the roots of all that has grown.[6]

His lengthy masterpiece, published in 1855, reflects an understanding far different from the discord and strife of the years immediately preceding the Civil War, and it is anticipating the reconciliation that lies beyond duality.

In our time, Buddhist monk Thich Nhat Hanh writes of the horrors of the war in his own homeland, Vietnam, which he knows firsthand. In his poem "Please Call Me by My True Names," this renowned master voices the very same theme at a time when the divisions of duality remain as stark as ever:

> I am the child in Uganda, all skin and bones,
> my legs as thin as bamboo sticks.
> And I am the arms merchant,
> selling deadly weapons to Uganda.

I am the twelve-year-old girl,
refugee on a small boat,
who throws herself into the ocean
after being raped by a sea pirate.
And I am the pirate,
my heart not yet capable
of seeing and loving....

Please call me by my true names,
so I can wake up
and the door of my heart could be left open,
the door of compassion.[7]

Duality is the nature of existence, and its alternating play of forms is eternal. It sets the stage for the universal spiritual drama, and it is the condition in which we discover our nakedness, self-conscious and separate from everything else. Just as we cannot know hot without cold, or up without down, it is only as individuals alone and vulnerable that we intuit the wholeness that is missing—our true nature. From this moment on, whether we realize it or not, our deepest desire is for this wholeness.

While we may dream of the day when the lamb will lie down with the lion and the clashing opposites of life be calmed, we will never find the way to that resolution in external events. The solution lies in our *relationship* to the events. We change the way we see, rather than what we are seeing. When we ultimately realize that all things are one, and no longer define ourselves within the limits of this and that, we find the peace, love, and compassion that come with the transcendent vision of wholeness.

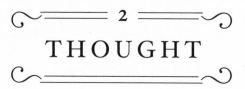

THOUGHT

**Most people don't inhabit a living reality,
but a conceptualized one.**

—Eckhart Tolle

Thought is not only the defining characteristic of our modern age, it is central to our very human existence. It is the tool with which we make sense of our surroundings, adapt to changing circumstances, and anticipate threats. It is also the basis for our relationships with other human beings, giving us the ability to understand the experiences and feelings of those around us. If we could not think, we would have no way to piece together the events of our lives. The world would be unintelligible.

Without this extraordinary and essential tool, our species would never have evolved at all. As a species, we have relied on thought—together with language and the ability to communicate and record our thoughts—to frame the accumulated experience of our past, describe the dimensions of our future, and lay the foundation for our progress in all the innumerable fields of human endeavor.

René Descartes understood this when he distilled the essence of existence into his famed proclamation "Cogito, ergo sum"—I think, therefore I am. With those words, he isolated the faculty of thought as the foundation of all knowledge, the one fundamental fact beyond question or doubt. In the wake of his pivotal work, this premise became the cornerstone of Western science and philosophy. But we don't need any knowledge of Descartes or his epistemology to grasp the truth in his words: unless we have practiced meditation and seen for ourselves how thoughts spontaneously arise and fall away, we too are likely to identify ourselves with our thinking. What we think becomes what we are. This is why we guard our ideas, opinions, and beliefs so tenaciously and jealously: we take them for the very core of our being.

Thinking is based on our minds' ability to isolate and compare patterns of sensory input and remember those that are significant for our lives. Observing the qualitative, spatial, and contextual characteristics of things around us in their infinite variety, we register the consistent ways in which those qualities differ, and from these patterns we discern the shape of an object or an idea. In this way, selecting but a small fraction of available input, we cognitively map our world. Our senses efficiently discern figure from ground, dividing and isolating particular patterns for threat or value while ignoring the details of the background.

Human beings have evolved to give the most attention to those aspects of the environment that represent the greatest danger to our survival. Animals, for example, were more of a danger than the savannah they roamed, so our eyes evolved to pick up movement out of stillness and our ears to note sounds out of silence. Over time, the patterns we discerned were labeled and classified, enabling us to exploit regular aspects of the environment (such as the habits of prey that we could use to track and trap it), to anticipate events before they happened, and adapt more quickly to unfamiliar surroundings. By recognizing and categorizing the phenomena we encountered, we became ever more efficient in responding to the challenges of our early environment. From these humble but crucial beginnings, the same extraordinary ability to codify experience into concepts has extended the dominance of thought into every aspect of human endeavor.

In a world of incessant flux, concepts lend a sense of constancy and predictability. Fixed and unambiguous, they transform chaotic and potentially overwhelming sensory input into a relatively consistent model of our world. The model is continuously being refined, with individual elements steadily proliferating as we make our understanding and our communication ever more nuanced and clear. Consider a tree, common to many of the world's environments and thus relatively easy to distinguish as a concept. From this one label, *tree*, thousands more concepts have arisen to differentiate between species of trees and the unique characteristics of each. At the same time, we conceptually dissect each individual tree into innumerable parts, from leaves and stems to branches, roots, and cells. These conceptual compartmentalizations are so clear, and so manifestly necessary to our understanding, that it is easy to overlook the fact that the elements we differentiate this way are not, in reality, separated at all. A tree is an organism, an integrated process of life that does not recognize the divisions and labels we impose on its components.

Thought may be indispensable to our existence in the world, but the efficiency with which it symbolically organizes that existence comes at a steep price. We communicate in words that condense experience into concepts, but when we forget that those concepts are arbitrary and begin to substitute our conceptual version of reality for actual experience of it, we lose contact with what is real. This is not problematic when we as children point out constellations in the night sky, because the conventional nature of constellations will soon become obvious to us; we will learn that a certain arrangement of stars makes up Orion only because we have given it that name. It matters far more when the same dynamic of conceptual isolation and division is at work in virtually every human activity. Confusing mental partitions with real divisions, we find ourselves in a world of racial stereotypes, religious fundamentalism, and nationalistic fervor, at odds with those who stand on the opposite side of any mental divide. It is like the leaves on one side of a tree attempting to annihilate their counterparts on the other, missing the fundamental oneness they all share. The living, breathing suchness of our world, the very ground of our being, is lost in translation to the language of thought. We take the map for the territory and can no longer see what is.

In the West, with its bias toward hard facts, the analytical approach to understanding has long reigned supreme. Science, for example, employs its related tools of reason and logic in a tireless exploration of the physical world, aimed at codifying it into ever more refined concepts. From the time of Descartes and Newton, we have seen the world as mechanical in nature and looked to science to illuminate its workings. For several hundred years this has been our prevailing paradigm, based in the belief that life itself can be dissected into parts in order to unravel its mysteries. We have dissected it more and more finely in a search for the smallest observable piece of the puzzle, the most elemental building block of the material world.

This approach has yielded remarkable advances in technology and medicine, surrounding us with comforts and convenience our predecessors could not have imagined. In this paradigm, though, things we cannot observe or measure become irrelevant, and the insights of the intuitive mind, because they are inaccessible by empirical means, are often dismissed out of hand. Religion scholar Huston Smith refers to the scientifically defined world as a "one-story universe," alluding to the fact that science's endeavors never extend beyond the self-imposed limits of a single ontological dimension.[1] Other dimensions of reality, which lie beyond the reach of quantitative measurement, have no place in this worldview, so we deny their very existence.

The scientific view is so dominant today, and we receive its edicts with such total faith, that its philosophic underpinnings perpetuate themselves. Its constricted gaze excludes all that could help us understand life's larger picture, and its successes, while often breathtaking, serve to keep the focus narrow. Entranced by the vast array of technological wonders that empirical investigation produces, we unwittingly sacrifice much of what gives our life meaning and purpose.

One of the most entrenched assumptions of modern life is that our perception, together with our extraordinary capacity for thought and reason, accurately describes the world we live in. Indeed, given the consistent features of our shared experience and the universal recognition of objects in our physical environment, our concept of the world seems accurate beyond question. We can hardly doubt that a chair is a chair. Nonetheless, there is another mode of perception, based on a profoundly different premise that is woven throughout the cultures and eras of human existence. *This* gaze takes in the qualitative aspects of life that are left out in the conceptual framing of our quantitative explorations. For millennia, humanity has cultivated this faculty, the intuitive perception of life unconditioned, accessing those ineffable feelings that speak directly to our human spirit. Intuitive perception is a different form of knowing, a nonintellectual form that *precedes* thought. This avenue to understanding yields an organic, unified model of reality devoid of all the usual divisions that thought imposes on our world.

Drawing on the insights that arise from an intuitive approach to experience, the esoteric spiritual traditions of all ages and cultures have challenged our most basic beliefs about reality with a startling vision in which thought and language are seen as *creating* our world rather than describing it. In this view, it is the very act of conceptualizing a "thing" that brings that thing into being, a power implicit in the very origin of the word: *concept* is derived from the Latin *concipere*, to take in, to become pregnant with, and its use in both the physical and the mental sense reflects an early recognition of thought's generative role.

Twenty-five hundred years ago, the Buddha declared that we construct the world with our thoughts. Azriel of Gerona, a thirteenth-century Jewish mystic, expressed the same idea differently: "Thought is like a mirror. One looking at it sees his image inside and thinks there are two images, but the two are really one."[2] It is a truth we can trace back to the beginnings of recorded history: the reality we see is self-created, fabricated with our thoughts, no more than a reflection of what we personally believe the world to be. Mystics have continued to assert the selfsame truth right up to the present day. Contemporary Advaita master Ramesh Balsekar finds concept and illusion to be synonymous, and Alan Watts asserts that it is through thought that we "thing" the world we see. But this truth is so alien to most people's ordinary understanding that few have recognized the wisdom it contains, especially in those parts of the globe where nonduality has no traditional roots.

In the early twentieth century, this began to change, even as science was stepping up its efforts to unravel the secrets of the universe. It came as a shock when cutting-edge research suddenly yielded support for the strange claims of esoteric spirituality. Einstein and his colleagues in the field of New Physics, though they belonged to the world of empirical investigation that had always dismissed the claims of mystics, were now conducting experiments that shattered the old assumptions. In their pursuit of the smallest individual particles of the universe, they ultimately found that nothing could truly be isolated. Instead, they found a web of infinite relationships, a world inherently indivisible. Thirteen hundred years ago, the Chinese master Fa-tsang stated: "An atom has no intrinsic nature—it involves all reality in its establishment. Since reality is boundless, so accordingly is the atom."[3] Ironically, through a process of endless division, dissection, and definition, twentieth-century science arrived at the very same truth.

Since the time of Isaac Newton, science has placed great emphasis on objective observation, using rigorous experimental controls to minimize external influence and promote confidence in the validity of research. It came as a great shock, therefore, when the groundbreaking work of twentieth-century physics proved that, after all, there was no world "out there" that our senses directly and accurately reported. For the first time, science recognized the participation of the observer in the determination of what is observed. In variations on a classic thought experiment of the nineteenth century, it was experimentally demonstrated that the behavior of a subatomic object—appearing either as a particle or as a wave—depended on *how it was observed*. The results at the quantum level could not otherwise be explained. Einstein made this remarkable statement: "Physical concepts are free creations of the human mind and are not, however it may seem, uniquely determined by the external world."[4]

More recently, in his book *Thought as a System*, quantum physicist David Bohm argued that our thoughts do not tell us the ways things are, but instead play an unconscious but creative role in determining the reality in which we live. Renowned American psychologist

Jerome Bruner agrees; he does not believe that the world is available for "direct touch," but concludes that we each live out our lives within our own representation of reality.[5] To each of these individual scientists, it became clear that the conceptual map was indeed not the territory.

New discoveries that radically revise old patterns of thought are always slow to take hold: look at the fierce resistance with which Darwin's evolutionary theory was met, or the decades of purgatory in which Freud's claims of a human unconscious languished, before either received wide acceptance. The findings of New Physics, already close to a century old and repeatedly borne out by new research, have only gradually penetrated mainstream thought. In the last thirty years, however, they have gained traction, and the fact that their findings parallel the deepest insights of the esoteric traditions has spurred new interest in ideas that had always hovered on the fringes of human understanding. The New Physicists themselves did not miss the convergence of these profoundly different modes of human perception, and their own spiritual writings are shot through with Eastern terms and esoteric views of consciousness. Now, at last, these two threads are coming together in a collaborative effort involving both spiritual adepts and scientists from many different disciplines in a dialogue of mutual respect and curiosity.

~

IMAGES OF THOUGHT

PROCESSED FOOD ~ We have often been told that we are what we eat, and now we are taking this truism more seriously than ever. During the last two decades we have grown increasingly aware of the artificial ingredients added to the processed foods we consume, many of which we now know to be unhealthy and even carcinogenic. For millennia, mystics have maintained a similar position, declaring that "we are what we think" (or what *we* process). Just as processing changes the nature of the food, the concepts we bring to our daily living alter experience to fit habitual patterns. We all know people who see the glass of life as half full or half empty, and the impact such thinking can have. Science now suggests that as much as 80 percent of our perception of reality is the result of mental conditioning and may have little actual resemblance to what is.

CLOUDS ∼ When we were children, we often amused ourselves by imagining faces, animals, or other objects hidden in the puffy clouds up in the skies. If we were playing the game with our friends or parents, the things we could identify were limited to the concepts we shared. Recognizing the conventional representations of such objects—a clown face, a rabbit—we could agree when one was found. Of course, the clown or rabbit existed in our eyes only and had no reality otherwise. The same is true for everything we perceive. The world is populated and furnished with things differentiated by our mental faculty from an organic process of ever-changing energy patterns. The "things" that seem to exist are created by thought in the same way that children find objects in the clouds.

CAT ∼ To shed light on the nature of thought, Alan Watts suggests the phenomenon of a cat walking on the opposite side of a fence, glimpsed in the gap between two boards. First we spot the head, then a less descript body, followed a second later by the tail. If the cat turns around and walks past again, we again see head, body, and tail in that same order. Given the limitations of this fragmentary perspective, if we had no previous knowledge of cats, we might conceptually divide the organic wholeness of the creature, take each part to be a discrete phenomenon, and infer from the apparently separate but consistently sequenced parts that the head is the cause and the tail the effect. In this same manner, thought divides the one into many, dismembering what is—a unity as indivisible as a living animal—and presenting us with the fragmented version that we then employ logic and reason to reconstruct. We observe our world as if through the crack in a fence, divide it into myriad disconnected "things," and interpret their interactions through the same paradigm of cause and effect, even though, in truth, these "things" are not separate at all.

BUTTERFLY ∽ The function of thought can be compared to the process of collecting butterflies. If an entomologist catches one of these colorful insects and pins its motionless husk on a board, he may admire the beautiful pattern on the wings and label the unique characteristics of its physical form, but he cannot apprehend its being anymore; that essence is lost. There is little in the display box that suggests the magic of its flight and the way it once fluttered from one flower to the next. Thought and its labels cannot communicate the ineffable. Like the butterfly, much of life resists the classifications and definitions we depend on to figure things out; it can be understood only by actual experience, by being and feeling, not through abstract thought. We know what green beans taste like, but to convey in words the experience of eating them is impossible. Likewise, when we think of the music of Bach, words cannot convey our own listening experience to someone who has never heard his music. Can a mother express in words the experience of giving birth to her first child? Life is in the living.

CANCER ∽ In an analogy some might find surprising, Bohm compared our system of thought to cancer, which he defined as a growth that is "incoherent" with the organism that supports it. Growing on its own in a manner inconsistent with the health of the body as a whole, cancer has destructive effects we cannot miss. The parallel with human thought is less obvious: it derives from what Bohm sees as the reflexive nature of our thinking. In the interactive process of experience, perception, and thought, he asserts, we are conditioned with a vast system of reflexes that, once set, resist alteration. Our thought patterns are relatively fixed, while the world around us changes unceasingly, and our mental rigidity can produce effects that no longer suit our circumstances or support our intended outcomes. The violence of some religious extremists today, and its glaring contradiction with the compassionate wisdom of their spiritual traditions, is just one striking example of such incoherence. If we are blind to our reflexes and take our thoughts as fact, our actions can become as disordered and destructive for our species as cancer is for the body.

CANDLE ∾ When you are in the dark, you light a candle. With the illumination it provides, you can see to get around without stumbling over the objects in your surroundings. With the rising of the sun, however, the candle becomes useless. The light it sheds now makes no difference at all. The same is true of thought when we use it to explore the mystery of life. When you are just starting on the journey of esoteric spirituality, nonduality seems very unfamiliar and strange, and you may well feel you are in the dark about the counterintuitive propositions it entails. At this early stage on your spiritual path, you will probably find it helpful to read and think through the teachings of ancient and modern masters. The concepts they lay out can illuminate your first steps and intimate deeper meanings. But as you delve deeper into the mystery of nonduality, thought becomes gradually less useful in unraveling its meaning. The understanding you seek will ultimately come from dawning insight, not from the dimmer light of deliberation and conjecture. An ancient Zen master once said that in the beginning of practice, a thousand books are not enough. In the end, a single word is too much.

Thought does not tell us what we are seeing but rather what *to* see. We inherit our vision of reality along with the language we are taught to speak, ensuring that we share the same version of life-translated-into-concepts as the other members of our society. We grow so accustomed to this culturally conditioned framing of our world, and so preoccupied with the images we perceive through its prism, that we never question the authenticity of what we are seeing. If, however, the conceptual lens is changed, the world changes accordingly.

A colorful example of this possibility is found in the work of Carlos Castaneda, an anthropologist and author who spent thirteen years with a Yaqui Indian shaman in Mexico. The experiences he shared with this enigmatic man, Don Juan, were disorienting, often dramatic, and well beyond the bounds of what most would consider normal. They were predicated on the teacher's ability to convince Castaneda of the arbitrary and plastic nature of his reality.

Like Castaneda, we all take for granted the "realness" of our world and presume it to be the only reality there is. The idea that it may not be is at best unsettling and can be terrifying. Movies or science-fiction novels that suggest a different paradigm for seeing the world may briefly captivate our imagination or spark casual conversation, but few dare to go too far down that road. However, the creative role of thought is entering our consciousness in other ways. The last several decades have seen a rapid increase in mind/body research, and its practical applications, such as the placebo effect or the use of hypnosis, are everywhere. Countless self-help programs now promise a healthier life through positive thinking. People faced with life-threatening diseases have access to resources that offer constructive ways to think about their illnesses and to imagine the healing process, and these approaches produce real results. It is not, however, the new patterns of thought themselves that bring about the healing, it is our *belief* that they will. From the laboratory to daily life, the advances have been so dramatic that it is easy to agree with the opinion offered by Norman Cousins, who declared, "Belief is biology."

For mystics, belief is *reality*. Nineteenth-century English poet William Blake asserted, "Everything possible to be believ'd is an image of truth."[6] Our unquestioning faith that our world is real takes the artificial structures of thought and gives them substance, makes them manifest. Imprisoned by our certitude, we pass our entire lives within the bounds our thoughts impose. We search for truth in an unfathomable maze of concepts and classifications, but we can never find the wholeness that is lacking. To follow a conceptual path is to go in circles, a venture not unlike the eternal inconclusiveness that so often characterizes philosophy. A concept has meaning only in the context of another concept; there is nothing absolute in it. The thinking mind is unsurpassed in resolving practical matters, but it cannot navigate the paradoxical dimension of nonduality. For the journey into the domain of spirit, we must transcend thought's fragmented vision and follow the intuitive path of mystical practice.

The story of the Flower Sermon, a favorite in Buddhist lore, points to this fundamental truth. In this wordless teaching, the Buddha is said to have pulled a single lotus flower from a pond and held it up to his disciples, with water and mud dripping from its roots. Since our human inclination is to think things out and make sense of our experience, the disciples proposed many explanations of the Master's meaning, but every conceptual interpretation missed the point. The Buddha was directing us to that which lies beyond thought. By saying nothing, he left nothing unsaid, and the disciple who did understand his intent simply smiled in the realization. The sight of the lotus unmediated by explanations and verbal discussion offers an opportunity to see beyond words, to directly apprehend what is. This same truth lies at the heart of the Taoist classic *Tao Te Ching*, with its insistence that the true way cannot be named nor the Unknowable known.

Thought is the loom on which the veil of duality is woven, concealing the pristine realm that we inhabited before we took on culture and concepts. It is a precious tool without which we could not learn, remember, or adapt to our surroundings, but we have placed too much of our faith in it. Behind this veil of words and divisions and distinctions, we live out our lives in the shadowy forms of a translated context and long for something we cannot express. Like tourists who let a beautiful vista pass them by while they read about it in a guidebook, we experience life secondhand. To find what we are looking for, to experience what the ancients herald, we must set aside our concepts for the moment, and open our senses to what is now. This is the only way we will see the miracles around us, really know what it is to be alive, and consciously be what we truly are.

3
TIME

Memory is time.

—Krishnamurti

In the earliest days of humanity, before our predecessors had attained the capacity for symbolic thought, they lived in a timeless world. Much like today's children, they existed in the moment, engrossed in their immediate physical surroundings, with no effort to plan or prepare for anything beyond it. Theirs was a realm devoid of hope or anxiety, and thoughts of past or future never interfered with their concentration on the object of their attention. During this hunting and gathering stage of our evolution, the actions of the group arose in response to immediate needs. When hungry, the group impulsively searched for food. When cold, they gathered wood and built a fire. There was no need to plan for the future, since there was no understanding of time—no concept of such a thing as a future.

In the next stage, the advent of language had brought with it the concept of time, and our predecessors had begun to farm. Acting without forethought was no longer an option, since a harvest depended on significant activity months beforehand to prepare the ground and plant the crop. People had to look ahead, anticipate needs, and identify necessary preparations. With the conceptual representation of events, they could recall things that had happened and project similar situations in the future. Combining memories and projections, the arms of time were gradually extended in a linear sequence of symbolic events, connecting those of past experience with those projected beyond the present. The lessons learned in the previous cycle of sowing and reaping informed the next season's planting and harvest as people refined their skill in cultivating, and thus the foundations of early civilization were laid. When humanity eventually learned to record significant events to ensure their recall, time took on an even more concrete form.

The same shift our predecessors made eons ago is repeated in the life of every human child. We are introduced to time at a very early age, and we assimilate it right along with language. When we learn to discriminate between one thing and another, and to associate the common objects in our surroundings with their proper names, we also begin to distinguish their sequence: as we learn to tell our socks from our shoes, we also grasp which to put on first. And we start early to apprehend before and after. Even before we can talk, family and friends compare us with the way we used to be, noting how much bigger and smarter we have gotten. We hear about things that lie ahead for us, and people wonder what we are going to be when we grow up.

By the time we enter school, we are living squarely in the world of time. Our attention is directed toward the future and the need to prepare for all that is coming. A fundamental shift has taken place, from our native preoccupation with *being* to a forward-looking focus on *becoming* something down the road. Failure to look ahead always comes with a consequence: if we don't clean our room, we can't go out to play *afterward*, and a dinner not finished may mean a television turned off *later*. As we grow, the consequences become more serious: the danger of being held back a year in school if we don't learn our lessons. At the same time, we are required to look back too, as when we're reminded of the way we behaved *before* and made to feel guilty for it. This orientation to past and future will define the rest of our lives and forever redirect our attention from the present moment to another time.

In the experience of early human beings as well as the children of every new generation, there is a dualistic distinction implicit in their turning away from the Now. Before that momentous shift, there is only the undivided timelessness of Eden, where no stress, worry, guilt, or regret exists. As Ken Wilber points out, the shift creates the illusion that we are separate from the present moment, *outside* the timeless Now. He adds that the role of memory in this process makes it seem as if we are *behind* present experience, a self standing apart and *having* experience. Think of what you say every time you introduce yourself: you recite virtually the same set of memorized facts that make up the story of who you are. You believe these personal memories to be fixed, while everything else seems to be passing by.[1] The recollections we have seem to confirm the existence of the self that *had* experience *then*, and implicitly does so *now*. Constantly repeated throughout our lives, each move away from the present reinforces this deceptive impression. To cross the boundary into the world of time is to be exiled in past or future, and thus to be separate from what is.

The role of thought in the development of the human experience of time is clearly critical. Once we attain the ability to conceptualize and label our sensory input, it becomes possible to remember events and sequence them symbolically. Thought divides unity into parts, and time gives meaning to their repetition, order, and duration. Both time and space are abstractions, products of the mind, and have no reality outside the conceptual framework we superimpose on our experience. When we sense the passage of time or movement in space, we are pulling unity apart into fragmented concepts. To create the possibility of a *there*, we have to contrast it with a *here*, dividing the wholeness of our immediate experience into discrete "places" separated by space. The same is true for what we call time, because to detect its passage or locate events in it, we must divide the timeless Now into a discrete *now* that is contrasted with a *then*.

Thought and its correlates of time and space function together to symbolically organize our sensory information, imposing arbitrary divisions on the oneness of what is. The original timelessness remains unchanged, but we perceive it through conceptual screens. These screens are conventions, with no basis in reality, but their practical value is unquestioned; we can only imagine the confusion and chaos that would result in the absence of our universally accepted measure of time. Coordinating anything at all—from household schedules and social calendars to air traffic control and international commerce—would become virtually impossible.

The dominant view of time that frames the events of the contemporary world is the one established by Isaac Newton in the initial stages of modern science. He proposed an "absolute time" that formed the background against which life played out. Unaffected by the events of the world, time was linear and constant, extending toward both an ever-receding past and an infinite future. More recently, this model was challenged when Einstein and his colleagues in New Physics conducted their revolutionary research and made the startling case for relativity—the idea that Newton's absolute time does not exist, but is relative to the motion of the observer. But there is no denying the influence of the Newtonian view or its applications in analyzing the universe and the life it sustains. We have used everything from the spectrum analysis of galaxies to the carbon dating of early human habitats to locate different periods of our evolving world on a straight, unspooling timeline. Archaeologists rewrite history when ancient manuscripts are unearthed, while psychologists study the stages of a person's past to diagnose present problems. All these methods are based on linear time, allowing investigators to order the sequence of events and assess their duration. Linear time is an arbitrary standard of measurement, a social convention with no more independent reality than that of measuring distance in meters or miles.

Despite this fact, the press of time is felt so strongly by modern peoples that few ever question or investigate its nature. The functioning of modern society is predicated on an obsessive relationship with time. Driven by our desires for a better life and the promise of fulfillment on the temporal horizon, we are stuck on fast-forward, in an unending rush hour that creates havoc in our lives. We put a premium on speed, but find ourselves more pressed the faster we move. Paradoxically, the e-mails, faxes, and overnight deliveries that punctuate our days and speed up our turnaround time leave less time than ever between the events of the day. In this manic rush to the future, we subject ourselves to unhealthy lifestyles, resulting in a host of "hurry sicknesses," including insomnia, heart attacks, ulcers, and migraines. Losing touch with the natural rhythms of life, we race through our lives with an ever-diminishing chance of experiencing what is real.

Many traditional belief systems have a similar relationship with time. In the conventional linear model, religious meaning is derived from historical events, and religious practice is preparation for a future redemption. Devotees strive for a better birth in the next life or eternal salvation at the end of this one, never imagining the existence of a dimension untouched by time. While mystics have long spoken of time as an illusion, and philosophers such as Immanuel Kant have made arguments for the subjective nature of our temporal world, these ideas are only lately coming into widespread awareness in the West.

∾

IMAGES OF TIME

RACE CAR ∾ Driving a race car is an activity that demands total concentration. Your life depends on it. With speeds sometimes exceeding two hundred miles an hour, there is no chance to reflect on what you are doing and no opportunity to second-guess yourself. With other cars jockeying for position, changing lanes, or trying to pass, everything is in flux, unpredictable, and risky. The countless adjustments needed to keep your car where you want it to be must happen instantly and spontaneously to survive the ever-changing circumstances. The ordinary sense of separation between experience and experiencer is absent—in a timeless flow of action, you become what you are doing. *Life* is the driver.

LIGHTNING BUG ∾ Under the cloak of darkness, the lightning bug illuminates the landscape, seemingly flashing in and out of existence with each display of light. Seeing it first in one spot, then in another, we cannot even know if it's the same bug. In many esoteric teachings, the world is portrayed as a similar manifestation, flashing into momentary existence in an unceasing series of instants between which there is no actual relationship. As the ancient Japanese Zen master Dogen explained, wood does not become ashes. Each instant is independent and unchanging and contains no movement toward the next. According to New Physics, the key role in producing these ephemeral flashes of manifestation is played by the "participatory observer." In other words, consciousness is instrumental in bringing the universe into existence. Mystics, more specifically, say that the *thoughts* of the observer play this role. Nevertheless, the agreement between scientist and mystic on this point is striking.

NOVEL ∼ Within the pages of a novel, the past, present, and future exist simultaneously; what was, what is, and what will be share the same space, literally, between its front and back covers. In the same way, we each hold our past, present, and future within our recollections, right now, as a novel contains all the events within its scope. Our worlds, according to the Buddha, are contained within us. We all have stories that represent who we believe ourselves to be, and it is from the perspective of these accumulated memories that we interpret the events of our lives. It is our thoughts alone that produce a sense of continuation and the belief that we have a past and a future. Like the story in a novel, our memories tell and retell our own personal story. But as with each passage we read in the book, the sense of time in our own lives unfolds from a series of mental images recalled in the *present moment*. We *never* have direct experience of the past or future—no sound, no sight, no taste, no sensation of any kind. Life is always and only now.

TELESCOPE ∼ The telescope is a marvelous instrument that allows us to gaze beyond the confines of Earth and its atmosphere. Since we cannot capture the whole of the night sky in a single glance, we position the telescope to scan the horizon one small section at a time.

As successive objects come into view, those we saw before are left in the past, while those yet to be seen are part of the future. And this is how we make sense of our world: we say that time moves, but the passage of time takes place solely in our perception. The view is framed by the way we see and is not inherent in that which we are seeing. As William Blake claimed, "If the doors of perception were cleansed everything would appear to man as it is: infinite."[2]

RIVERBANK ∼ When you think of a river flowing alongside its bank, the juxtaposition of change and changelessness evokes the common experience we all share of time passing us by. When we are self-conscious, we have the sensation of being stationary and separate from the events unfolding around us. The sense of contrast stems from our memories, which anchor us like fixed points on a riverbank. We develop a sense of stability that seems to stand outside of present experience, apart from the cascading flow of appearances that pass by in the Now. However, if we become captivated by the beauty of the river, as sometimes happens, the apparent gap between subject and object dissolves and we lose all sense of self in what is. This is the realm of the holy, the sacred. We are not bystanders by the river of life; it is what we are.

THE WORLD'S HIGHEST MOUNTAIN ∼ There is a metaphor found in Hindu and Buddhist cosmology that evokes a sense of eternity, which is measured in what is referred to as *kalpas*. A kalpa is metaphorically described as the time it would take a bird with a silk scarf in its mouth to wear away the world's highest mountain by passing over it once every hundred years. The image of this light, soft cloth brushing over granite peaks yields a sense of the Unknowable, of the unfathomable for which no beginning or end can be imagined. Our ordinary experience of time is very different, as the days of our lives seem to pass in a fleeting present sandwiched between the immensity of past and future. However, on those occasions when we lose ourselves in a favorite activity like painting, gardening, or playing music, the press of time disappears. Eternity, and the feelings of the unfathomable evoked by an image such as the kalpa, are not to be found in an immeasurable future, but in this very moment: *that* is what has no end.

~

The mystical understanding of time is a polar opposite to the one with which most of us are familiar. For millennia, the sages of the world have maintained that time is an illusion that separates us from what is. They have urged a return to the moment, the unceasing Now, outside of which they say nothing exists. In declaring that enlightenment cannot be found in the world of time, spiritual masters show us how urgently we need to understand time's paradoxical nature.

When we read the words of these mystics, a flood of memories arises to contradict them. These memories can be so vibrant and palpable, so real in our experience, that the past they assert by their presence is hard to contest. How can anyone deny time when presented with such vivid images of the past? Yet, on closer examination, we recognize that memories themselves occur nowhere but in this very Now. We have never returned to the past, nor have we traveled to the future. The entire universe of our experience forever takes place in this very moment.

To unravel the mystery of time, it is essential to make a clear distinction between the linear model, employed by scientists in the physical realm, and the psychological model. The flow, the succession of appearances, is unquestioned. That is actual. What is not is *entities* that continue. Psychological time is subjective and is founded on a belief in the self, an entity with which we identify and through which we perceive time. It is the presumed continuity associated with this conceptual identity that creates the frame of reference within which life is measured and understood. The subjective clock that measures the passage of our lives is set at birth and determines the limits of our personal time zone. This idiosyncratic point of view colors all our experiences, placing them in context, and draws our attention to personal goals and dreams for the future.

But when we recognize the conventional nature of the self, and intuitively see its unreality, then we free ourselves from the grip of time-based emotions like guilt, resentment, worry, and fear and even transcend the boundaries of life and death. These imagined limits, and the measuring of life by expected life span, fall away as we reenter the flow of the timeless. We realize that the past, present, and future are all contained in this instant and have no existence apart from it. Our palpable sense of their reality arises from thought, from our remarkable ability to remember previous events. What we overlook is the fact that memories of those events only exist in the moment.

Living in the Now means to be where you are, going with the flow of life without dualistic divisions of any kind, no longer separating experience into past and future, nor being drawn by memory or anticipation away from the present moment. To say that there is no time, or that time is an illusion, is not to deny its usefulness in its conventional role. Instead, it is to see it for what it is: a social agreement on a system of arbitrary divisions superimposed on the flow of life to coordinate our human activities.

When the mind is still and the din of thought has calmed, there is no experience of time or concern for it. The kaleidoscope of inestimable detail that forever awaits our attention, the rich tapestry of our moment-to-moment experience of life to which we have ready access, has no need for time's generic categories and classifications. Most of us, in quiet moments of solitude or immersed in activities we love, have experienced this timelessness and tasted the essence of what is.

KNOWLEDGE

**As long as you are certain about things
you are living within boundaries.**

—Deepak Chopra

I n the last two chapters, we saw how thought, reason, and memory
shape our experience of reality and our sense of time and give us a
conceptual map by which we navigate the world. The product of that
reasoning process is the body of tradition and shared assumptions that we
call knowledge—the bedrock on which human society is built. Knowing
the same language, heritage, and culture, the members of a society have
a common basis for communication, cooperation, and all communal
activities—indeed, for their very survival. The accumulated knowledge of
one's native community, its infrastructure of facts, expertise, and accepted
truths, sets the boundaries within which all members are expected to
function. At an individual level, too, our stories and experiences—our
personal store of knowledge—define the way we see our own selves.

Knowledge perpetuates itself through the process of acculturation,
in which the socially ordained worldview is fostered in its members
through the collaborative effort of all those around them. Children begin
to learn this conceptual blueprint almost as soon as they are born, and
the facts and conceptual understandings that they acquire are stabilized
and logically integrated as their reasoning ability develops. At this stage,

information or experiences inconsistent with such "reality-adjusted" thinking are typically dismissed—such as the "imaginary friends" that young children often play with and talk to—or never recognized in the first place.

From the very beginning of our lives, we are taught the importance of learning about the world and mastering the ideas, facts, and figures that are the currency of social interchange. As first teachers, parents try to expose their children to experiences that will start to lay the knowledge base for the future. In school, the process continues in earnest as children and then adolescents refine their cognitive abilities and learn to use reason more effectively to acquire new information. We have all seen how the explanations for Santa Claus, which the very young accept without question, come under increasing scrutiny as children get older. Students are evaluated on their retention and comprehension of an ever-growing body of knowledge, as well as on their ability to communicate their understanding to others. And this mastery of information is an indispensable stage in the life not just of the individual, but of the whole society, preparing it for the tasks that lie ahead. Building on the accumulated knowledge of past generations, the modern world has made startling advances in medicine, technology, and innumerable other fields of endeavor. All these developments grew from the fertile soil of past experience and the lessons learned and passed down by our forefathers, and our ever-increasing knowledge continually pushes the envelope of possibility.

But while knowledge has yielded profound benefits for adaptation and advancement, it is also profoundly limited and limiting; by its very nature, it divides up the unity of what is into multiplicity, filling our perception of reality with untold phenomena that we consider discrete entities. Our habitual ways of seeing the world are not as valid as we assume; they are narrow and misleading representations that create far-reaching problems for us when they come into conflict with other views. The history of our species stands witness to terribly destructive, yet endlessly repeated patterns of behavior that all arise from what we think we know. We are the only species in the world whose members destroy one another in a persistent, systematic way, acting out of deeply conditioned yet delusional belief in the arbitrary divisions that separate us. While we need access to the knowledge of the past for its pragmatic applications in the present, we must also recognize its sobering inadequacies. Otherwise, the inherited template we use to make sense of our surroundings, and the conditioned reactions it produces, blind us to the truth of what is and to our own true nature.

You've probably seen or heard stories about people under hypnosis behaving in strange and amusing ways. In the hypnotic trance state, they may become blind to objects right in front of them or see things that are not there. They may be unable to lift their arms or even to remember their names. Such behavior is the effect of a psychological phenomenon in which the person's ability to think critically is bypassed and a selective perception is established. The subject becomes responsive to whatever the hypnotist suggests and nothing else. This process is a bit like a scale model of a much larger phenomenon, something that psychologist Charles Tart, a renowned expert in altered states of consciousness, refers to as a "consensus trance." We start to enter it in infancy: in the most formative period of our lives, we are taught the socially acceptable way to do things, much the way a subject under hypnosis is taught to quit smoking, and when we diverge from the path, we are corrected, disciplined, or loaded with guilt. Our family, our schools, and our society in general continue to train this selective attention over a lifetime of repetition, backed by physical or emotional force—a powerful hypnotic immersion.

All human beings inherit their worldview through the same process of immersion, but what they learn depends on the time and cultural circumstances into which they are born. Though the homogenization of global commerce and exchange, the spread of television, and the ever-increasing reach of the Internet have erased some of the most striking contrasts, the world's peoples do not all share the same knowledge of the world. In the modern Western environment, for example, with its strong bias for information scientifically gathered and verified, many people (and certainly the establishment) question the existence of extrasensory perception or deny it out of hand. Even the universal human experience of consciousness is something most Western scientists hold to be little more than an epiphenomenon of matter, a side effect of brain chemistry. In sharp contrast, indigenous tribal populations, untouched by modern ways of thinking, commonly inhabit a world that is both alive and conscious. Their rituals are designed to promote respect for and balance with the natural surroundings. The spirits of trees, animals, ancestors, and other elements of their world can be offended, appeased, or appealed to for guidance. Though such behavior might be dismissed as childlike by city dwellers, the extraordinary abilities of aboriginal peoples to adapt to their surroundings defy such facile explanations. Their sensitive relationship to the land is often reflected by their ability to find water in the desert, track animals in rocky terrain, and perform other such feats with a success inexplicable to outsiders.

Just as the society into which we are born sets the overall backdrop against which our lives unfold, our conditioning as individuals creates other patterns of selective attention that further restrict what we experience. We each see through a unique lens of knowledge, beliefs, values, and expectations accumulated over a lifetime of schooling, relationships, work, routines, health and illness, gain and loss. The world we know is our unique version of reality, sometimes profoundly different from that of others. People who are generally friendly and good-natured are likely to perceive others as pleasant and non-threatening. By comparison, people filled with anger are apt to encounter conflict and disagreement in their social encounters. The character of our everyday lives is a function of the way we see the world, and not the result of external events or circumstances, as most of us assume.

Even empirical science, which so many take for absolute, is shaped by selective perception, as Thomas Kuhn forcefully argued fifty years ago in *The Structure of Scientific Revolutions*. To the surprise of many in the scientific establishment, his main assertion was that scientific theories do not evolve as the logical, inevitable consequence of accumulated research, but rather depend on the dominant paradigm and intellectual climate of the time. Even in a scholarly environment that prides itself on objectivity, the limitations of conditioned thought and societal expectations hold sway.

Religious faith and spiritual teaching, too, partake of this cultural conditioning; then, handed down as absolutes, they divide us deeply from other beliefs and believers. In most societies, the dominant forms of religion are passed down almost automatically from one generation to the next and woven into the very fabric of everyday life. For millions of people, the way to approach the Divine is something simply taken for granted. And in societies where centralized religious authority rules, people or groups diverging from official doctrine are often, sometimes harshly, repressed.

This was clearly the case with the believers responsible for the now-famous texts found at Nag Hammadi, scriptures thought to have been written in the period immediately following the death of Christ. As Elaine Pagels explains in *The Gnostic Gospels*, sectarian struggles for control of doctrine were rife at the time, and those who gained the upper hand retained their position by repressing all competing views. Anyone who strayed from the dogma espoused by the dominant sect was at risk. It was for this reason that the scrolls containing the esoteric teachings of Jesus were buried—hidden from the authorities to keep them from being destroyed—and not uncovered for almost two thousand years. In the centuries that followed, before the separation of church and state, governments in the West commonly took their own measures to keep alternative views in check—often extreme, as is vividly illustrated in the notorious reign of terror under the Spanish Inquisition. The scarcity of spiritual sages in the West who espoused mystical ideas or took non-traditional paths to spiritual truth shows just how chillingly effective this repression was and how deep the divisions created by the dualistic template of knowledge could go.

~

IMAGES OF KNOWLEDGE

OCEAN ~ Japanese Zen master Dogen declared that everything in life is seen from a reference point—that all our judgments are made from a limited perspective. To convey this key fact to his students, he used the analogy of sailing in the middle of the ocean. When one can no longer see the shore in any direction, the ocean appears to be a perfect circle. Yet when we get up close to the shoreline, its infinite features and irregular configurations contradict what we seemed to know. Dogen explained that the truth of our limited perspective applies to all things, not only to familiar manifestations but to those whose dimensions we cannot even conceive of.

POST AND TETHER ∼ It's common for a dog owner to use a rope or leash to tether a dog to a post or some other fixed structure, allowing the animal to enjoy the out-of-doors within safe confines. When the dog's attention is aroused by something beyond the reach of its restraints, it barks and pulls violently against the rope, but to no avail. Its range of motion is defined by the post to which it is tethered. Each of us has a fixed point, determined by genetics and experience, that functions to restrict what we can see and understand as surely as the post restrains the dog. A third-generation Palestinian youth raised in a refugee camp would undoubtedly interpret the conflict in the Middle East differently than someone of the same age raised in a Jewish kibbutz on the West Bank. Thus the exact same events can be seen from positions so starkly different that there is no common ground at all. Closer to home, we find that the same phenomenon determines the quality of relationships with our own family members and closest friends. Each of us is restrained by our unique conditioning, and we communicate with others only to the degree that our circles of understanding overlap.

REARVIEW MIRROR ∼ When we learn to drive, one of the first skills we develop is using the rearview mirror to monitor what drivers behind us are doing. This practice is indispensable for making the many decisions necessary to safely navigate through traffic. At the same time, it is equally important that we keep our eyes on the road in front of us. Common sense tells us that to rely exclusively on what we know from looking in the rearview mirror would be disastrous. The same is true of navigating through life, but it is a truth much more easily forgotten. There are endless examples of how our attention is so rigidly fixed on what we already know, so blinded by conditioning, that we miss the terrain that lies directly ahead and the wonder that unfolds around us in every moment. Jesus alluded to this limitation of our understanding when he said, "No one who puts his hand to the plow and looks back is fit for service in the kingdom of God."[1]

OPTICAL SCANNER ∿ Many large stores use bar codes and optical scanners to monitor inventory and keep the checkout line moving. Printed or pasted on virtually every item for sale, bar codes are sequences of vertical lines and spaces that optical scanners instantly translate into product names and prices. In a similar way, our brains affix labels and values to everything we perceive, automatically and without any conscious effort on our part. Modern studies have confirmed that the brain identifies objects or experiences in the first milliseconds of perception, before we are aware of them.

According to Buddhist teaching, every perception, whether of a sight, sound, touch, taste, smell, or thought, is accompanied by a corresponding feeling: pleasant, unpleasant, or neutral. We react to those values in one of three ways—grasping at those that are pleasant, resisting those that are unpleasant, being generally indifferent to those that are neutral—every bit as automatically as the optical scanner reads a bar code. If, however, we train the mind as the Buddha taught to be consciously aware of our sensory perceptions and the feelings associated with them, we can take control of our behavior and thus short-circuit the mind's conditioned reactivity.

ROLLED-UP POSTER ∿ To protect posters from damage, dealers often roll them up and package them in cardboard tubes. While this strategy works well for the posters, it creates a challenge for us when we attempt to unroll and display them. As hard as we try to hold a poster flush against the wall, it rolls right back up again. This struggle parallels the way our own conditioning keeps us "rolled up" in habitual patterns of thinking and behaving. Like the poster, we get used to a certain position—philosophical, political, or religious—and tend to snap right back to it after we stretch briefly to consider other possibilities. Such is commonly the case when we are exposed to new spiritual teachings, or when we attain brief insight into the nature of things, glimpses of something we could never grasp before: once the excitement of the breakthrough subsides, we revert to our old habits, to what we know. It can take years of practice to stabilize new ways of seeing.

RUSSIAN NESTING DOLLS ∼ Russian nesting dolls, long popular as souvenirs from that country, are hollow wooden figures carved in graduated sizes, so that one fits inside another. Children watch with amusement and wonder as each figure opens up to reveal another, even smaller one underneath. So it is with our knowledge of the way things are. Each time we grow confident in our understandings, some new scientific discovery shocks us out of our complacency. In the face of life's unfolding pageant of change, the only tenable position is the recognition that all human truths are soon replaced by new versions that make the same impressive claims the old ones once did. We live in a universe of incomprehensible dimensions; our perceivable domain of existence ranges from the hundreds of millionths of an inch used to measure the nuclei of cells to the light-years that gauge the vast distances of the cosmos. And who is to say that the dimensions of reality are fixed or the limits of human potential are predetermined? With the development of new instrumentation, from the electron microscope to the Hubble telescope, we are able to probe ever more distant frontiers. We do not know what we do not know.

E arlier in this book, I talked about the danger of taking the map for the territory—of forgetting that what we experience as real is actually conceptual and subjective. As we've seen, the practical value of knowledge for our lives may be neutralized if we assign that kind of reality to the fragmentation and division inherent in our conceptual maps. Ultimately, the wisdom, peace of mind, and freedom we yearn for will forever remain beyond our reach.

In the last century, though, knowledge and our means of attaining it have been seriously brought into question. The importance of the subject in the exploration of any phenomenon was established with the "participatory observer" paradigm of quantum physics. The role of this subjectivity in the determination of what we experience as real, along with the cultural relativity of worldviews, was to become the central theme of the entire postmodern movement. The traditional dualistic division of subject and object has been challenged, and, by implication, the entire framework within which we make sense out of what is. And the subjective nature of what is "out there," now taken as a given in disciplines from literary criticism to international relations, is consonant with the esoteric teachings that have pointed to the same truth for millennia.

The nature of human spiritual endeavor varies widely across cultures and eras, but it is safe to assume that in every time and place there have been those who have explored their religious questions and expressed their religious feelings in ways that ran counter to the dualistic divisions of inherited doctrine. In early times, such individuals were often recognized as shamans, prophets, or sages, and the members of their communities looked to them for guidance—especially where no single religion dominated and there was less pressure to conform. In India, a country with an extraordinary diversity of spiritual expression, individual exploration of the Divine continues to flourish. Those who seek their own truth, often in unusual or exotic ways, are known as *sadhus* or holy men and are tolerated, supported, or even revered by those around them.

In Europe, the dominance of doctrine began to wane in the sixteenth century with the onset of the Age of Reason. Reacting to centuries of superstition and the dogmatic rule of the Church, and inspired by the earlier courage of Galileo and Newton, people felt growing disaffection with divine law and revelation as the primary sources for human knowledge. The thinkers of the day grew increasingly bold in their efforts to unravel the mysteries of the world around them.

As literacy spread, those for whom conventional religious formulae failed to resonate had more places to look for answers to life's deepest issues. The most common alternative avenues depended on the use of reason and the accumulated knowledge of the past. Some seekers made this their only approach, and critical analysis and skepticism typically guided the choices they made.

Reason and knowledge play a crucial role, of course, even on the paths of those who look inward for spiritual understanding. For many, it's the wisdom of past masters that kindles their yearning for truth and starts them on the long and arduous investigation of their inner lives. Often the first step in this journey is the selection of a suitable teacher, which requires some analysis and critical judgment to evaluate his or her character and clarity.

Then there are the techniques used in the various traditions of inner exploration, which seekers must also master in order to navigate the realm that has remained unknown to so many. Some forms of meditation require years of practice to hone one's concentration and skill—a longer and more intense preparation than that required for an advanced degree in science or medicine. In most traditions, teachers closely examine both students' methods and their understanding of their interior experiences in order to guide them in the proper direction. And while introspective spiritual approaches usually preclude the kinds of controls you might find in a science experiment, the results (intuitive insights) are still scrutinized and verified by others who have gone before—typically in a private interview. Those who practice alone may have true insights, but it can be difficult for the uninitiated to distinguish them from novel and creative means of expression, such as the writing of James Joyce or the art of Robert Rauschenberg. Both produced bold, unconventional breakthroughs in their respective fields but still remained firmly in the world of thought and knowledge. Such creativity revises our maps, while spiritual insight works to remove them.

Still, there comes a point on the spiritual path when everything we have learned comes into question. Just as we have to pursue the materialistic dream to discover its emptiness, we must likewise pursue the path of knowledge to discover that there are no answers. As we have seen, our worldview is inherited. Conventional knowledge gives us the information from which our world is constructed, and society nurtures the belief we need to make it real. The conceptual maps we are given function reasonably well when we are seeking answers in the material world, but they fail us when we turn to the mysteries that lie within. There are pointers along the way, but eventually we must leave our maps behind for our journey home.

Only by letting go of the habits of conditioned thought and inherited knowledge can we regain the innocent vision with which we were born, now informed by our more mature reason and intelligence. This is the essential step that Jesus was pointing to when he assured his disciples that they must approach the Divine as children. In the esoteric traditions, all our knowledge is ignorance; it is seen as the most basic obstacle to the unraveling of divine mysteries. Since knowledge is inherently dualistic, based on the discriminative process of thought and language, everything we know is characterized by division and fragmentation. Spiritual truth cannot be realized through these cognitive processes, and all that is learned in this manner must be unlearned in the end.

Over five millennia, the mystics of all ages have sought a different form of knowledge in a direct, intuitive apprehension of our true nature. Ultimately, one who seeks truth must enter the process completely naked of mental constructs. Even the precious techniques, from meditation to mantras, and teachings of practice itself are jettisoned at the end. Rather than memorizing the words of the noble ones who have gone before, we are to experience what they experienced. Rather than desiring spiritual realization—for the very desire divides us from the object of our longing—we are to allow understanding simply to happen, without attempts to manipulate or hasten it. We cannot do without knowledge at the start of the path, but in the end, until we put aside critical judgments and conceptual distinctions, the gateless gate remains forever closed.

5

SELF

Why are you unhappy? Because 99.9 percent
of everything you think, and of everything you do,
is for yourself—and there isn't one.

—*Wei Wu Wei*

The self, or ego, is the only part of us—indeed, the only aspect of life in any form—that experiences itself as separate from everything else. It plays the lead role in the drama of our lives, and it is the favorite hiding place of the Divine, since it's the last place we would think to look! It is as a self that we find our place in the physical world of daily existence. It is as a self that we experience confusion, suffer, and discern that we are lost. It is also as a self that we intuit what is missing in our lives and start on a path toward rediscovery. Lacking connection with a tribe or with nature, links that gave meaning and solace to early humanity, we struggle to understand our isolation and eventually begin our search in earnest.

On the cyclical journey of Exile and Return that we examined in the introduction, it is in the first phase of the cosmic hide-and-seek that we lose track of the Divine through its diffusion into manifestation and multiplicity. In this period of the odyssey of life, the unity of the whole is hidden in the myriad divisions and parts of the virtual world of concepts. And part of this division is the separating out of our individual self as we learn to perceive the concepts that make up the world. For most forms of life, devoid of reflection or self-consciousness, there is simple awareness of what is happening in the moment. In the human being, however, with its extraordinary intellectual ability, there is something else: an awareness of being aware. What is originally infinite and unbounded Awareness, present and inherent in all that is, narrows down into the particular perspective from which each of us sees the world. This creates the appearance of countless separate individuals, each with its own separate consciousness. Life, in effect, puts masks on and forgets its true being in a cosmic game of make-believe.

What we all consider to be our own personal awareness is really the Awareness of Life, contained within the tenacious habits of thought and endless stories that tell us who we are and what is real. In what Eckhart Tolle calls a "monstrous act of reductionism," the vast unity of life as a whole finds itself identified with and bound within the finite personality and perspective of a human being.[1] We behave like people at a masked ball, so obsessed with the beauty of the masks that we forget what lies hidden behind them. But unlike the ball-goers who by custom remove their masks at the end of the dance, we never take ours off, thereby missing the point of the whole affair.

The idea that our separate self simply conceals our innate oneness with the Divine may seem counterintuitive, to say the least. There is clearly little hint of anything exalted in the behavior that characterizes much of human activity. Watching the evening news, with its daily dose of murder and mayhem, drives this point home with extraordinary effectiveness. And there is nothing in the sacred literature of the nondual paths that implies the divinity of the conventionally recognized ego-self. Rather, this self is described in terms of ignorance, a veil of confusion, blinding us to the truth of what is and producing the suffering so characteristic of human existence. The nondual view, by contrast, offers a glimpse of the divine wholeness concealed behind the mask of the separate self.

When times are good, we get comfortable in that mask, complacent and well hidden in the game of hide-and-seek. This is why it is said that success is more dangerous than failure. But when the events of life crowd in with distress and suffering, melancholy surfaces and committed seeking begins. In our quieter moments, we sense our isolation and intuit a wholeness that is unavailable in the circumstances around us.

When we are born, our vision is fresh. The world as we first experience it is undifferentiated and timeless, and we have no real perception of self or other. We can see the magic of life without filters and become totally lost in fascination, one with our surroundings. But then we are educated, and we eat from the Tree of Knowledge. As we are taught language and the lessons of good and evil, our vision becomes restricted. We start to see the world through the dualistic filter of concepts, with the grid of borders and boundaries it superimposes on everything. The holistic wide-angle lens view of our birth is transformed, and our vision refocuses on the sharply defined piecemeal view of reality that makes up our modern culture. Conceptual habits become unconscious assumptions that automatically frame our reality. We live within the confines of a hand-me-down view of the world that everyone around us shares, and we never even suspect the possibility of seeing in another way.

We begin to see ourselves as separate from everything and everyone, and the structure of language itself deepens the delusion even further. Every verb requires a subject, articulated or implied, and personal pronouns are necessary to communicate within the rules of grammar. "I" is not the same as "you," and everything that we say or read or hear reinforces the division. We say *I*, *me*, *my*, and *mine* almost every time we speak.

The process of identification with self is initiated by our parents when they name us and, in effect, tell us who we are. As we grow up, the idea is reinforced and endlessly repeated at every age and in every setting. Whenever we meet new people, for example, from kindergarten to retirement, introductions begin with our names. Likewise, we identify ourselves in nearly every phone conversation we have. As if the enculturation of language were not enough, our sense of identity is further solidified by an extensive paper trail, beginning with our certificates of birth. With each year, more documents accumulate around us: school records, medical histories, credit reports, legal agreements, tax statements—just to name a few. As adults, whether we are making a purchase, visiting the doctor, casting a vote, or doing any number of other common things, we are routinely asked to show proof of who we are. The process goes on and on.

Modern modes of thought strengthen the idea of the isolated self at the deepest levels of our awareness. Science, for example, sets the standard for knowledge in the developed world, and it places great value on empirical objectivity. From science's early beginnings, any connection between subject and object was thought to invalidate whatever results were produced. The self that observes and measures the world must be totally detached from the object being observed, eliminating the possibility of any bias or influence, so as to understand it accurately. And this principle, inherent in the scientific method, has filtered into our understanding of the whole world, our collective view of who and what we are. Any time there is a difference of opinion, no matter how insignificant the subject, someone is likely to invoke objectivity: "Looking at it objectively..." we might say, or "Leaving our personal feelings out of it..." We watch for any prejudice in others' arguments, as well as our own, and are quick to recognize when someone is too close to an issue and therefore unable to divorce his or her personal view from the debate. The idea is that facts, like scientific findings, are most valid when we keep the self sealed off from them.

Accompanying the delusion of self and our perceived separation from everything else is the assumption of personal responsibility, a phenomenon that as far as we can tell is unknown in the vast remainder of the animal kingdom. We first come up against it when we are toddlers with that growing sense of *me*. It is at this point that we begin to be judged *as* good or bad based upon our behavior. As we grow older, whether we get a star on our first-grade spelling test, are voted the most popular in high school, or win Employee of the Month, we typically feel a sense of personal pride and accomplishment. Sooner or later, such judgments from others lead to self-judgments, and this suggests the existence of a division within each of us. Are there two different selves—a self that thinks and acts and a self that observes and judges? Questions like this derive from humankind's unique capacity to be aware of its own awareness: to be both the knower and the known, both the figure and the ground of our being. The same division found in every aspect of our external affairs, self separated from everything else, clearly has a parallel within us as well. This is the reason for our concerns about such concepts as self-control, self-restraint, or self-improvement. It is amusing to think of our dogs or cats doing anything to improve themselves. Their contentment and sense of peace in being just as they are, so apparent in their daily behavior, is the envy of our kind. It offers stark contrast to the torment and regret in which so many people live out their days.

Perceiving this split in our own personal being, we may begin to feel incomplete, inauthentic, and unfulfilled. Some of us experience this as a need for purpose, involvement, personal accomplishment, or material gain. But none of these things can really fill the gap, because they address our conceptual identity rather than our true nature, leaving the hollowness at the core of our being untouched. As we saw in the introduction, the Perennial Philosophy makes clear that the fundamental drive of humanity is to rediscover the wholeness that we intuit as missing, and nondual practices offer a path to get us there.

But realizing the wholeness of our true nature comes at a high price: it asks us to relinquish our conventional image of self, which we can hardly help but hold dear. After all, our selves seem like more than ego-masks to us; they are our thoughts and feelings, our physical body and our distinctive mind, our talents and desires and dreams—in short, everything that makes up the content of our daily life and our inner life. It is as a self that I am writing this book and it is as a self that you are reading it, bringing to it your particular intelligence and unique perspective. So, naturally, our instinct for self-preservation is strong. Once the danger to self is sensed in our practice on the nondual path, or encountered in another of our endeavors to unravel the mystery inherent in life, many of us turn away. Our ego, in which we have masqueraded so long, seems too dear a price to pay.

Consequently, with our efforts deflected, we seek fulfillment by enhancing and embellishing the familiar character of the ego, rather than transcending it. As Ken Wilber explains in his book *The Atman Project*, we distort the correct intuition that "one is all" into an ego-centric desire to possess everything. Instead of realizing timelessness, we try to live forever. Rather than being everything, we aspire to have everything. In lieu of being one with God, we try to play God.[2]

These substitutes that Wilber describes are easily recognized in modern society. Millions of people are obsessed with getting ahead, and being number one is many people's primary goal in life. We sense competition with others and feel a need to stand out. We all have stories that accentuate the singular nature of our person, and we take these dramas seriously. We chase fame, power, and wealth relentlessly, with insatiable appetites for something fame and power and wealth can never deliver, forever unable to fill the void we sense within. In the Buddhist tradition, the metaphorical image for this drive is the *hungry ghost*, commonly pictured with a huge belly and a tiny mouth, unable to eat fast enough to ever be satisfied. Even in religious life, we can fall victim to self-aggrandizement, a problem all too apparent in the lives of some prominent television evangelists of our day. Any seemingly significant purpose or cause—even our search for meaning itself—can be seized by the ego as a ploy to be bigger and more important. But no matter how we attempt to achieve satisfaction or to demonstrate mastery, over all, our efforts are in vain. We yearn for the infinite, but even incredible fortunes and worldwide fame perpetually fall short. They are weak simulacra for our true nature.

~

IMAGES OF SELF

FLAME ~ We all know what fire is: the light, heat, and flames produced by something that is burning. We can picture a fire in our imagination with no difficulty. We also know what flames look like; we have watched their flickering movements and colors around the burning logs in a campfire or on a hearth. A flame is defined as a glowing body of burning gas. While the difference between flames and fire can be found in any dictionary, in our actual experience the distinction between the two is difficult to detect. We cannot separate in life what is so easily divided in words. The same is true with our sense of self. When we try to identify our deepest self by eliminating all the nonessential elements, it is elusive. Is there one who feels in the absence of feelings or who thinks in the absence of thoughts? When we dream, is there a dreamer, or is the one who is dreaming only found within the dream? When we first encounter such questions, they seem rhetorical. But they lie at the core of nondual spirituality and, if seriously investigated, lead us directly to the paradoxical nature of our being. It gradually dawns on us that it is as impossible to separate our self from what we are experiencing as it is to separate a flame from the fire.

CLOCK ~ It is hard to imagine how we would make it through our days if we did not have access to clocks and the schedules they keep us on. But the system of telling time, which we all take for granted, is nothing more than an agreed-upon method of classifying and dividing into intervals the daily and seasonal cycles of the earth's relationship to the sun. It is an arbitrary convention, as imaginary as the designations of equator, latitude, and longitude. The ego is exactly the same kind of convention. We couldn't live without an identity; social security numbers, driver's licenses, professional credentials, passports, and the like are necessities for anyone trying to navigate life in modern society. Nonetheless, spiritual growth requires that we understand the arbitrary nature of this phenomenon we call the self. We can use it for convenience and for the everyday social interchange of modern life, but we must remember that it is just a convention, no more real than the concept of midnight or noon.

PRISON CELL ~ Someone who is incarcerated for many years may keep pictures in his or her cell that are cheerful and reminiscent of the outside world. Photographs of old friends and lovers, mountains or open fields, may evoke sensations no longer available in any other way. But regardless of how the physical environment is manipulated, it cannot set the prisoner free. This image points to the futility of trying to escape our discontent by redecorating the ego. People who feel boxed in by life may change the furniture, buy new cars, or move into bigger houses. They may enroll in acting classes, learn judo, or take public-speaking courses to dress up the images they project to others. Such cosmetics for the ego have little effect on the real issue, though. Just as new decorations in a jail cell leave the reality of imprisonment unchanged, the problems inherent in the human condition cannot be remedied with self-improvement activities. We are locked inside a conceptual identity that precludes the freedom that is our birthright. Only by realizing our true nature will we get out of this prison.

RORSCHACH TEST ∽ You may be familiar with the Rorschach test, which is sometimes used in psychological evaluations. It uses abstract black images, like inkblots, starkly silhouetted against a plain background. The tester asks the client to describe what he or she sees in each image; the answers are thought to be useful diagnostically. A person who is peaceful and well adjusted will probably see something pleasant and nonthreatening. Someone filled with anger or emotionally disturbed, on the other hand, is apt to find violent scenes in the figure. The nature of the reality we experience every day is like a Rorschach response—a function of a very similar relationship between the world we perceive and the way we perceive it. The self is a reference point, a set of hopes, fears, and expectations based on our unique life history and conditioning. This determines what we notice, value, and reject. The observer is not separate from what is observed, but participates in shaping what is seen.

CLOUDS AND SKY ∽ The relationship between the self and the vast being that it sometimes obscures can be compared to the way clouds can block our view of the sky. The clouds represent the egos we parade through life: some are large and impressive, others meek or insignificant. Some have beautiful forms that capture our interest, and others flaunt the power of their dark, threatening thunder. Behind the play of these numberless, ever-changing forms lies a sky forever the same. This unchanging presence symbolizes the Absolute, the truth behind all phenomena, and we can see it clearly only when the clouds have drifted away. With us it is no different. Only when our concepts of what we are dissolve in realization, such as we may find in the practiced attention of meditation, can we see the truth so long obscured.

SURF ～ For many of us, walking along the beach is a favorite activity. When we arrive at the shore for our vacation or weekend getaway, most often the first thing we do is walk down to the water, take our shoes off, and test the water temperature. Then we walk along the edge of the surf, holding our pants legs or skirts up to keep them from getting wet. When a wave suddenly comes up higher than the rest, we quickly retreat a step or two up the sand. This common experience sheds light on our approach to the Divine. When we advance in our practice and touch upon the vulnerability of our egos, it is natural to pull back to protect our old sense of self. If we wish to realize the deepest insights of spiritual maturity, we must take off the ego that has covered us up for so long and dive naked into the refreshing waters of the Divine.

CLAY POT ～ The ubiquitous clay pot has been used since early times to explain the self to students of life. Its clay is the memories that make up the entity we believe ourselves to be. Our names, our parents, our childhoods, and our early years at school are mixed with the recollections of our more recent life experiences to create a rich medium to work with. Add the many beliefs, expectations, and fears everyone has, and you have the makings of an effective ego. In the hands of a capable potter, in this case the mind, the clay is skillfully worked and molded into the individual self we believe we are. We use it as a vessel to hold the moments of each new day, giving them context and meaning. But as the fragile clay pot is inevitably dropped and broken into pieces, there is a climactic point when the idea of self is fractured by insight as we suddenly understand our real nature. While some attempt may be made to glue the pot back into its original form, the shattered delusion of the ego will never again hold water.

~

We are born of two mothers, given existence in two radically different ways. Our actual mother is life, and we are conceived in the human womb and nursed with the milk of wholeness. Our virtual mother is language; we are conceived in the thoughts and words of our people and nursed at the breast of our cultural and intellectual heritage. Ever after, we struggle with the conflicts and confusion that have plagued us all since our species learned to divide up what is and give names to its separate parts. The key to our spiritual dilemma is not to find God, but to find our true Self—to solve the riddle of our conflicted existence and to return to wholeness.

While the limitations and problems of our concept of self are manifold, this is not to say that personality has little value or must be eliminated. The importance of a *healthy* ego has been widely recognized for many years, and the difficulties that prevail in its absence are well known. Teacher-training programs, for example, have long emphasized the importance of being positive with students, even while correcting mistakes they make in class. A fundamental goal in the educational profession is to strengthen the concepts children have of themselves, for this is recognized as a significant factor in effective learning and social development. Business is finding this out as well, and many companies have replaced punitive kinds of motivation with positive ones.

For our sacred journey, the benefits of a healthy ego are even more important. In the authentic exploration of nondual spirituality, a strong sense of self is essential in order to successfully negotiate the formidable obstacles that we will encounter. Such obstacles have been delineated in the sacred writings of all cultures, and have been graphically represented in human mythology as dragons and demons that must be overcome.

To cross the threshold of transformation and enter the realm of the unknown can be terrifying. With one glimpse of the unconditioned, our sense of reality becomes ambiguous, the certainties of tradition are shaken, and the fear of nonexistence grows strong. Perseverance, courage, and intelligence are indispensable for safe passage beyond what appears at first to be our demise. The ego doesn't actually die or disappear in that journey. We continue to exist in the conventional sense we always have, but no longer *identify* with it. Nothing is changed but our understanding of what is real. We can now act from the context of transcendent wisdom, while continuing to manifest in the limited, immanent form of our old self—experiencing life with the same spirit reflected in Jesus's direction to be in this world but not of it.

In the Buddhist tradition, a question that teachers often pose to students is: "What is your original face before your grandparents were born?" This koan, or paradoxical riddle of sorts, insinuates a reality far deeper than the surface characteristics with which most people are preoccupied. It points past the common obsession with our bodies and the extraordinary lengths to which we go to improve how we look. The enigma likewise bypasses everything we have learned, the personality we have developed, all the wealth we have amassed, and the many accomplishments we so eagerly show off. The perceived content of our lives is given no quarter in this question, and for that reason its meaning is beyond the reach of most who try to fathom it. But once our personal stories are dropped and our perceived importance forgotten, we can see that this ancient query is directing us to what we are, to what is—to life itself.

6

ATTACHMENT

When the heart grieves for what is lost,
the spirit rejoices over what is left.

—Sufi saying

At our most basic, we humans are reactive creatures. The human body is endowed with a nervous system in which sensory receptors respond to stimuli in the environment. We react instinctively to our contact with the world according to the pleasant, unpleasant, or neutral sensations elicited by each new stimulus. As these feelings arise, we unconsciously cling to experiences we find agreeable and push away those we find disagreeable.

All forms of life have some such stimulus/response system, essential for the survival of the species at the most basic level—seeking food, avoiding pain. But as humans, we are subject to stimuli that affect us at the level of our moods, minds, and hearts. At the mercy of our instincts, we are pulled back and forth between the poles of pleasure and pain, gain and loss, and praise and blame. We can be cheerful about an improving sinus infection one minute and have our spirits completely turned around the next by a malfunctioning computer. Saving money at a wonderful sale can excite us, only to have our mood plummet when the car runs out of gas. We might feel elated by a compliment from a coworker, then deflated by criticism from a supervisor.

For humankind, this biological mechanism has spiritual implications as well. The Buddha taught that craving and aversion are the root causes of suffering. We become attached to those things we find pleasant, and we suffer when we cannot have or hold on to them. Likewise, we suffer when we cannot avoid experiences or sensations we find to be unpleasant. We struggle perpetually to have things be other than the way they are. Because we are taught to see the world dualistically, with fixed boundaries everywhere, we have no awareness of the unity of life; we attempt to attain the good while avoiding the bad, but our obsessive drive to have one without the other proves forever beyond our reach. As we saw in the chapter on duality, ceaseless change and alternating fortune are the very nature of life. To become attached to the way things are, or the way we think they should be, is to guarantee disappointment and emotional turmoil. It is with this in mind that the teachings of nonattachment must be seen—as a wise and healthy relationship with the way things are, not an aloof, uncaring, or cynical posture toward life. This becomes clear when we read about the sages from the various nondual spiritual traditions and find their lives filled with compassion, generosity, wisdom, and equanimity.

Our consumer culture promotes a particular form of attachment: a craving for material things that contains the promise of a deeper fulfillment. It is normal for people to desire the things they need, and to store provisions for an uncertain future is simply our survival instinct doing its natural work, but the intrusive presence of advertising systematically amplifies our inherent attraction for such material goods. We are told that they will enhance who we are and encouraged to think ourselves incomplete without them. The message is always the same: we are what we drive, what we wear, or what we have, and clearly we need and deserve more of everything.

Fulfillment and completion, the ads tell us over and over, lie in the external world. The effectiveness of these messages is reflected in the contagion of fads and the rush to get the newest gizmo. We are convinced of the importance of the treasures displayed in every store window, and we can dream away our lives wistfully surveying what we

are missing. Barbara Kruger, an American conceptual artist, provoca-
tively expresses our modern attachment to "more" in a photographic
collage entitled *I Shop, Therefore I Am*. Madonna conveys the same
idea somewhat differently when she sings of being a material girl in
a material world. No matter the mode or medium, few of us would
deny the consumerism of modern society to which both Kruger and
Madonna allude.

A worldwide network of production and commerce churns out an
incomprehensible volume of new products, and yet the appetite of con-
sumers seems to remain insatiable. People pursue each new acquisition
as if it will fill an inner void, yet they cannot truly find satisfaction that
way, because they are looking in the wrong place. Just as a whale could
never be filled on the diet of a minnow, even if it believed itself to be
one, we can never find fulfillment through the accumulation of material wealth. Though we mistakenly identify ourselves with our physical
body and mind, and adapt in this way to our fragmented world of duality, the wholeness of our true nature can never be found in externals.

Our attachments to people may seem, at first glance, to have less
to do with externals and more to do with our true nature, and yet they
can be even more problematic. We often mistake attachment for love,
and in such cases, when the dynamics of material possession generalize
to our relationships, the effect can be devastating. What we typically
mean when we declare our love for someone is that we are attached to
the good feelings we get in his or her company. To make matters worse,
our craving is often for the way things *used* to be, the way our partner
or spouse looked and acted when we were dating or first married.

This attachment is so unyielding because it is based on an *idea* to
which we hold tightly and has little relevance to the ceaseless change of
what is. Marriage is an abstract noun, a concept, a set of legal arrangements and personal expectations, but life with another person begins
anew each morning. The two people living together today are very different from the individuals who committed to each other years earlier.
To insist that their partners remain the way they were before, or to
pressure them to conform to an ideal held in the mind, is to destroy

the living magic of sharing daily experience as it unfolds in its always unpredictable way. The emotional turmoil associated with such controlling attitudes can have a smothering effect on the recipients. We see this play out over and over in the lives of those around us, all too often leading to guilt, resentment, infidelity, or divorce. Modern society is deeply lonely because we are unwittingly controlled by our attachments and relate to each other as objects of craving or aversion rather than living, changing human beings.

Our cherished opinions and beliefs may be the most difficult attachments to relinquish—more closely held even than our relationships with others—and the vigor with which we react to those who think or believe differently clearly reflects their strength. Our positions on everything from politics to global warming to the best vacation spots tend to be fixed and entrenched, even when the subject is something we might readily admit to be trivial. Some are attachments established early in life and others are recent additions, but if we listed them, there would likely be as many things we love to hate as things we hold dear. When we argue about such issues, our need to be right can be so strong that it blinds us to facts, even convincing ones, that contradict our position. It can also make us vulnerable to the most painful of assaults; ridicule directed at our physique may be hurtful and upsetting, but comments that impugn our ability to think are much more threatening to our sense of self, whose power we saw in the last chapter. The identification with our mind is so deep that we go to great lengths to prove our point or have the last word.

Since the earliest times of our species, the fight-or-flight syndrome has been elicited by physical danger. In the presence of a perceived threat, our sympathetic nervous system primes the body for the intense activity needed for either defense or escape: adrenaline courses through our bodies, the pupils of the eyes dilate, the action of heart and lungs accelerates, blood flow to our muscles increases, and so forth. These simultaneous physical responses enhance our physical abilities and may indeed save our lives when the situation warrants. Today, unfortunately, the same reactions that might once have successfully parried the claws and fangs of a wild animal are frequently triggered by provocations that represent no such danger—threats to our attachments rather than to our physical survival. We have all seen situations in which someone reacts to a remark or insult as if it were a life-threatening event. When flare-ups like this become a pattern, they can do more harm than they prevent, causing a multitude of problems in our relationships and our health. Whereas such instinctive responses occurred only in life-threatening situations for our early predecessors, they kick in with regularity in the pressured lives of millions today.

Spiritual traditions such as Buddhism teach the dangers of attachment and offer precepts and practices that counteract it. The key to understanding attachments, and the reason for their prominence in the nondual teachings, is the recognition that letting go is a necessary prelude to liberation. But it's worth noting that spiritual matters are, ironically, where some of our deepest attachments are anchored. We lose our freedom when we are shackled, no matter the type of restraint. When bound even by the golden chain of our cherished spiritual beliefs, we lose our freedom and become prisoners of our own minds. Deeply entrenched in our beliefs, we can become so identified with certain views that we reject all divergent perspectives. When we become so certain about our own understanding, we close the door to true insights. It is for this reason that Thich Nhat Hanh says that, ultimately, "all views are wrong views."[1]

❧

IMAGES OF ATTACHMENT

TRAP ❧ In Southeast Asia, villagers employ a simple device to catch wild monkeys. They make a hole in an empty coconut shell, just big enough for a monkey to get its hand through. Then they fill the shell with candy and secure it to a tree. Eventually one of the curious animals is attracted to the smell of the sweets and, reaching its small hand inside, eagerly grabs the tantalizing prize. But when the monkey tries to pull its hand out of the coconut shell, it cannot—the hand grasping the loot is too large to pass back through the hole. When its captor appears, the monkey could easily escape simply by releasing its hold on the candy; but, paralyzed by desire, it cannot. Such a tableau offers a classic parallel to our human inability to let go. Like the monkey, when we allow our desires and attachments to dictate our behaviors, we too lose our freedom. Unable to let go, we are trapped by our own desires.

BAGGAGE ∼ It is common knowledge that traveling with excessive baggage can be burdensome. Those who learn to travel light have less to worry about and often enjoy their trips more. Few people, however, generalize this lesson to the rest of their lives. Many people become so encumbered with possessions that managing them all can be overwhelming. If one of the dozens of products we purchase malfunctions, we may have trouble simply finding the receipt to return it. When the things we own have significant monetary value, security systems and multiple insurance policies come into play. Maintenance is an additional and ongoing concern, as any owner of a home or car will attest. The more we have, the worse it gets, until we may feel ourselves virtually enslaved by our possessions. Sages are consistent in their admonition to travel lightly on the journey through life: they know that freedom from material distractions frees the traveler to attend to what is most important. As Socrates said, "Those who want the fewest things are nearest to the Gods."

MONOPOLY ∼ The popular board game *Monopoly* engages us in a process of buying and selling real estate with the goal of acquiring more property than the other players. Depending on a combination of luck and shrewdness, we sometimes amass a fortune and establish control of the board. Other times we watch our money disappear. In those times of financial calamity, the game is not much fun to play, and we get irritated with those who gloat over our misfortune. But suddenly we remind ourselves that it is all a game and we really do not owe anything to anyone. All our worries and disappointments vanish in the realization, and we can smile and even be amused at our situation. This common experience sheds light on the effect of letting go of our attachments and all the concerns that go with them. When our understanding of the dynamics of attachment begins to mature, we see life in a very different way and can begin to look at our circumstances without clinging or fear of loss. Eventually we realize that in the truest sense human existence is a kind of make-believe, or *lila*, as the Hindus call it, just as imaginary as the games we play for fun.

PICKPOCKET ⁓ There is a traditional saying that when a pickpocket meets a saint, he sees only his pockets! This is a humorous image that makes a very important point about attachments. What we are attached to determines the world in which we live. When we go to the mall, the things we look at are those we have an interest in. One person may see only the bookstores, while another is attracted to the sporting-goods outlet. A child will look for the toy stores and his grandfather will see only the bench. Our attachments direct our attention. When someone in love confesses that he or she only has eyes for you, in a very real sense it is probably true. As we mature spiritually and start to let go of some of our habitual cravings and aversions, our world begins to expand. We notice more around us and see with eyes less bound by conditioning. It is with such vision that we are more likely to catch a glimpse of the world of nonattachment heralded by mystics for thousands of years.

SCULPTOR ⁓ A sculptor working with wood or stone will typically chip away at the surface to gradually reveal his vision. As the artist carefully removes material from different areas of the surface, the nondescript block of stone is slowly pared down into the intended image, as if that were its true form all along. In spiritual practice, there is a process of transformation that likewise steadily unfolds. As we sit in meditation, study mystical teachings, or listen to the words of a teacher, we begin to loosen the grip of the multitude of attachments with which we so strongly identify. In time, we may chip away at our deeply held cravings and aversions and, just like the sculptor, slowly begin to reveal the beauty and truth that lies hidden beneath.

LOTUS FLOWER ～ The lotus is a timeless metaphor used in the East to symbolize a life free of attachments. Growing in mud and surrounded on all sides by the murky waters of the pond, it remains clean and dry with its beautiful white bloom untouched. Similarly, those who attain spiritual maturity can live in the material world without becoming encumbered by attachments and the suffering they bring. The lotus suggests that it is possible to let go of attachments while continuing to live in the midst of the temptations that abound in human existence. It does not require a retreat to a mountain cave or monastic life. There are untold numbers of individuals who fully engage in life without succumbing to the pull of attachment.

In our contemporary world, with its extraordinary advances in technology, the speed with which things change is stunning. Our children cannot remember a time without computers, digital cameras, or cell phones, while fewer and fewer adults have much recollection of things like black-and-white television sets, record players, or rotary phones. The cars of our youth, of which we were once so proud, offer a quaint contrast to the computerized vehicles of today. We accept astronauts living aboard the International Space Station as a matter of course, and organ transplants are now commonplace. Those of us in the middle or latter part of our lives reminisce about the comparatively simple times of our childhood, remembering toys far less sophisticated than the games and gadgets that fascinate our offspring. The reality of change is all around us, and its inexorable progress threatens everything to which we are attached. Clinging to the old ways of doing things and protecting the treasured ties of our past is an enterprise doomed to failure.

With aging come daily lessons in letting go, though most of us are slow learners. For many, the most alarming aspect of change is readily apparent when we look in the mirror each morning. It has been said that we die on the installment plan, continually noticing more wrinkles and less hair despite our most strenuous efforts to retard their advance. With the passing years, we also commonly experience a downsizing of possessions and activities. Whereas in the first half of life we focus on what we don't yet have, in the second we attend to what we haven't yet lost. Friends die, memories fade, and with retirement many relinquish a major aspect of their identity—their careers. Despite the obvious theme that emerges in this process, people still may fail to understand that external possessions and accomplishments have no lasting importance and nothing to do with their true being. Many hold on to all they can until the very end, relinquishing their attachments only when their wills are read *post mortem*.

Lama Surya Das, in his book *Letting Go of the Person You Used to Be*, recommends that people keep a journal and name their losses. Recognizing the common inclination to reject or repress such realities, and consequently to miss the opportunities for healing and inner reconciliation that they offer, Surya Das suggests we record the attachments that hurt us the most to lose. This exercise is not meant to encourage us to dwell on the painful aspects of life; rather, it is designed to help us examine and face our losses in a manner conducive to spiritual growth. When we contemplate the loss of these cherished attachments and review the aftermath of each of these painful events, we open the door to a new relationship with change. Looking back in this way at the loss of a spouse or partner, for example, can reveal unresolved feelings, lessons learned, or healing that has already occurred. It is at this point that we can begin to understand the nature and value of the mystical teachings on nonattachment.

The practice of nonattachment is not the same as "detachment"; it does not suggest that we avoid having preferences, nor does it require that we renounce all our possessions or the aspects of daily life we enjoy. Instead, it points the way for changing our *relationship* to our experiences.

When we no longer grasp or resist the various aspects of our lives, our eyes are opened to the magic of what is. We realize that our efforts to control the ceaseless flow of life are as futile as trying to hold a best-loved note in a musical composition in order to enjoy it more fully, only to realize that its very transience is an essential element in its beauty. The untiring human determination to control things, to get and keep what is pleasant and avoid or eliminate all that is not, flies in the face of reality. We have no control over the way life unfolds. By engaging in hopeless attempts, we sacrifice the very peace we wish so deeply to attain.

Accepting the natural unfolding of life, we learn to be present with what is, to let go of our innumerable agendas, and to relinquish our determination that life conform to our will. Changing our relationship to the attachments we accumulate in life, and modifying the habits of resistance we meet in the process, are formidable challenges, but the insight we gain in the effort can be transformative. When we accept life as it is, with an open gentle spirit, we are able to taste what Pema Chödrön calls "the wisdom of no escape."

KARMA

**Although my view is higher than the sky,
my conduct regarding cause and effect is as
meticulous and finely sifted as barley flour.**

—Padmasambhava

Karma has insinuated itself thoroughly into the modern vernacular in recent years. "It's good karma," you may hear someone say, as reason for a friend's recent successes. In the media as well as in private conversation, comments like "You reap what you sow" or "What goes around comes around" have become commonplace. Yet many people who use the concept of karma casually have no more than a superficial understanding of its true nature. Some associate it with a relentless system of cosmic retribution for past transgressions, while for others it is linked to the social injustice of the Hindu caste system, in which suffering is blamed on misdeeds in past lives and a better life depends on faithful acceptance of present circumstances. Some use the term in the context of another person's suffering, insinuating blame and judgment: "So-and-So must have bad karma." But these oversimplified views of karma reflect none of its real subtlety and nuance. The popular portrayal of this ancient principle as a rigid, mechanical system of reward and punishment obscures the real insights that it holds for those who fathom its truth.

Karma is a Sanskrit word meaning action or deed, and in both Hindu and Buddhist teachings on the subject, it is our actions that are believed to determine our destiny. Karma, in its truest sense, is predicated on the principle of interconnectivity and the interdependence of all existence. It is a self-balancing, self-regulating law of causality according to which every action, whether of thought, word, or deed, exacts a consequence. Indeed, we can see why it is often compared to Isaac Newton's Third Law of Motion: for every action there is an equal and opposite reaction. Karma shares the same kind of universality that we associate with such laws of physics.

It does not, however, imply a lockstep, deterministic system of forces such as those that play out between energy and matter. Operating on physical, mental, and spiritual levels, the multidimensional back-and-forth flow is constantly responding to input from myriad sources that modify the manner in which it unfolds in the present. The endless play of karmic dynamics is kept in equilibrium by the unceasing adjustments of the whole; everything does everything. In addition to physical laws, we must remember the role of consciousness, intention, and the organic flow of life. As we learn from experience, and our understanding of life grows more discerning, our motives change, as do the unfathomable workings of karma itself.

Nature seeks a balance, and disparity has a limited shelf life. As Ralph Waldo Emerson put it, "The dice of God are always loaded. The world looks like a multiplication-table, or a mathematical equation, which, turn it how you will, balances itself."[1] The *Tao Te Ching* expresses the same truth: "The Tao of Heaven / Is like bending a bow / Lower that which is high / Raise that which is low / Reduce that which has excess / Add to that which is lacking."[2]

We struggle with the consequences of karma in one way or another every day. Those of us who strive to lose weight, for example, are always in search of an effective diet (or sometimes a quick fix), but we often fail to control our ill-advised eating habits. The proliferation of fast-food establishments and our culture's legion inducements to unhealthy eating have no doubt contributed to the problem, but most of us know the foods we should and should not eat. When we plan our meals wisely, the outcome—healthy weight loss or maintenance—is predictable, as are the consequences when our resolve weakens. While some people have health problems that complicate this equation, for most of us, a careful and determined effort to eat skillfully each day can produce physical effects that become ever more apparent.

Another common example of everyday karma is found in the modern use of credit cards. Millions of us, by choice or necessity, live on credit. Banks, as a rule, are eager to increase their lucrative business of lending money, and so they readily extend credit to almost anyone who has an income. People who use credit cards as a quick and easy means to get the things they need or desire sometimes face consequences they have not adequately considered. The shopping frenzy that precedes the Christmas holidays is notorious for encouraging excess, and the mountains of debt that overextended shoppers face in January can be overwhelming. Credit arrangements allow us to buy now and pay later, but ultimately the bill for unskillful choices always comes due.

The karmic results of our eating and spending habits are fairly apparent, but not all of our behavior translates so obviously into consequences. The effects of our actions in life are often delayed; some might not even show up in this lifetime, and thus we may find innocent people suffering severe misfortune or individuals of great cruelty enjoying seemingly undue prosperity. As Aldous Huxley declared, "God is not mocked, but also let us remember, He is not understood."[3] Karma's unfolding is often perplexing from our limited perspective; though we can sometimes discern the apparent effects of earlier years on our situation today, and anticipate consequences that may result from our conduct today, it is guesswork.

Still, the momentum of our actions continues uninterrupted, like the ripples from a pebble dropped in a pond. Long after the stone has disappeared, the disruption spreads across the surface in every direction, leaving no part untouched. This intricate, interlacing pattern of movement continues unceasingly until the energy is fully expended and the pond returns to quiescence. Similarly, human behavior disturbs the harmony of the whole and its repercussions continue until equilibrium is restored.

Such karmic repercussions are all too clearly illustrated in the devastating environmental problems we face today. The industrialized world has acted with careless disregard for the well-being and integrity of our planet over the better part of a century, and global warming, acid rain, polluted waters, and deforested landscapes are but a few of the effects that this behavior has caused. Such habits are difficult to correct, given our self-serving orientation and our attachment to our accustomed way of living; the far-reaching action required to resolve the ecological crisis will tax our courage and commitment. The same kind of challenge confronts us personally when we try to change our habitual behavior in other domains of our lives. Karma develops a momentum that is difficult to reverse.

The play of karma unfolds among nations as well, as they too act from the same delusion of separateness. Like the egocentric motivation that propels the unskillful actions of individuals, patriotic fervor or righteous indignation can lead to collective actions that are inharmonious with the whole. One country acting against another does harm not only in terms of the destructive impact on its enemy, but also in the form of negative karma for itself. At the same time, given the interconnected nature of the universe, the effects of conflict in one region are felt throughout the world. The Buddha made very clear that as like creates like, so violence produces more violence. Only when such unskillful actions are met with the opposite kind of behavior is the cycle broken.

Reversing the momentum of human behavior at any level is never easy, but some individuals of remarkable courage give hope to all those who seek skillful solutions to injustice. Mahatma Gandhi gave the world a stunning example of the possibilities that karma offers each of us to change the direction of our lives: against the most powerful colonial empire of the world at that time, his courage and vision brought about a bold new direction for the resolution of human conflict and established nonviolence as the path that India would follow in winning its independence. Martin Luther King, Jr., did likewise when he led the fight against injustice in America's civil rights movement, and Thich Nhat Hanh exemplified nonviolent action through his grassroots relief program for villagers caught in the middle of the Vietnam War. The Dalai Lama's steady opposition to the Chinese oppression of Tibet, and Myanmar dissident Aung San Suu Kyi's unshaken resistance to repression in her country, offer equally inspiring examples today.

Virtually every spiritual tradition incorporates the karmic paradigm in one form or another to encourage good behavior and keep the faithful in line. While different faiths espouse different codes of morality and virtue, and their system of rewards and punishments likewise vary, they all envision some kind of ultimate justice that promises significant consequences for human behavior. In the exoteric traditions, virtuous living and faithful adherence to the holy teachings may lead one to prosperity in this life and salvation, nirvana, eternal life, or propitious rebirth after death. In contrast, evildoers may expect to face illness and misfortune in coming years, followed by an undesirable rebirth or everlasting damnation beyond this life. In many religions, the consequences of either merit or transgression may be passed down to future generations, yielding, respectively, abundant blessings or a harvest of distress for one's progeny.

In esoteric forms of spirituality, behavior is similarly understood to have consequences, but the motivation that spurs devotees is of a very different sort: not a desire for some form of afterlife redemption, but the yearning to return to wholeness. The ultimate purpose of mysticism is to discover one's true nature; to do so, we are obliged to remove any obstructions that retard spiritual maturation, and our transgressions place just such obstacles in our path. To paraphrase Gandhi, we will fail to find the truth we are looking for if the slightest impulse to violence informs our actions. He insisted that life is an indivisible whole and people doing wrong in one aspect of life cannot expect to do right in another. When we are engaged in competitive, selfish, and unethical behavior, we are not in alignment with the way things are. Blinded by our actions and dissipating our energies through competition and intrigue, we let our spiritual vision become hopelessly obscured.

Though the details vary from one culture to another, the guidance of nondual traditions in this area of morality and virtue has the same goal: to conserve our energy and shield our concentration from the centrifugal effect of selfish behavior. It is in this context that karma plays a central role, guiding each practitioner through the insistent teachings of cause and effect to develop the virtuous behavior that characterizes spiritual maturity.

When we are acting from the delusion of self, our motives are not in concert with the rest of creation. Blinded by desire, we in effect act "alone" against the whole, and frustration and suffering inevitably result. No other form of life attempts such foolish behavior: the myth of separation is unique to human beings. There is no intention to be found in the organic unity of nature, nor does it pursue objectives or have a purpose. Humans have long recognized a profound difference between nature's effortless harmony and their own frenetic efforts to arrange life according to their personal designs. Of course, this does not mean that intentional behavior must be avoided. The key is to recognize what is happening and act mindfully from that understanding.

Over two thousand years ago, in his *Yoga Sutras*, Indian sage Patanjali made clear that each one of us has memory traces or inclinations that are vestiges from previous thoughts or behavior, but that we can choose whether to act on them or not. By our present actions, we strengthen or negate these karmic dispositions and determine how we progress on the path to spiritual understanding. Author Joseph Goldstein, cofounder of the Insight Meditation Society, has compared this process to that of an artist in the process of creating a painting. Envisioning our lives as the canvas, he sees us fashioning our own image by choosing from a palette containing either love, generosity, and wisdom, or greed, hatred, and delusion. With clear comprehension of the intentions that precede each action, we can avoid unskillful behaviors that obscure our understanding and choose skillful actions that promote realization. Far from consigning us fatalistically to a course we cannot change, the ancient principle of karma empowers us to modify ingrained habits and prepare the way to freedom.

While we cannot unravel the numberless causes of our current problems, it is possible to observe the unfolding of the karmic process in the present moment and interrupt its development. This is a key aspect of Buddhist meditation, and the Buddha spelled out very carefully how to accomplish it. In the *Visuddhimagga*, or *Path of Purification*, a standard commentary on the Buddha's teachings, we are instructed to "guard the sense doors" by watching the rising and falling of each feeling that is elicited by incoming sensations and mindfully avoiding the unskillful actions that such feelings so commonly generate. As Matthew Flickstein explains, we can place "a wedge of mindful awareness" between these feelings and the cravings for sense objects that follow.

When we understand the patterns of mind that are responsible for our unskillful actions, we have the chance to interrupt the karmic chain reaction and reduce behaviors that retard our spiritual growth. Longtime practitioners often comment that they have a "longer fuse." For example, when they are on the receiving end of rude comments, they are less likely to respond in kind. With mindful awareness of the sequence that leads from an unpleasant feeling to a sharp reply, they gain an opportunity for transforming the relationships they have with such people.[4]

～

IMAGES OF KARMA

ELECTRICITY ～ If we are working carelessly with wiring and we get shocked, we are unlikely to think that the bolt of electricity was punishment from God for our negligence. Rather, we see right away that we have no one to blame but ourselves. Certain behaviors are paired with certain predictable consequences. If we are not careful in the way we handle live wires, we will learn hard lessons in the process. It is simply the nature of the work. Similarly, esoteric spirituality emphasizes personal responsibility rather than ideas such as sin and divine judgment. Karma is called the great teacher, and while its consequences can be dire, it is through the pain and suffering our mistakes produce that we ultimately become seekers on the path to freedom.

CEILING FAN ∾ Those of us who live in warm climates often have ceiling fans that quietly, but efficiently, circulate the air and make our homes more comfortable. When the fan is turned off, the motor stops propelling the blades, but they continue in their circular motion for several minutes before they come to a complete stop. It is the same with karma. Even when we are able to refrain from behavior that has produced suffering for us in the past, we may not find ourselves immediately free from that suffering. The momentum of our previous actions must often play out in our lives before the fruits of our new behavior become apparent.

SPIDERWEB ∾ Spiderwebs have decorated the nooks and crannies of our lives as long as any of us can remember. The delicate interweaving of the silken threads is designed by nature to alert the spider to the slightest disturbance. If the web is touched in any part, the entire structure vibrates. The world we live in is similarly intertwined. Nothing is separate, and a disturbance in one area is felt throughout the whole. The principle of karma is based on this kind of reciprocity and balance. Our individual behavior does not occur in a vacuum, and no matter how insignificant our actions may seem, they produce an effect in the world around us.

FACTORIAL ∾ When we are suffering, we often want to isolate the causes and identify the sequence of actions that led to our current conditions. We continually obsess over particular actions, our own or others', as the genesis of our personal and societal problems today. But nothing is that simple. Consider factorials—mathematical calculations of the number of ways in which a certain number of things can be sequenced. The factorial for 10 exceeds three and a half million possible sequences! If just ten physical objects can be sequenced in so many different ways, it should be obvious that any attempt to analyze the karmic chain of causation in human behavior is futile. Everything causes everything; even the minor daily events in our personal lives are infinitely complex.

CUE BALL ∾ In the popular game of pool, the object is to strike the cue ball in such a way that it hits the target ball and knocks it into one of the six pockets placed around the table. The trajectory of the cue ball is critical because it determines the path of whatever balls it hits, and a skillful player can predict the path of the target ball accordingly. As human beings, the habits and patterns we develop in our lives build a certain momentum that predisposes us to act in certain predictable ways. Just as the trajectory of the cue ball affects the course of all the other balls it encounters, so too do the habits of our lives impact behaviors yet to come.

Recognizing that karma is essentially imponderable, the Buddha refused to discuss its intricacies or the way it unfolded in one's life. He spoke of the cause-and-effect relationship between actions and consequences and emphasized the value of mindful scrutiny of each thought and behavior in controlling negative karma, but beyond this, he avoided abstract discussions on the issue. In the ensuing millennia, not all seekers have followed his example, but those who have attempted to unravel karma's complexities have been singularly unsuccessful.

Why is karma so inscrutable? The foremost reason has to do with the unity of life and the impossibility of explaining unity from the perspective of separateness. The mystics of the world tell us that the world is interconnected in ways that defy linear analysis. As we have seen in previous chapters, the dualistic divisions that are possible in thought have no parallel in reality, and the conventional boundaries we impose in order to communicate with one another conceal the oneness of what is.

Another reason why we cannot disentangle the workings of karma lies in the relationship between spiritual practice and spiritual transcendence. Exoteric forms of religion offer models of reality that lie squarely within a dualistic framework, and the link between virtuous living and promised rewards is clear. In nondual spirituality, however, between beginning effort and eventual transformation there lies an intellectually impassable breach. The categories of cause and effect carry no meaning in the nature of what is, and the concepts of self, time, and karma likewise no longer have relevance. Such conceptual differentiation is a necessary starting point in practice, as it is necessary in daily life, but it holds no more truth than distinctions between stem and flower or chicken and egg in the timeless flowing change that is the fabric of all life.

We must make every effort to purify our minds and actions in preparation for spiritual practice, but we can never perfect our behavior enough to gain enlightenment. Good karma is not an end in itself, and no amount of chastity, sacrifice, and refinement can produce real insight. In the words of Advaita master Ramana Maharshi: "The more you prune a plant, the more vigorously it grows. The more you rectify your karma, the more it accumulates. Find the root of karma and cut it off."[5] Maharshi is pointing to the idea that an action has a "doer"—which is valid only within a dualistic framework—and reminding us that when selflessness is understood, the ownership of karma disappears along with the delusion of the self. Such enigmatic teachings are bound to result when sages speak of dualistic reality from the perspective of oneness. We cannot use logic to navigate the abyss between the two, any more than reason can reconcile the relative and the absolute, self and selflessness, destiny and freedom, or the other pairs of contraries that populate the mindscape of history.

We awaken to the truth of nonduality only when our eyes are opened by grace or enlightenment and we see our true nature. At that moment, the Ten Commandments, the precepts of the Buddha, Islamic law, and all the other traditional codes of morality fall away. The duality of "an eye for an eye" is eclipsed by the opening of the mystical "third eye" of wisdom, which sees the resolution of good and evil in the unity of what is. In the *Bhagavad Gita*, Krishna counsels Arjuna: "As the heat of a fire reduces wood to ashes, the fire of knowledge burns to ashes all karma. Nothing in this world purifies like spiritual wisdom."[6] Twentieth-century Christian mystic Joel Goldsmith echoes his words when he declares, "Though our sins be scarlet, we are white as snow in the very minute we realize our true identity."[7]

It is important to emphasize that this idea—that karma is ultimately transcended—must not diminish the importance of ethical behavior nor obviate our human obligation to act with compassion and understanding. When Jesus says, in the Sermon on the Mount, that he has come not to abolish the Law of the Prophets but to complete it, biblical authority Geddes MacGregor finds a reconciliation of these two levels of truth and concludes that the notion of grace without law is "like talking of literature without language," but much worse: it is "like talking of love without sacrifice."[8] We find a very similar stance in the teachings of Buddhism, where failure to recognize both levels of truth is disparaged as a "one-sided" view. In all the mystical paths, realization is accompanied by compassion. Sages behave selflessly, even though the traditional injunctions no longer hold. No longer blinded by the delusion of separateness, the enlightened understand their individual behavior as the action of the whole. As the mystical teachings assert, it is not goodness and virtue that we *have*; rather, it is goodness and virtue that we *are*. Compassion flows freely, given without judgment of those receiving it, as shade from a tree touches all who sit under it without distinction.

It is in this transcendent context that we make sense of the esoteric teachings on karma and morality; they are the words of wholeness. From Rumi we hear: "Out beyond ideas of wrongdoing and rightdoing, there is a field. I'll meet you there. When the soul lies down in that grass, the world is too full to talk about. Ideas, language, even the phrase *each other* doesn't make any sense."[9] In the *Tao Te Ching*, we find a similar thought: "When benevolence was lost, righteousness appeared; and when righteousness was lost, the proprieties appeared."[10] In other words, when we forget the oneness of our origins, distinctions and judgments multiply, and we need to create codes that tell us how to act. When we awaken from our dream of duality, however, and see things as they are, our natural goodness flows freely.

Throughout the mystical heritage of humankind, this theme emerges over and over in the lives and words of the world's sages. When human activity is not obstructed by delusion, life flows unimpeded, spontaneously and unselfconsciously, manifesting compassion and self-less service. When we see others as our self, our "me-first" view of life becomes irrelevant, and right and wrong lose their meaning. To help or harm another is to help or harm oneself. Perhaps St. Bernard expresses it best: "Love seeks no cause beyond itself and no fruit; it is its own fruit, its own enjoyment. I love because I love."[11]

8

SUFFERING

Grant that I may be given appropriate difficulties and sufferings on this journey so that my heart may be truly awakened and my practice of liberation and universal compassion may be truly fulfilled.

—Tibetan prayer

If you have ever seen *The Scream*, the famous painting by Norwegian expressionist painter Edvard Munch, you know that the image can have an indelible effect. In its viscerally affecting portrayal of an anguished face set in a landscape of distorted forms, it has been said to represent the burden of melancholy and existential angst that humanity carries in the modern world—the pall of suffering that hangs over modern life. Even with the extraordinary advances we in the developed world have made in the quality of daily life, few would deny the suffering that continues to dominate our horizons. In addition to the endless conflict, starvation, and natural disaster we see on the nightly news, most of us need look no further than our own neighborhoods or even our own homes to find human misery in abundance.

Our well-being has not kept pace with our material progress. While such horrors as slavery and the subjugation of women are largely things of the past in most modern societies, and advances in medicine and technology have alleviated many of the forms of disease and hardship that ravaged our predecessors, such scourges as suicide, depression, and substance abuse still wreak havoc in the lives of millions. Even the wealthiest of us, surrounded by splendor and extravagance, may find ourselves emotionally impoverished and alone. If Jesus, the Buddha, or Lao Tzu could see us now, they would not be surprised by this fact, while they would no doubt be amazed by the technological prowess of our contemporary world. They would see that the same fundamental reasons for suffering that prevailed thousands of years ago remained unchanged.

The key to understanding suffering is our delusion of self. As we have seen in several of the preceding chapters, our entire lives revolve around this entity we believe ourselves to be. Through our mistaken identification with this separate self, this tiny fragment of what is, we see life from a very narrow perspective, with fixed ideas about the way things should be. We struggle all our lives to force the vastness of being to conform to our ideal, but our efforts are futile. The world does not bend to our personal agendas. And when we cannot let go of the way we think things ought to be, we suffer. This was the heart of the Buddha's Four Noble Truths, and it is the key to the wisdom and understanding we need. Suffering is like rope burn: when we hold on too tightly to our attachments and desires, as to a rope slipping through our hands, pain is inevitable. Until we recognize that life is change, our actions will continue to oppose the very nature of reality as we attempt to protect what is "ours" from the inexorable flow of existence.

To deal with the stress and confusion inherent in the human condition, we may seek solace externally, in doing more, owning more, even eating more. Many people deaden their pain through compulsive activity, thinking that if they keep busy enough at work or at home, they will keep angst and fear at bay. Others lose themselves in meaningless forms of entertainment and hours of mind-numbing activities. But we cannot find peace if we are seeking it in the wrong place. Looking outside ourselves for solutions to suffering is doomed from the outset, because the ceaseless nature of change leaves nothing untouched, not even those supposed solutions. This truth in turn creates fear, a major component of suffering. We strive all our lives to protect the things we cherish, yet our world can still come crumbling down in a single day. So we worry about everything, continuously shifting our concern to what seems most vulnerable at any given time—be it the health of a loved one or the well-being of the planet—and we spend billions on tranquilizers and antidepressants to deal with the pandemic of anxiety that this nagging apprehension creates.

Our suffering is increased by the fact that we identify not only with our body/mind, but also with a constellation of people, objects, events, and ideas that extend our concept of self. We define who we are through the groups we join, the relationships we form, the communities we live in, and even the cars we drive. As we saw in chapter 6, our attachments are manifold, and any perceived attack upon them or downturn in their fortunes can trigger suffering as strong as if we were in physical pain.

Consider our modern obsession with sports and athletic competition. The teams that populate the local, regional, and national landscape are the objects of deep identification for their multitude of fans. A popular sports show on television, ABC's *Wide World of Sports*, used to open with a short video of memorable moments of elation and dismay, as the commentator spoke of "the thrill of victory and the agony of defeat." In truth, this is a pretty accurate description of the experience of millions of loyal sports enthusiasts who passionately follow their favorite teams. The fans' moods typically rise and fall with the fortunes of the teams with which they identify: a big win is cause for celebration, and a loss can plunge them deep into gloom. The same dynamics affect us all, even if we do not follow football or baseball. Our lives play out as an endless series of wins and losses, resulting from the ever-changing circumstances of "our" relationships, "our" careers, "our" possessions, or "our" ideas.

A critical feature of this phenomenon, and of all suffering, is the role that thought plays in the process. Whether it is a rehashing of a favorite team's performance, or the brooding we do over something potentially life-threatening, it is our *thoughts* that are the problem—the second-guessing, the consternation over missed opportunities, the memories of last year's failures, the perceived lack of fairness in the world, the endless mental replay of critical moments in our lives, and the thoughts of what friends will think or say. We can obsess over these things for weeks, months, or even years—and it is, often literally, all in our minds. As Mark Twain once quipped, "I have been through some terrible things in my life, some of which actually happened."

Most people experience this kind of thought-mediated suffering almost daily. Though there may be nothing happening in the moment to cause discomfort or concern, there are "tape loops" in our heads that torment us continually—running commentaries based on a complex blend of accumulated memories, conditioning, and karma that play throughout our waking hours. For many people, these tapes play a consistently gloomy or cynical tune, and for them, the glass of life is always half empty. They experience their lives according to their expectations, so if their past was filled with pain and disappointment, their misery continues even when there is no cause for it in the present.

This dilemma is much discussed in the mystical teachings of various traditions, and practices such as meditation offer us a window into the reflexive nature of these endlessly recurring thoughts. When we recognize the difference between our mental constructs and the reality of what is, we can begin to change our relationship to suffering. Instead of trying to tamp down distressing or destructive thoughts, or learning to think more constructively, it is possible to alter our *responses* to our thoughts simply by observing them mindfully. Seeing the way our thoughts spin out of control, with no volition on our part, can transform our reactions to them. Through the practice of mindfulness, in which we learn to be present without judgment, decision, or even commentary, the lifelong identification with our thoughts begins to loosen.

~

IMAGES OF SUFFERING

ARROW ~ The Buddha told a story about a man shot with a poison arrow. When others tried to help him pull the arrow out, he insisted that they first answer questions he posed about the shooter. Who was he? Where did he live? Why did he shoot the arrow? All the while, the poison was draining his life away. The parable illustrates how human beings spend years exploring irrelevant or unanswerable questions, while all the time their suffering continues. The story highlights our habit of focusing all our attention on *why* it is that we suffer, when the solution hinges on the question of *who* it is that suffers. As the Buddha made clear, there is suffering, but none who suffer. The solution to human travail lies in the unraveling of this enigmatic paradox.

SNAKE OF ROPE ⌇ It is common enough in life to mistake one thing for another. If we think of a campsite in the mountains, with evening falling, it is easy to imagine how a coiled rope lying on the ground could be mistaken for a snake. A camper startled by the illusory snake might stumble backward in fright and land painfully on a rock (or fall off an inconvenient cliff). In life, our fears and anxieties are similarly produced by our misperceptions of what is. In an absolute sense, the things we most dread have no more reality than the snake made of rope, but the suffering we experience is very real indeed. The freedom that the world's mystical traditions teach is freedom from such delusion, for with understanding, suffering loses its bite.

CHESS PIECES ⌇ The pieces of a chess game make no decisions; they are only (sometimes literally) pawns in the process, pushed from square to square until the game is over. Can you imagine if the game pieces identified with the outcome of the action and became elated when they were moved skillfully or depressed when they were captured by the opponent? It would be like a tragic comedy, with the little knights and bishops dancing with joy or crumpled in agony as the tide of the game turned. At a very deep level, this is what our own suffering is like. While we must learn from our mistakes and apply the wisdom we gain to the unfolding circumstances each day presents, the events of our lives have no more to do with us than the events in a game of chess have to do with the pieces. As one Zen teacher has put it, "Your life is none of your business." The mystics of the world agree. Though a difficult truth to discern, it is life that makes the moves, not we.

SHOES ～ An ancient Buddhist parable compares the human approach to solving life's problems to a person who would cover the entire countryside with leather in order to protect his feet from the sharp rocks. Clearly, it would be far simpler for him to wear a pair of shoes! As ludicrous as such a plan appears, it actually parallels the way in which most people strive to alleviate their suffering: they seek to reform the world, endlessly modifying external conditions to suit their desires instead of the other way around. Given the impossibly complex challenge of controlling the ever-changing circumstances of life, would it not be better to simply change one's outlook instead?

FISH IN THE OCEAN ～ Zen teachers tell a timeless story about a fish in search of the great ocean of life. Oblivious to the water all around it, the fish swims great distances in its quest, with no results; it cannot find the ocean anywhere it looks. The fish is living in the ocean, but doesn't realize it. If the fish were rudely yanked out of the water on a fisherman's hook, however, the elusive goal would suddenly become obvious: water is its very life. Our experience is quite similar. We are immersed in life, in the flesh and blood of our existence, but blindly seek fulfillment elsewhere. We spend most of our lives in mental games and abstractions, puzzling over what life means, while the truth is all around us. We simply need to wake up and smell the proverbial roses. This is it! Just this. Yet we often don't realize it until, like the hapless fish, we find ourselves out of our element, gasping for air. When suffering abruptly interrupts the normal flow of things and shakes us out of our routines, it is an opportunity to see life from a deeper, more substantive perspective—but one we often miss. How many of us fail to see the truth of life until we are close to death? Then the simple sound of a bird's song or the smell of baking bread can bring us to tears. Some fish are thrown back and get a second chance, but it is very risky for us to count on such a reprieve.

～

As much as we all strive to avoid it, the simple truth is that humanity *needs* suffering. Throughout the ages, mystics have taught a consistent lesson: it is through hardship and reversals of fortune that we are roused from our complacency and the unconscious patterns we are prone to settle into. It is suffering that shakes us up and clears our vision. For this reason, the Buddha referred to suffering as the Holy Truth. In a similar vein, twentieth-century Zen master D. T. Suzuki asserts that the painful struggles of life are "providential," for they crack the "ego-shell" and open us to life's secrets.[1]

Rumi expresses it poetically, declaring, "Darkness is your candle."[2] When everything in our lives is going well, we can become so engrossed in trivial preoccupations that we lose touch with what is important. Success strengthens our identification with the self and keeps us from transcendence. We have no motivation to find something better. But if we are suddenly and unexpectedly confronted with our mortality and the transience of all we cherish, we are forced to recognize life's preciousness and seek its meaning. As it is said, we are jolted awake by nightmares, not by pleasant dreams.

When someone close to us dies or we are given a terminal prognosis of our own, the priorities of our lives abruptly shift. The need to redecorate the house, so pressing yesterday, fades quickly into the background. Friction with friends over petty irritations is forgotten. Bank accounts and promotions at work lose their relevance in contrast to our new life-and-death challenges. The explanations we were given by our parents to make sense out of things, though they satisfied our previously superficial inquiries, often come up short in life's most difficult times. We seek answers to what seems so wrong about life. Why is there suffering? How can a loving God allow this to happen, especially when the victims are innocent children or people who are kind, gentle, and good?

In the Bible, when Job cries out against the cruel and seemingly senseless suffering visited on him, God answers him thus: "Where were you when I laid the earth's foundation? . . . Have you ever given orders to the morning, or shown the dawn its place . . . ? Does the hawk take flight by your wisdom and spread its wings toward the south?"[3] It's hard to see what comfort this could be to one who is faced with losing everything; nevertheless, it is the very answer we are given in nondual spirituality. Job is directed to a larger picture, beyond the narrow-gauge perspective of the ego. Before we realize and understand our true nature, such words are little solace. With the wisdom of insight, however, we come to see suffering as the suffering of life itself, rather than that of the individual alone. We discover that we are *not* alone, separate and cut off from everything else. There are no boundaries that quarantine us from each other, and when we see this clearly, we can understand the hurts of personal experience within a much larger context.

The existence of suffering is not in question; it is the supposed existence of *one who suffers* that we need to examine. Just as it makes no sense to think of each organ of a body as suffering through its own illness alone, the presumption that pain is somehow "ours" misses the fact that all of life is organically one. This is the transcendent perspective of mystical practice, and we often glimpse it for the first time when circumstances force us to. In the context of nonduality, the hardships of life are not things happening to us. As counterintuitive as it sounds, we are the happening itself. We are not experiencing life; we *are* life.

St. Teresa of Avila likened suffering to the darkness of the cocoon that precedes the emergence into the butterfly. It is the cup from which we must all drink for our eyes to be cleansed. Once beyond unskillful emotions such as the anger and blame that are characteristic of the way many deal with trauma, people begin to see the world in a very different way and to notice things they never did before. Perhaps we have long been oblivious to the suffering of those around us or too busy to consider their plight, but when we are deeply shaken by our own dramas, our eyes can be opened to the misery that surrounds us all. Ironically, it is often an exposure to personal pain that kindles our love and compassion for others. Though different people manifest very different reactions, some dark or embittered, others clearly experience a common bond with the rest of humanity for the first time. Recognizing our own vulnerability in a deep and visceral way, we are connected to all of life as it too faces pain, calamity, and death. It is no longer "our" suffering, but that of life itself.

While suffering is endemic to the human condition, there is a way to short-circuit its effect on us. The key lies in changing our relationship to our mind so that we see through our thoughts, beliefs, and judgments and effectively discern the difference between our perceptions of reality and reality itself. Consequently, the remedy for suffering lies not in analysis or changing attitudes, but in being present with what is. To paraphrase insight meditation teacher Sharon Salzberg, we must drop our defensive reactions and have faith to open ourselves to the truth of what is happening in the moment. It is only with that unconditioned awareness that we can see what is actually unfolding and respond as the moment dictates.

We cannot avoid pain. It is a fundamental and necessary aspect of existence. What is unnecessary is the confused and misguided reaction we have to it. When we think of ourselves as isolated and alone in our plight and unfairly singled out by life, anguish is a natural result. And so, in the cult of individuality and intense self-consciousness that characterizes our society, it is only natural that suffering will dominate our lives. The existential dread so vividly reflected in the philosophy and art of modern culture—the silent horror we see on the face of *The Scream*—is a product of this delusion. On the first half of the hero's journey we are charting, this suffering is the defining characteristic and driving force, and that is according to plan. As we go farther into our exile from wholeness, it is the pain of separation that impels us to search for answers and seek a way back to the Source. Jarring us out of our stupor of selfhood, it sets the stage for resolution and starts us on the path of return to our true being.

9
MEANING

It takes an honest heart and mind to acknowledge
that we don't really know what purpose there is to
existence or that there is any purpose at all.

—*Catherine Ingram*

Viktor Frankl points out in his seminal work, *Man's Search for Meaning*, that we must find significance in our suffering if we are to successfully endure it. But for millions of people, even living in an age of opportunity and abundance unparalleled in history, meaning seems to be in short supply, and it gets more and more difficult to find import in the midst of travail. It's as if we have become disconnected from the things that give the most significance to human existence and lost our place in the greater scheme of things.

As we've seen in previous chapters, there are many reasons for our modern malaise. Thought brought separation; self laid the groundwork for attachment and suffering and led to the situation we find ourselves in today. The traditions that once gave us a sense of belonging are dying out as our ties with family, community, culture, and religion weaken, leaving us parts without a whole, adrift in a universe that sometimes seems hostile to our very existence. Until we reconnect with the Source and find our place in the whole of creation, meaning, happiness, and well-being will elude us. This is the central truth expounded in all the wisdom traditions and myths of humanity, and according to Huston Smith, our current crisis derives from the fact that those ancient teachings have been largely ignored. Modernity, he argues, with its scientifically derived emphasis on the finite, has demeaned the human potential. As he puts it, "The issue is simply that of balance and proportion, the balance that derives from a sense of proportion, infinite matters being accorded infinite regard and finite ones being regarded conditionally."[1]

Joseph Campbell once said that we are all scrambling up a ladder, only to discover when we reach the top that it is leaning against the wrong wall! It's not hard to see the relevance of this powerful image. In Campbell's view, we are majoring in minor subjects, experts in the mundane but existentially directionless. We spend our lives accumulating the money we mistake for wealth, while sacrificing opportunities to gain what is truly priceless—but even the most extraordinary success in the secular realm does not translate automatically into happiness or spiritual fulfillment. Peace and unity are elusive, and in their place we find the burgeoning violence of clashing cultures, radical movements, and patriotic fervor. Greed remains unabated even where affluence abounds, revealing the profound inadequacy of conventional success to satisfy our hunger.

The modern view of reality is a narrow one, bounded by the limits of empirical analysis and scientific reductionism. Science was born in a time of widespread superstition and religious dogmatism; the introduction of scientific inquiry brought with it a massive infusion of fresh thinking and new theories that paved the way for unprecedented growth in our understanding of ourselves and the world. The subsequent development of radio and television, satellite technology, the Internet, and, most recently, social media has made available an ever-expanding panorama of ideas and cultures previously unknown to most of us. In their wake, the traditions and beliefs of our parents have come under increasing scrutiny, and millions have begun to look elsewhere for the elusive meaning of their lives.

Nevertheless, science in its meteoric rise has taken on an arrogance and bigotry of its own. While opening the door to a vast array of improvements in society, the scientific movement has largely excluded any aspects of life that do not fit neatly into its empirical paradigms, and it steers clear of intangibles not measurable by instruments or controlled experiments, invoking the authority of research to dismiss anything that lies beyond their scope. The truth is simply that science's principles, so successful in making sense of the physical world, do not generalize to concerns of the spirit—but people for whom science *is* a religion often miss or ignore this fact and take the absence of empirical evidence as proof that such things are nothing more than superstitious holdovers from an earlier age. The tail is wagging the dog; the magnificent tool of modern science is too often mistaken for the zeitgeist of human society and a paradigm for human life.

In the world's modern societies, millions find themselves struggling with nostalgia, melancholy, and depression, many of them trying to fill what Sartre referred to as a "God-shaped hole" in the human consciousness. Even those brought up on the scientific method may be haunted by the sense of something missing. Modern life has produced great ingenuity and cleverness, but the rational analysis that has been so essential in other areas of endeavor has proven incapable of reconnecting us with the wellspring of life's deepest meaning. Carl Jung once declared that virtually all his patients over the age of thirty-five had issues related to the spiritual aspect of life. He maintained that the modern world was in crisis because it had been "desacralized." In a similar vein, religion scholar Karen Armstrong argues that the rise of fundamentalism throughout the world is a direct response to this loss of the meaning and connection that had traditionally been at the very center of the human experience.[2]

With the thundering revelations of Copernicus, Descartes, Darwin, and Freud, we jettisoned many outdated superstitions, but along with them our very sense of place in the world around us. We are told we are no more than thinking animals fending for ourselves in a hostile world, and the horrors of the Holocaust, the gulags, Pol Pot, and Darfur only seem to prove the point. We are killing each other in record numbers and taking our own lives in dark desperation. We are even destroying our own planet.

We have lost our bearings, replacing our old guideposts with the intense self-consciousness that characterizes modern life. Our belief in our separateness is what blocks understanding and precludes any meaningful connection with the rest of life: we cannot hope to find meaning when the premise from which we begin our search for it is a delusion. And this meaninglessness defines the nadir of humankind's fall from grace.

Ironically, in our alienation and turmoil there is a historically unique opportunity. With the developed world now freer from hunger, disease, and exhaustion than ever before, the door is open for more and more people to investigate the deep mystery of life. True spirituality has been called the ultimate luxury, requiring, as it does, time and solitude and some measure of freedom from the encumbrances of daily existence. In the past, inner examination of the deepest spiritual realities was left to a few monks, nuns, wandering mendicants, and cliff-dwelling yogis released from the requirements of daily subsistence by supportive communities that provided for them. Today, however, many people find it possible to go on a retreat or set at least a little time aside for contemplation. At the same time, those drawn to the spiritual search have unprecedented access to the sacred literature of the world and, more than ever before, can find inspiration in the wisdom it contains.

And modern life offers one more reason—perhaps the most significant—why the time is ripe for a return to spirituality: the fact that so many people today have the opportunity to experience the shallowness of material success firsthand. Until they see it for themselves, those who have not yet achieved the luxury and prestige that prosperity promises cannot imagine its vacuity, so they can hardly be expected to renounce its allure. But when people attain whatever material goals they have set and still find themselves succumbing to despair, it drives them toward something more lasting and real. It reminds one of Siddhartha Gautama, son of a king in northern India some twenty-five hundred years ago. Raised as a prince in a world of wealth and privilege, Gautama hungered for something more. Driven to discover the ultimate truth of existence, he relinquished his claim to the kingdom he was to inherit and commenced his search in earnest for the meaning that resonates deeply within all of us. When he discovered it, he was called the Buddha, the one who is awake.

~

IMAGES OF MEANING

PAGE OF A NOVEL   ~   By itself, a single page torn out of a novel tells us little. It is a small fragment of a much larger whole, disconnected from everything that once gave it meaning. Until we find the book it came from, we can make no sense of it. If, however, the page is put back in the book and its words read in that larger context, the meaning it holds is instantly clear. We find ourselves in a similarly baffling situation, lost amidst the unfathomable scale and incomprehensibly vast numbers with which modern science describes our reality. We can hardly escape the perception of our insignificance when we consider how small the orbits of our daily lives appear against that infinite background and a cosmos measured in billions of light-years. Until we realize our fundamental identity with life itself, the "book" that gives a context to all our stories, it will be as difficult to find meaning in one brief life span as in one loose page.

ALPHABET   ~   It is interesting to recall our early years when we first learned the letters of the alphabet. Each letter was a separate challenge with its unique name, shape, and sound. Our teachers or parents would point to individual letters, guide our stubby fingers over their outlines, and praise us when we recognized or reproduced them, but we had little idea of why those shapes and sounds were so important. As we grew, and came to see the relationship of the individual letters to each other, we increasingly understood the power and magic they held. When combined, they were transformed into words, sentences, paragraphs, whole books—they were the keys to a fabulous world of meaning. Sometimes, in the anonymity of modern society, our lives seem as inconsequential as a solitary letter. When, through spiritual practice and insight, we come to see our deep interdependence with everything else, our world can be transformed as dramatically as that of the young child who first realizes the wonder of reading. When we see that we belong, when we understand the intimacy and depth of our bond with everyone and everything, a new and beautiful vision of life unfolds. We have come home.

LOST KEYS ～ There is a well-known story from the Sufi tradition about a man who lost his keys in an alley one night. He was searching for them under a lamppost when a neighbor asked him what he was doing. He replied that he was looking for his keys. Asked where he lost them, he pointed to the other end of the street. "Why aren't you looking over there?" the surprised neighbor wanted to know. The man responded, "The light is better over here." We are just as foolish today, searching for meaning and answers to the deepest mysteries of our lives where the light is best, though we know in our hearts that we lost the keys to truth somewhere else. The spiritual wisdom for which we yearn is not to be found under the bright light of science or reason. We must follow the advice of the mystics and search for it within.

WATER CYCLE ～ In the global cycle of water, moisture evaporates from the ocean, then falls back to the earth's surface as rain or snow and eventually flows back to the sea. Running downhill from every direction, water gains momentum for its journey of return. A trickle becomes a stream, then a creek, and then a river, until it rejoins the ocean. The names we give to bodies of water imply that they each have a separate existence, but in truth they are a process without destination—no end in sight, just evaporation, rain and runoff, perpetually recycling. There is always movement, but never progress. Is this not the model for all of nature? Where is there progress or purpose in the natural world? The seasons come and go, the planets spin indefinitely, and the galaxies circle endlessly without apparent purpose or any sight of journey's end. Scientists even suggest that the universe as a whole may be a cycle of ceaseless contraction and expansion. We are no different. As the title of a book by the Buddhist nun and author Ayya Khema puts it, we are all "nobody going nowhere." Deluded by our belief in a separate self, we have forgotten our oneness with all that is, and we needlessly look for meaning in our individual lives, as if we were trying to isolate a raindrop from the ocean.

～

Are we truly insignificant? Are we specks of intelligent life adrift in the vastness of an indifferent cosmos, or do our lives mean something after all? There are no simple answers, but in the Biblical parable of the prodigal son we do find clues to the resolution of this perennial human concern. When the son claims his inheritance and abandons his father's fields to seek excitement in the outside world, he confronts the lessons that life holds for us all. His fortune thrown away in reckless and dissolute living, he is faced with the bewilderment of separation and homelessness that, until then, he has never known. Is the suffering that results from his selfish arrogance and impulsive departure meaningless? Is his experience inconsequential? To the contrary, they are essential to his eventual recognition of truth. As so often in life, we don't realize what we have until we lose it—or almost do.

The rest of us endlessly repeat the same story. All over the world, the young feel the urge to venture out on their own and see life for themselves. Parents watch with dismay as their children make the same mistakes they themselves once made. It is a spiritual rite of passage: like the prodigal son, we must first squander our birthright chasing the dreams of pleasure, affluence, and fame that so mesmerize modern society before we can recognize their emptiness, realize our real nature, and reclaim what we never really lost.

When we were very young, we were one with life, but didn't know it. That was the brief period of our lives that preceded the entry of the ego and the sense of a separate self. To have remained in this blissful absence of self-consciousness (had that been possible) might have kept us from our eventual suffering, but it would have relegated us to an unconscious life, not unlike that found in the rest of the animal kingdom. While we may admire the spontaneity, naturalness, and worry-free disposition of the animals that share our environment, we recognize that self-awareness is the unique blessing of our human birth and remains the *sine qua non* of spiritual awakening.

It can be difficult to appreciate life's lessons when we are faced with the cruel torment of a chaotic world and the apparent meaninglessness of our existence, but it is from this place of farthest exile that the journey of return begins. As the Advaita master Ramesh Balsekar once asserted, it is only in the state of duality that the desire to know what we are will arise. When our world is fragmented into self and other, the resulting self-consciousness produces suffering that spurs the search for wholeness. It has been called spiritual labor pain, and, like the physical kind, it holds the promise of a new birth.

If our ultimate purpose is to return to wholeness, does this mean that we have no more immediate purpose to serve? Can our individual lives make no difference in the lives of others? The answer depends on your frame of reference. From the perspective of duality, we do make a difference. Our efforts to improve the lives of our fellow human beings and alleviate their suffering create good karma and nurture spiritual growth. The importance of good works in our spiritual development is emphasized repeatedly in the sacred literature of many traditions. On the other hand, purpose and significance can be self-aggrandizing and may carry little import beyond the limitations of our personal agendas. It is always important to ask *who* it is that is seeking significance or quests for purpose. Recognition from others or even pride in yourself for altruistic accomplishments can further conceal the very "self" we are trying to unmask.

Seen from the perspective of unity, questions of meaning appear in a very different light. As I have said before, it's not a matter of some individual doing some thing; *everything* does *everything*. There is no credit or blame, because there is no agent to assign it to, no separate self that demands its own significance. When an individual realizes that his or her actions are in truth the actions of the whole, life is infused with the strength that derives from this insight. In the Ten Oxherding Pictures of the Zen tradition, the search for our true nature is depicted metaphorically as a man seeking his ox. In the final phase of realization, the man is pictured returning to the marketplace with the wisdom and compassion of awakening.[3] This same principle is embedded in the Bodhisattva tradition of Mahayana Buddhism. After realization, the master remains in the throes of the manifest world and devotes himself or herself to relieving human suffering.

In the coming chapters, we will see it is this truth that informs the lives of the world's saints and sages and empowers them to engage the world with such extraordinary benefit to others. In the words of Mother Teresa, Martin Luther King, or Mahatma Gandhi, for example, there is never a suggestion of personal credit taken for, or meaning assigned to, anything they have done, nor personal attachment to results. Instead, they share a vision of themselves as instruments of the Divine: *Thy will be done*. We find a clear parallel for this in Taoism, with its core principle of *wu wei*, meaning "non-doing" or "action without action"; it conveys the idea that the individual plays no role, but "acts" in alignment with being, in harmony with what is. In all nondual traditions, we find this shift from the duality of self and other to the unity of what is.

In a world that places such emphasis on meaning and purpose, the teachings of nonduality challenge all spiritual seekers who attempt to unravel their paradoxical wisdom. When we hear that our lives have no significance, we can easily start to see life, bleakly and nihilistically, as meaningless altogether. When we read in the *Tao Te Ching* that "the world is a sacred instrument / One cannot control it,"[4] our cherished ideas of progress, improvement, and making a difference immediately come into question. We must understand, however, that our qualms arise because we are looking at all of this from the perspective of the doer in a world of divisions. Without the ego that reigns in this reality, there would be no fear of a meaningless life.

Does a flower have meaning? Standing naked and fragile for the short span of its existence, the flower makes no pretense of playing a role or making a contribution. When we look at its delicate form and catch the light scent it unreservedly shares, we don't ask what purpose it serves; the question of meaning does not arise. The flower is perfect as it is and need make no apologies. Alan Watts argues that only words and concepts have meaning, because they point to something other than themselves; they are symbols, significant only as a conduit for communication.[5] This is not the case with life. As Watts would say, the flower doesn't *have* meaning. It *is* meaning.

Wayne Teasdale would add, however, that the unfolding of a seed to the perfection of a blossom, and its subsequent decay, reveal a deep truth about all life. There is nothing haphazard in the process of nature, and according to Teasdale, the comprehensive purpose reflected in a flower suggests a similar truth embodied in our own spiritual pilgrimage to the source and origin of all that is. As he makes clear, this purpose is not of the parts but of the whole—"the divine drawing all things to itself first by the interconnectedness of everything, then through its cosmic symbolism, and finally through the communion and union of the mystical journey itself."[6]

People go round and round looking for meaning, never realizing that the seeker is the sought. Meaning is found in being, nowhere else. As long as there is one who is chasing it, the chase will never end. Like the flower, we *are* meaning. We cannot find it in objects or accumulate it through accomplishments. We can only *be* it. For this reason, Jesus declared that those things hidden from the wise and learned have been revealed to little children—and watching young children at play shows us just what he meant. They are so fully intent on what they are doing, so caught up in what Zen calls the "isness" of being, that the question of meaning never occurs to them. With the innocence that precedes the appearance of the ego, they *are* the truth so often repeated: life is in the living. When as adults we can return to this oneness, with the wisdom gained from having thought it lost, we will have closed the circle of life.

PART TWO ~ THE RETURN

In everyone's heart there stirs
a great homesickness.

—*Rabbi Seymour Siegel*

This insofar as they have learned to become one from
many, and again become many as the one grows apart, to
that extent they come into being and have no lasting life;
but insofar as they never cease their continual change, to
that extent they exist forever, unmoving in a circle.

—*Empedocles*

No problem can be solved from the
same level of consciousness that created it.

—*Albert Einstein*

When we stop regarding the unreal as real,
then reality alone will remain, and we will be that.

—*Ramana Maharshi*

YEARNING

O friend, understand: the body is
like the ocean, rich with hidden treasures.
Open your inmost chamber and light its lamp.

—Mirabai

I n the opening pages of this book, we explored a theme central to the mythology of humankind and woven into the wisdom traditions of our species. Joseph Campbell called it the journey of the hero and described it as a return to our true nature—to the realization of our oneness with life itself. When we have reached the lowest point on the journey, that state of suffering and meaninglessness that we are led into by our delusions of duality, what propels us back up toward the light is a profound longing arising from the depths of our souls. But what is it we are really yearning *for*?

Various spiritual traditions have explained this cosmic mystery in terms of the Divine playing a solitary game of hide-and-seek. First it loses itself in the multiplicity of seemingly separate phenomena that make up the world we know; then it remembers the truth and is drawn gradually out of hiding, back toward unity. It is in this context that the inner teacher is to be understood: the Divine is hiding in the heart of each of us. The longing we feel for wholeness is the Divine calling to itself, hoping to be found. As God says in a sacred Hadith, a traditional

saying passed down from the time of Muhammad, "I was a hidden treasure and I wanted to be known: That is why I created the world."[1]

In the literature of esoteric spirituality, across all times and cultures,
there is universal recognition of this fact—the idea of an inner teacher
comes up again and again. To read the words that echo through the ages
is to witness the fervor the world's mystics have shared for this understanding and the certainty they have felt of its truth. They knew, as the
modern sages likewise know, that the answers to our most fundamental spiritual questions are very close at hand. The Buddha said, "Look
within, thou art the Buddha," and in the Hindu classic *Bhagavad Gita*,
Krishna tells Arjuna, "I am the true Self in the heart of every creature."[2]
The same idea is reflected in the words of Jesus: "The kingdom of God
is within you." Rumi, the thirteenth-century Sufi poet, wrote, "The
entrance door to the sanctuary is *inside* you";[3] in the same epoch, half
a world away, the Japanese Zen master Dogen said, "Don't follow the
advice of others; rather, learn to listen to the voice within yourself."[4]

The Quakers based a whole faith on the belief that the human heart
held the presence of the Divine: this "Inner Light," as they called it, was
the authority by which they could each pursue their individual paths
to realization. And the great sage of the Oglala Sioux, Black Elk, tells
us that "the heart is a sanctuary at the center of which there is a little
space, wherein the Great Spirit dwells, and this is the Eye. This is the
eye of the Great Spirit by which He sees all things, and through which
we see Him."[5] Over and over in the spiritual endeavors of humankind,
the same message is heard: Look within and trust the authority of your
own heart. It is a storehouse of wisdom, truth, and love.

But this message does not often resonate with modern seekers,
especially in the West. There are several reasons for this. One is the
common perception that the spiritual realm is something transcendent, otherworldly, and far removed from the turmoil and confusion
of this earthly existence. Martin Luther taught that each believer was a
"priest" unto himself and argued that spiritual experience should not be
mediated by agents of a religious hierarchy. Even so, many worshippers
today seem to view themselves as followers rather than agents, their

role limited to prayerful petitions directed outward and upward to a heaven-based deity, depending on ordained intermediaries to bridge the chasm they perceive between themselves and the Divine.

Our modern conceit presents another serious obstacle to spiritual truth. As we saw in the last chapter, modern science has us puffed up with our apparent ability to unlock nature's secrets, leading us to put a premium on hard facts and conclusive evidence even in matters of the spirit.

As formidable as these factors are, the biggest obstacle between us and the truth within is the fact that we feel unworthy to claim it as our own. This is a view that finds support from several quarters. For many raised in traditional Christianity, the idea of original sin burdens us like a spiritual version of inherited debt: in the story of the Garden of Eden, the expulsion of Adam and Eve is seen as a loss of innocence, an entry into a "fallen" state, leaving humankind in need of redemption. (By contrast, as we saw in the introduction, Joseph Campbell's interpretation of the same story presents our "fall" as a matter of forgetting our true nature and needing only to remember.) A different but likewise substantial cause for our skepticism is found in Sigmund Freud's theories of the unconscious and his portrayal of the murky realms that lie beneath our awareness. And the meaningless cruelty and selfish behavior that dominate local and world news only serve to drive this impression home. No wonder the teachings of innate goodness so consistently found in esoteric spirituality often fail to penetrate our conventional appraisals of human nature. How *could* the divine wholeness we yearn for be contained in such flawed vessels?

Given the emphasis that the dominant religion of the West places on the sinful nature of humanity, people are often surprised to discover that esoteric teachings occur with some frequency within the Christian tradition itself. Over the two millennia since Christ, innumerable mystics and sages of the Church have spoken of the presence of the Holy Spirit within us all, reflecting the same fervor seen in other spiritual traditions. John the Evangelist tells us, "The spirit you have received from him remains in you, and you don't need to have any man teach you; but that spirit teaches you all things, and is the truth."[6] This same conviction is reflected in the words of Julian of Norwich, Symeon the New Theologian, St. Bernard, St. Bonaventure, St. Teresa of Avila, St. John of the Cross, and St. Catherine of Genoa, to mention only a few. In what may be the single most arresting expression of this truth, four-teenth-century German theologian Meister Eckhart declares, "The eye through which I see God is the same eye through which God sees me."[7] But because such appeals to inner truth threaten established authority, they have often been ruthlessly suppressed. The Spanish Inquisition may be the most notorious example of the possible consequence for unorthodox views, but throughout the Middle Ages in Europe many mystical seekers ran such risks.

How are we to understand this stark divergence between the views of conventional wisdom and those of the esoteric teachings—the view that sees the truth somewhere outside and the view that locates it within? It's simply that these are the views of different eyes. Before spiri-tual illumination, we see the world dualistically; we perceive ourselves as separate, vulnerable, and deficient, and we look outside ourselves for completion. After awakening to our true nature, we realize there is only wholeness and we are That. We are already where we need to be. So the esoteric teachings are bound to meet skepticism and confusion. Search-ing for truth through the eyes of a self, we can never see what is. And when we identify mistakenly with this small-minded persona, a kind of internal civil war can break out in which we are constantly at odds with ourselves, with emotional torment and self-loathing the result.

Eckhart Tolle recalls a time in his life when he struggled with this contradiction within. It brought him to the verge of suicide. As he thought over and over that he couldn't live with himself any longer, it suddenly came to him how strange the thought was. He wondered: "Am I one or two? If I cannot live with myself, there must be two of me: the 'I' and the 'self' that 'I' cannot live with." Then a light dawned: "'Maybe,' I thought, 'only one of them is real.'"[8] This realization opened the door to his spiritual awakening.

The Divine within is an essential aspect of the esoteric vision and it has never been more relevant than it is today. In a world that idolizes the superficial, and too often skims the surface of life, the issues most deserving of our attention often go unrecognized. The mystic sages redirect us back to what is real—our own being. They are telling us that the truth we yearn for is close at hand. We need only look in the right direction.

~

IMAGES OF YEARNING

GRASS GROWING IN CEMENT ~ How many times have you seen a blade of grass pushing up through a crack in a sidewalk or patio? It happens everywhere, and even when steps are taken to subdue the growth, over time the grass usually wins. For such a tender little plant to overcome such overwhelming odds is amazing. Cement is a substance designed for hardness and durability, and structures built with it can last indefinitely. Yet thin green shoots of life yearning for air and light find a way to breach this formidable barrier, needing only the smallest of openings to poke through. The divine seed buried deep within each of us does the same, as it pushes through many years and many hard layers of conditioning. A small crack in the thick shell of the ego, deliberately created by reading and meditation or inadvertently opened by crisis, is often all that is needed for this living wisdom to find its way into our consciousness. Sharon Salzberg tells how some Hiroshima survivors had their faith rekindled when grass began to grow among the ruins. Witnessing this simple resurgence, they knew that the natural law remained intact even in the wake of such cataclysmic horror. Salzberg encourages us to find our center of gravity in this fundamental aspect of our nature, our innate awareness and love that lies beneath the painfully constricting layers of the ego, yearning to break through.[9]

HOMESICKNESS ~ Our first experiences away from home as children are often hard to forget. Whether it was our first summer at camp or a few days spent with relatives, we probably felt homesick.

During our waking hours we may have been sufficiently distracted to forget it, but at the end of the day, the longing for home returned. There is within each of us a similar yearning to return to the Source. In the noise of life and the pressure of our days, we seldom perceive it, but in those moments when we are still enough, it makes itself felt. We may not be able to put into words why we begin our spiritual search, but most likely it has something to do with being homesick: with having a vague sense of being incomplete, separate, and alone. Sooner or later, we hear something—what the Bible calls the still small voice within—calling us home.

HOMING INSTINCT ~ Many species are known for their homing instincts—the extraordinary ability to find their way home. Dogs, for instance, left behind in moves or lost on cross-country trips, often turn up on the front steps of their joyful owners' homes weeks and even months later. Homing pigeons, with their almost infallible sense of direction, have been used as message carriers since as far back as 5000 BCE. From their wide-ranging tours of the oceans, salmon instinctively find their way back to their native streams to spawn. In the insect world, each autumn millions of monarch butterflies intuitively journey thousands of miles to specific destinations they have never seen. Is it so far-fetched to believe that we too have a homing instinct? We may have forgotten who we are and whence we come, yet, like strangers in a foreign land, we sense that we are separated from our origin and long to return. This yearning comes from our deepest level of being, and we intuitively know the way home.

THE HOUSEPLANT ~ Many people decorate with potted plants, putting them in different places around the house. Wherever the plants end up, within a few days, their stems begin to lean toward the nearest window, and after a couple of weeks their bias for the light becomes obvious. In the same way that vegetation is phototropic, or light-seeking, we are drawn to the spiritual. When we read a line that strikes a familiar chord or hear a talk that resonates long afterward, this inclination to the truth is making itself felt. Although our minds can easily become numbed by the hectic rush and complications of modern living, our hearts recognize the truth and lean toward it. When we can bask in spiritual light, we grow and thrive, but deprived of it, we shrivel like a plant in the dark.

ICE ～ Water seeks its own level—this is well known. Unless obstructed in some way, it will naturally gravitate to the lowest level and come to rest in that position. This is true of all water as long as it is in the liquid state. If it is solidified into ice, however, its movement is "frozen" as well, and it cannot return to a natural state of equilibrium. The same is true of the innate wisdom at our core. When unobstructed, it automatically seeks the wholeness of its natural state. It cannot flow in this direction, however, if it is conceptually frozen into the mistaken identities we call our egos. With devoted practice on a nondual path, such as Zen Buddhism or the Hindu tradition of raja yoga, we can let awareness melt the rigid construct of who we think we are. Like an ice sculpture in the sun, that static persona can thaw and the water of our being can return, formless, to the incredible ocean of life.

The inner teacher is the deep intelligence of our true being, what we are, what is. There is no need to go elsewhere to find it, no need to wait for a better time. Ajahn Chah, the Thai Buddhist monk, once said that we are searching for the horse we are riding: the means of our journey home has been with us all along. Unfortunately, many people seek the truth afar, never realizing that what they yearn for lies in their own being, closer to them than they are to themselves.

Even when we begin to look within, we tend to think in terms of some *thing* that is being sought. After all, it is our belief that something is lacking that spurs us into action. Psychiatrist and contemplative theologian Gerald May, in his *Dark Night of the Soul*, explains that when we use words like "God" or "Divine Presence," we make our goal into an object and imply a separation that does not exist. Since our normal procedure in everyday life is to act from the stance of the ego and seek outside ourselves for happiness and fulfillment, it is easy to transfer this way of thinking to spiritual practice. Doing so, however, only perpetuates the dualistic distinction between subject and object and diverts our attention from what is real.

In fact, it is the unnamable that we approach in our spiritual quest. We cannot begin our search for this truth with fixed ideas of what to expect or mental images of a goal. Whatever maps we have of this hidden realm are just that—maps, not the territory itself. To assume otherwise will keep us from shifting our focus from the figure to the ground of our being and experiencing for ourselves the truth of which the masters speak. The techniques that different wisdom traditions have used to make the journey within are many and diverse, but ultimately, the conventional paradigms do not apply. They must be left at the door along with our shoes.

Though we may draw inspiration from teachers we admire, and glean wisdom from their guidance, imitating their actions will not help us in the long run. There is no vicarious realization, no enlightenment by proxy, and there are no shortcuts: we cannot reach the Promised Land we long for by adopting prescribed rituals or taking a set of beliefs on faith. We must make the journey ourselves. Over a thousand years ago, Zen master Yunmen declared, "As long as you aren't your own Master, you may think you have gained something from what you hear, but it is secondhand merchandise and not yours."[10] Centuries later, Sufi mystic Abu Yazid al-Bistami expressed the same idea: "Men learn from the dead, but I learn from the Living One who never dies."[11] Modern master Jack Kornfield makes the same point when he asserts that rote practice is little more than "acting spiritual" and cannot substitute for the deep knowing and basic goodness that is our own.[12] Taoist teacher Deng Ming-Dao puts it this way: "Those who follow Tao are their own instrument of divination."[13]

This is not to say that *self* is the way, for our egos must take a back seat on the journey within, though they will announce their eagerness to lead the way. The ego is quick to see the opportunity for increased self-importance in such an august endeavor. Ironically, the more effort we make to find the elusive inner teacher that will show us the way to wholeness, the stronger the sense of a separate self pursuing it becomes, and the further we get from realization. In this paradoxical realm, we must find without seeking.

When we are advised to "go within," does it mean that the answer is actually found within the confines of our body/mind? It does not; the Unknowable does not abide by such dualistic distinctions as inside and outside. As we approach the realm of the spirit, the grip of concepts and the divisions they impose begin to loosen, boundaries grow transparent, and we fall into our natural state—wholeness. Symeon the New Theologian, a fourth-century abbot in Constantinople, reflected this understanding: "I, a frail, small mortal in the world, behold the Creator of the world, all of him, within myself. And I know I shall not die, for I am within Life, I have the whole of Life springing up as a fountain within me. He is in my heart, he is in heaven: both there and here he shows himself to me with equal glory."[14] When we go within, we find nothing and we find everything; by losing ourselves, we find ourselves, and the seeker becomes the sought. Such is the paradoxical truth of esoteric spirituality. For this reason, we must let our hearts, instead of our minds, guide us to our true nature.

We have been attempting to control the nature of things with our minds for millennia, but the suffering and meaninglessness that characterize our modern existence bear witness to the futility of our efforts. Buried beneath all our patterns of egocentric thinking and behavior, there is something vast and fully capable of accomplishing the task: life itself. If through spiritual practice we can gather the courage to relinquish control, the spiritual odyssey begins in earnest. With an open heart and an empty mind, we discover that we are not alone on this adventure. As Deepak Chopra affirms: "Seekers are never lost because spirit is always beckoning to them."[15] Describing her own journey within, St. Teresa of Avila expresses it this way: "The feeling remains that God is on the journey, too."[16] Hidden under the mask of the ego is a Presence that longs to reveal itself, if we will just step out of the way. Once we clear the path, the inner teacher will do the rest.

PATHS

Religion is the creation of people and cultures.
Spirituality is the direct personal relationship with Tao.

—Deng Ming-Dao

I f you were to ask a new acquaintance about his spiritual path, he would probably respond by telling you what religion he was or what church, synagogue, or temple he attended. But these facts, while quite adequate to casual conversation, describe only one dimension of the spiritual life. To understand the true trajectory of people's spiritual lives, we need to look to their approach to spirituality. Do they take comfort in the beliefs and rituals of mainstream religion or are they drawn to the mystical points of view in esoteric traditions? While both approaches offer to show the way to truth, they take very different routes to get there, and to move between them entails a fundamental paradigm shift in the way we perceive the world and our place in it.

Today, exposed through travel and media to once-distant lands and cultures, we have an unprecedented opportunity to explore diverse spiritual traditions from around the world—both the orthodox belief systems of organized religion and the inwardly directed practices of the mystical tradition. Frithjof Schuon, acclaimed as one of the greatest experts in comparative religion, labels these paths *exoteric* and *esoteric*, a distinction I touched on at the start of the book. In his 1957 book *The*

Transcendent Unity of Religions, Schuon characterizes exoteric belief as a fundamentally dualistic understanding of reality, in contrast to the more rarefied esoteric branch of human spirituality, which rejects dualistic divisions in favor of a more holistic view.

As its name implies, exoteric religion is engaged in the manifest, outer aspects of doctrine and observance, giving prominence to historically revealed truth and a hierarchy that prescribes and mediates its followers' approach to the Divine. Arising in specific cultural contexts and tied to specific historical figures, exoteric traditions usually frame their chosen form of worship as the best, if not the only, path. And the sharp distinctions they draw—between right and wrong, believer and nonbeliever, dogma and heresy—often lead to intolerance for other forms of worship, even for different branches of the same basic faith. This dualistic worldview tends to discourage inclusive thinking and effectively rule out any suggestion of a universal truth that connects us all. Such an idea is a visceral threat, implicitly undermining believers' assurance of salvation as the chosen or favored people of God.

In dualistic religions, built firmly on the presumption of selfhood, one's individual existence is seldom called into question. According to Ken Wilber, such forms of religion use myths, rituals, and ceremonies to give their followers a new and sustaining way to think about life and helps them make sense of their suffering. In this paradigm, faithful observance wins divine favor, while conduct not in compliance risks retribution. Through prayer and ritual, devotees petition the deity for guidance or strength in handling the events of their lives, as well as for divine intervention on their behalf. In the long view, acceptance of the requisite beliefs and ethics is usually paired with some promised reward in the afterlife, ranging from eternal bliss to desirable rebirth. Wilber explains that spiritual doctrines of this kind serve to *translate* the unceasing conflicts, paradoxes, and dilemmas of life into a form that gives meaning and hope to the individual. In contrast, he finds that esoteric forms of spiritual expression act to *transform* the individual, opening the door to the deepest insights into the true nature of human existence and of life itself.[1]

For the untold millions who face a daily struggle to survive, there may be little time or opportunity to attempt the radical engagement with life that this realization of nondual reality requires. In these circumstances, traditional religious practice can be a source of indispensable solace. Indeed, organized religion holds great wisdom and truth, just as mystical practice does; but much of it lies hidden beneath the trappings of form. As the parables and metaphorical teachings in sacred scripture are codified into creeds and dogma, spiritual intuition and discernment are stifled, and transcendent truths get lost in the accretion of doctrinal embellishments over thousands of years. As the German theologian Rudolf Otto argued in his seminal work, *The Idea of the Holy*, the efforts of religion to reveal the *mysterium tremendum* that lies at the heart of existence serve instead to conceal it. He maintained that institutionalized versions of the secrets of life only tended to divert us from the experience itself. The Danish philosopher Søren Kierkegaard added that dogma can become a form of idolatry, an end in itself with little connection to the intuitive spark that ignited the religious flame at its origin. These modern thinkers echo the wisdom of the sages of nonduality, with their shared conviction that to name the unnamable is to close ourselves off from truth.

Seekers who are new to the mystical traditions are often taken aback when they first discover that some of these spiritual paths make no mention of God. But the lack of the familiar concept of a supreme being is not the same as the denial of the Divine found in the theories of some modern thinkers, such as Marx or Nietzsche or Freud. Nondual traditions, lacking any concepts for the holy, nonetheless have no lack of holy awe; they simply explore and interpret the indefinable without attempting to attach labels to it. It reminds one of Victorian author and thinker Samuel Butler's remark about God, "I cannot tell which is the more childish—to deny him, or to attempt to define him."[2]

This book is about the return to wholeness, going back to the source from which all manifestation evolves. The return entails a perceptual shift from the dualistic reality of our conventional world to the nondual, where boundaries no longer divide what is. In our everyday experience, concepts create in our minds a world of seemingly separate objects and events, which we then organize and make sense of through the framework of space and time and the dynamics of cause and effect. When the dualistic paradigm is applied to the spiritual realm, the deepest feelings and concerns of humanity often find substance in the *concept* of God. Concepts shape our deepest yearning and intuition into an image of God that is separate from us. The particular image to which we respond depends on our conditioning and capacity, but it is a fundamentally dualistic relationship. The pantheon of world religions is filled with personal gods, sometimes described with very human attributes and emotions—but between the worshipper and the object of worship there is an unbridgeable ontological divide.

In esoteric traditions, such conceptual schemes are considered a function of conditioning, not an inherent part of what is. Nonduality abides no contrast or comparison, no distinction between this and that, and no sequence of before and after. Beneath the surface play of phenomena, there is a formless, undifferentiated realm invisible to the naked eye; devoid of all parts, there remains only the unceasing flow and energy of life. Any concept of the Divine, therefore, is misleading, as it stands in the way of the deepest insights into the nature of reality. "God" is a concept, and, as such, is considered a misguided attempt to capture the infinite in the finite—to limit that which is limitless. As Mariana Caplan points out, "it is our imagination of God that fails," not God who fails us.[3] St. Augustine voiced the same insight sixteen hundred years ago when he said God was not what we imagine or think we understand.

Thus, there are no images or descriptions of the Divine in the esoteric literature that play more than a metaphorical role. Just as assumptions of individual existence dissolve in the ascent to the nondual, the traditional images of God likewise cease to be relevant. When we talk about the source of those aspects of life considered most holy and sacred, those which fill us with wonder and awe, only abstract ideas or terms can convey a sense of their boundlessness. Whether we say the Tao, the Unborn, Being, or any of the numerous other designations, there is no division, either explicit or implied.

Interestingly, this is true not only in Buddhism and Taoism, whose theology makes no mention of a supreme being, but also in those traditions in which God is most prominent. Considering the longevity of nondual truth in India, and the countless teachings and scriptures that have proclaimed the boundless, indefinable nature of what is in the Hindu culture, the esoteric practitioners there were able to openly express such an understanding, but for mystically minded seekers embedded in Judaism, Christianity, and Islam, explications of such insights about the Divine have always, of necessity, been more veiled. To affirm this same radical transcendence of a personal God, students of the Kabbalah speak of *Ein Sof* (infinity) or *Ayin* (Nothingness), asserting only what the Divine is *not*. As twelfth-century rabbi and mystic Maimonides puts it, "With every increase in negations regarding God, you come nearer to the apprehension of God."[4] Meister Eckhart, the fourteenth-century German theologian, and Ibn Arabi, the thirteenth-century Sufi mystic, both refer to a similarly abstract and all-inclusive "One." Contemporary thinkers reflect the same understanding. Paul Tillich, one of the most influential Protestant theologians of the twentieth century, expresses it this way: "God is being-itself," as opposed to a "being."[5] Rabbi David Cooper, an authority on the Kabbalah, captures the same idea quite effectively in the title of his book on the subject: *God Is a Verb*.

Over and over, the mystical teachings tell us that we cannot *know* the truth intellectually, but we can *be* it. Experiential as opposed to conceptual, esoteric spirituality has been compared to falling in love—something else that's impossible to adequately express in words. It is a matter of union with what is—with what we *are* in the deepest sense. In contrast to the exclusivity associated with worship in different exoteric faiths, esoteric spirituality consistently draws us back to the inherent wholeness of all that is. Judgment, good and evil, heaven and hell, and the myriad distinctions that make up our conventional worldview fall away when we realize what is. It comes with the shift from figure to ground. Recalling our discussions in the chapter on duality, we cannot see both figure and ground at the same time. Only when our focus shifts from the external trappings of spirituality can we discern the ground of our being.

~

IMAGES OF PATHS

PATHS UP A MOUNTAIN ~ Most mountains have many paths that wind up their slopes. They start at different points, lead up in every direction, and vary widely in the skill and strength needed to climb them. Many climbers reach the lower elevations, but the constraints of time, skill, or courage keep most from pressing on. And the views from the lower elevations can be very different, depending upon the climbers' vantage points: one sees the pine forest covering the south slope, another the rocky outcroppings on the north. The few who climb higher get an ever-widening perspective, seeing more and more of what others are seeing from other sides of the mountain, until all the paths converge at the summit and the jubilant climbers share the same spectacular view. In spiritual endeavors, seekers of truth do not all begin their journeys on the same path. Any number of traditions, methods, and teaching styles are available to prepare and initiate them, and there is insight to be gained on any such path. In this sense, we can say that all paths lead in the same direction: wholeness lies at the heart of all great wisdom traditions. Seekers who mistake the concepts for the truth can only climb so high—but those who reach the summit share the same realization: the unimaginable freedom inherent in their true nature.

FINGER ~ The sacred writings of mystical traditions are often likened to a finger pointing at the moon. It would be ridiculous to imagine that the lone digit was the moon itself—this is obvious. Yet throughout the history of spirituality, the faithful have pored endlessly over the words of the sacred texts, all the while missing the brilliance of the divine truth they point to. Scholars have spent whole lifetimes debating the intent of the most obscure details, as if the dogma were the Divine, but never catching sight of the experience they describe.

SUNLIGHT ⌒ When sunlight shines into our homes, it illuminates everything touched by its rays. As it moves across the grain of a hardwood floor, a flowered pattern on the couch, or the light-green paint on the wall, its appearance changes constantly, but everyone understands that all the light emanates from the sun. In the same way, the world's great religions, often strikingly different in dress, rituals, ceremonies, and beliefs, are ignited by the same yearning in the human breast and the same intuitions of the human heart—but the shared vision and insight that brought them into being has largely been forgotten. Followers who focus on the external manifestations of a religion—who argue that the floor has nothing in common with the couch—will often find themselves in strident disagreement with believers of other traditions, but those who understand the shared basis of all religion rarely quarrel with those of other faiths.

ART ⌒ Human beings have represented their world in art for thousands of years, but the modes of representation have shifted dramatically over time. For much of human history, figurative art was the dominant style; then, in the last century, people became attracted to increasingly abstract, subjective forms of expression. Religion, too, has moved from concrete, anthropomorphic representations of the Divine to increasingly abstract thought that recognizes our inability to capture spiritual truth in concepts. Which is best? The answer depends on the individual in both art and religion. Just as aesthetic beauty is in the eye of the beholder, the Divine is in the heart of the devout.

PHYSICS ⌒ The laws of classical physics have served us well for centuries and continue to do so in innumerable ways. Nonetheless, their truth is not absolute; the discoveries of New Physics have revealed a deeper reality. Extensive research on the properties of the subatomic realm has produced breakthroughs that have led directly to many of the breathtaking innovations we use all the time. From cell phones and microwave ovens to the ultrasound that provides images of our unborn children, the invisible reality of New Physics has yielded many technological miracles once considered impossible. Similarly, the world of the spirit lies on the fringes of our comprehension but contains powerful truths. For millennia, mystics have explored its depths and revealed insights previously unimaginable. Like Newtonian physics, with its well-understood and readily exploited laws, conventional religion improves the lives of devotees in countless ways. Nevertheless, there is a deeper level of truth that underlies it. As Huston Smith points out, theism is true, but it is not the *final* truth.[6] Just as the breakthroughs in New Physics opened new vistas, the wisdom of esoteric spirituality holds the key to the most pressing human problems that face the world today.

RAFT ∿ If you need to get from one side of a river to the opposite shore, you might use a raft. The Buddha chose this image, as common in his day as in ours, to convey a very important point. He asked his followers if, after they had crossed the river, they would continue to lug the raft around. They replied that it would be senseless to do so. The Buddha then explained that the same was true of his teachings. Once we have followed the spiritual path to realization, it makes no sense to worship the vehicle that got us there. It would be far more reasonable to leave the raft on the riverbank for others to use.

We have a foot in two very different worlds, one of numberless divided parts and the other of the whole. No wonder we struggle with doubt. It is our minds that have guided us thus far through the maze of a finite human reality, while our hearts continue to call us back to the infinite. To realize the truth of existence and our own nature, we must bridge the two seemingly incompatible halves of our being, uniting them into one magical expression of what is. For this we need a path that offers a method instead of a dogma and yields experience untrammeled by belief. For too long, the innate wisdom in our hearts has been suppressed by the aggressive dominance of our minds. To find our way out of delusion and plumb the depths of life's mystery, we must still the mind and its insistent dualism. We must discern the difference between the transcendent truth and its multiple forms, or, as Huston Smith once put it, find its essence as one would find the poetry in the poems.

The journey home to our true nature is extraordinarily difficult. D. T. Suzuki, one of the first to introduce Zen to the West, asserts that the realization demanded of all who complete the journey is the most profound transformation humanly possible. He asks: "How is it possible for the human mind to move from discrimination to non-discrimination, from affections to affectionlessness, from being to non-being, from relativity to emptiness...? How this movement is possible is the greatest mystery not only in Buddhism but in all religion and philosophy."[7] It is a challenge few individuals accept. It is an adventure that demands such an investment of time and energy, and such single-minded devotion, that for the millions encumbered with the relentless demands of modern existence it is all but impossible. Nevertheless, the universal experience of being "called" has for millennia preempted people's best-laid plans and irrevocably altered the direction of their lives.

We often use the language of "paths" and "journeys" to talk about humanity's spiritual quest, as in fact I have throughout this chapter, yet this is another subject that proves the inadequacy of conventional language to convey what is inherently paradoxical. The path we must find is, in truth, no path at all. We are not seekers, though we use the term constantly. No matter what we think we are about when we set out on our spiritual exploration, we are not going anywhere, nor is there anything we need to find. The pursuit of spiritual truth has nothing to do with fixing ourselves. It is a matter of discovering what is and always has been. It is simply awakening to what we already are.

While mainstream faiths lay out specified beliefs, rituals, and behaviors as the means to divine reward, in esoteric spirituality no one earns a better rebirth or advances toward salvation through good works. Instead, it is a different way of *seeing* to which we are directed again and again. In the Gospel of Thomas, for example, when the disciples ask Jesus, "When will the final rest for the dead take place, and when will the new world come?" he replies: "What you look for has already come, but you do not know it."[8] In the same vein, the Buddha repeatedly asserted that the only thing we need do was to simply open our eyes.

We are born whole and forever remain that way. Our spiritual odyssey from wholeness into an existence in exile and back home again is a mental one, every step of the way. To get where we are going, we go nowhere, returning to the place we never left. We do this by following a "path" that leads us through the dream world we take for reality, clearing away the confusion of our conceptual habits, and opening our eyes to a world without boundaries. Putting aside the maps of the mind, we follow the compass of the heart and the yearning within back to the territory of our true nature.

Esoteric spirituality strives simply to awaken us to the fact that we have never left home, except in our minds. Of course, from a conventional point of view this makes no sense, so the uninitiated readily dismiss it. Modern society, with the emphasis it places on logic and conceptual thought, has little patience with anything that does not add up. Given our culture's obsession with productivity and the bottom line, a process that produces nothing and a path that leads nowhere attract few customers. But this rejection of esoteric truth just makes it all the truer. In the *Tao Te Ching* we read: "Lower people hear of the Tao / They laugh loudly at it / If they did not laugh / It would not be the Tao."[9]

ALIGNMENT

It is in the silence of the heart
that God speaks.

—*Mother Teresa*

When we enter a place of worship, be it a temple, synagogue, mosque, or church, we often perform some customary act of reverence, meant to prepare us for the comfort and wisdom we hope to receive within. Whether we take off our hats or shoes, bow or kneel, or cover our heads with prayer shawls or yarmulkes, such actions are attitudes of humility that open our minds and hearts. Similarly, when we embark on the journey toward self-realization, we must adopt an attitude that prepares us to receive the truth of what is. When we align our actions with our spiritual aims, we eliminate any separation between our daily life and our practice. By living in accord with our true nature, we cultivate a peaceful mind and heart and, in turn, an openness and receptivity to spiritual transformation. No matter what path we follow, these first steps bring us into alignment with truth.

Every aspect of our behavior that is not in harmony with the way things truly are only acts to obscure the truth. Our efforts cannot be divided; as Jesus warned, we cannot serve two masters. Sufi mystic Ibn Arabi taught that the quintessential element of man's form was the heart, fashioned in the likeness of God. For the heart to be the receptacle of

pure being—the pure consciousness of God—he said it must be emp-
tied of those "imaginations" of the ego that veil and negate the real.[1]

Buddhist monk Amaro Bhikkhu would put it another way, noting
that we must attune our "outside" attitudes and behaviors with those
"inside," or what he calls the immanent manifestations of that transcendent reality. As he says: "As we practice loving-kindness, our heart automatically comes into accord with reality and we feel good. . . . Goodness feels good because the attitude resonates with reality. Lying and
harming feel bad because they are dissonant with that reality of what
we are."[2] Frithjof Schuon also speaks of the need to conform to divine
law and to "anticipate morally" the transcendent reality we aspire to
know, that is, to behave in accordance with the yearning in our hearts.
Alignment with this higher order is seen as the *conditio sine qua non*
for mystical practice. While Schuon emphasizes that such alignment
in no way guarantees the coveted spiritual breakthrough, it is necessary
in order for practice to bear fruit. "Will for the Good and love of the
Beautiful," he writes, "are the necessary concomitants of knowledge of
the True, and their repercussions are incalculable."[3]

It is through the daily practice of virtue that we begin the shift
from our conventional view of ourselves as separate beings toward an
awareness increasingly permeable and receptive to the whole. Virtuous
living lays the foundation for all that follows, and virtuous living at its
most essential, reflected in mystical wisdom across time and culture,
recognizes no distinction or boundary between self and other. To do for
another is to do for yourself. To harm another is to harm yourself. We
are one. So often manifest in the lives of the world's spiritual masters,
this selfless behavior offers stark contrast to the "me first" orientation of
contemporary society and the seemingly unbridgeable chasm it opens
between self and other. Selfish and immoral actions unceasingly reinforce the dualistic view of reality, and until they give way to selflessness,
there is little hope for success: they are incompatible with efforts to
quiet our thoughts and penetrate the secrets of nonduality.

This emphasis on moral and ethical behavior is not unique to esoteric spirituality. From the earliest beginnings of religion, the precepts

or commandments of *every* tradition have defined those behaviors believed to promote harmonious living and prohibited those that would disrupt or fragment social stability. Nevertheless, there are significant differences between exoteric and esoteric views on virtue. In contrast to exoteric forms of religion, and their emphasis on *afterlife reward* for virtuous living, the esoteric practices see virtuous living as the foundation of all that happens *now*. They find a direct connection between our behavior toward others and the unfolding clarity of our spiritual insight.

For serious seekers of truth, realization demands ever more strict and subtle levels of compliance. In Buddhism, for example, the five precepts against killing, stealing, sexual misconduct, lying, and use of intoxicants become far more comprehensive for those who aspire to the higher levels. As Matthew Flickstein explains, the prohibition against killing is broadened to mean reverence toward all forms of life; the precept of no stealing is expanded to include the cultivation of generosity; and the rule against sexual misconduct dictates, more broadly, responsibility and consideration in intimate relationships. The ban against lying is widened to discourage embellishment or exaggeration of personal claims and encourage sensitivity to the impact of one's speech. The fifth precept, the avoidance of intoxicants, is generalized to encompass any highly stimulating or potentially toxic sense experiences taken in through the five physical senses or the mind that can lead to heedless or unskillful behavior.[4] Books, movies, video games, and even popular music with graphic depictions of violence or sexual content exemplify what is to be avoided.

While the specific directives concerning virtuous conduct vary according to cultural setting and historical period, all the mystical traditions clearly share the same intent: to free the seeker from the delusion of self. The ninth-century Indian sage Shankara stresses that liberating knowledge is accessible only to one whose mind has been calmed, for whom such things as pride, hypocrisy, cruelty, impatience, and insincerity are no longer allowed to perpetuate *samsara*, the cycle of life and death riddled with pain and sorrow. Humility, he asserts, is a moral

quality that prefigures the extinction of the ego and makes one receptive to transcendent truth.[5]

According to the early-twentieth-century Sufi master Hazrat Inayat
Khan, the restrictive view of the *nafs*, or ego, disrupts the harmony
that is an elemental aspect of life and an essential condition of realization. "The further we advance," he maintains, "the more difficult and
the more important becomes our part in the symphony of life; and
the more conscious we are of this responsibility, the more efficient we
become in accomplishing our task."[6] Khan assures us that it is those
who are happy and untroubled who are able to break through the barriers that imprison them and attain at-one-ment with the Absolute.
Thomas Merton frames it this way: to enter the inner sanctuary of our
being, we must let go of our dependence on sensual pleasures, self-
gratification, and all the unskillful behaviors that come with them.[7] The
ethical behavior we strive to increase at the beginning of our spiritual
search facilitates concentration and mindfulness and opens our hearts
to deeper insights.

In this preparatory stage of practice, we must also align our awareness along the lines of faith. This involves a shift from our head to our
heart, from the seen toward a reality that is unseen, from the priorities
of the material world to the peace and contentment of the spiritual
realm. We must begin to yield our desire for control, follow the longing within, and trust those who have gone before. Faith is the courage
to move from assertiveness to humility so that we might be receptive
to the teachings of the sages. For some, this advice may evoke painful
memories from younger years, when we were told to take doctrinal
teachings on faith, even those we questioned. Others may reject the
counsel of faith because it goes against the grain of the scientific mindset that informs so much of modern life: it seems to connote a lack of
rigor, even intellectual laziness. But faith has a very different meaning
in the mystical traditions of the world.

Higher levels of mystical practice transcend the world of the mind,
and thus they require that we relax our usual hold on reason when we
embark on the spiritual adventure. St. John of the Cross instructs us

to "love and have delight in that which thou canst not understand or feel concerning Him, for this, as we have said, is to seek Him in faith."[8] Sharon Salzberg, in her book entitled *Faith*, defines this quality as "the ability to move forward even without knowing."[9]

In the beginning stages of our practice, we have as yet no direct knowledge or experience on which to base our conviction or build a sense of purpose; without faith, we could not muster the energy and commitment to pursue a goal that is so subtle and elusive. An ancient simile compares the novice on the mystical path to a fish asking a turtle what land is like: esoteric truth is so foreign to conventional understanding that the uninitiated can no more grasp the deep levels of insight than a fish can conceive of the nature of land. To make the eventual leap, we have to trust the guidance of those who have gone before us. "When there is faith," Shankara assures us, "the mind can be concentrated on the point one wishes to know about, and this enables one eventually to know it."[10]

Faith seen in this light is fundamental to Aldous Huxley's view of spirituality as well. For him, faith is "a pre-condition of all systematic knowing, all purposive doing and all decent living."[11] He considers it a synonym for trust, as the scientist might base his or her research efforts on a faith in the reliability of the universe. In the context of mystical practice, Huxley maintains that faith in those "whose selflessness has qualified them to know the spiritual Ground of all being by direct acquaintance"[12] is likewise a prerequisite for committed engagement. He sees it as belief that can, with devoted practice, be *confirmed* through personal experience. Such trust is very different from belief in ideas or religious doctrine.

For Salzberg, the difference is that faith is immanent. She says that whereas "beliefs come to us from outside—from another person, or a tradition or heritage—faith comes from within, from our alive participation in the process of discovery."[13] Merton puts similar emphasis on the guidance and reassurance we can find within, assuring us that "our inmost 'I' is the perfect image of God."[14] While stressing the fact that they are not talking of the ego, great teachers from many traditions point to the same idea: when the Divine within is awakened, the experience of its presence is ample confirmation for our faith.

In the *Bhagavad Gita*, great emphasis is placed on *shraddha*, a quality of soul that, although not synonymous with faith, carries a similar meaning. In chapter 17 of the *Gita*, a short but self-contained chapter devoted to the topic, Krishna says: "Our faith conforms to our nature.... Human nature is made of faith. Indeed, a person is his faith."[15] Spiritual teacher Eknath Easwaran explains that this is not an intellectual abstraction, but one's very substance, in the same sense as expressed in the Bible: "As a man thinketh in his heart, so is he." Easwaran goes on to say that according to the *Gita*, "Right *shraddha* is faith in spiritual laws: in the unity of life, the presence of divinity in every person, the essentially spiritual nature of the human being."[16]

The final alignment requires shifting our focus from the noise and complexity of everyday life to the stillness and simplicity that our endeavor requires. To engage in mystical practice, with its subtle and paradoxical nature, we must find respite from the chaos and concentrate the mind. As the Buddha made clear, concentration is essential for the suppression of what he called the hindrances: without it, mental factors that prevent insight, such as sexual attraction, ill will, lethargy, restlessness, and doubt, can easily derail one's practice. And if concentration was considered important thousands of years ago, when the pace of life was much slower and distractions far less intrusive, how much more do we need it today?

Concentration training is best undertaken in a conducive context, free of distractions, and from the beginnings of human spirituality, seekers have sought peace in solitude. The Buddha's years of seclusion in the forest preceding his enlightenment, or the forty days and nights of Jesus's sojourn in the wilderness, are merely the most prominent examples; some form of withdrawal from the distraction and conforming pressures of collective existence has been the choice of countless individuals responding to the yearning within, and wandering hermits, ascetics, and shamans abound in the lore of many mystical traditions. The search for solitude eventually led to the establishment of monasteries and convents, spaces set apart and consecrated to the contemplative life. Today, spiritual retreats offer periodic escapes from hectic lives for individuals and groups seeking inner peace and a chance for contemplation. And to reduce the distractions that come from within, spiritual teachers have long advocated tactics from working on one's virtue—a form of alignment we have already examined—to confession, apology, forgiveness, loving-kindness meditation, and association with like-minded people. When we adopt behaviors of this kind, the personal conflicts and festering emotional wounds of the past have space to heal, and the chattering mind can begin to quiet down. Such steps can open our hearts to more compassion and understanding and nurture the sense of peace and well-being so beneficial to practice.

Once the inner and outer environments are made conducive to concentration practice, the different esoteric traditions employ a wide variety of specific exercises to bring the mind under control. Typically, the practitioner is trained to focus on a single object, using it as an anchor to hold awareness fast amid drifting thoughts. Different traditions prefer different objects: the breath, a candle, the midpoint of the brow, visualization, chanting, the repetition of holy names. By gently but firmly returning the wandering mind to the chosen point of interest, one gradually shapes one's attention into a tool of precision, absolutely essential for the investigation of the subtle workings of the mind, like the rise and fall of individual thoughts. Just as a magnifying glass can be used to focus the light of the sun on a small spot so intently that the object bursts into flames, refined concentration can direct all the energy of one's attention to a chosen object, sometimes with similarly powerful results—a stunning flash of insight.

≈

IMAGES OF ALIGNMENT

OX MOUNTAIN PARABLE ∼ There is a parable from the time of Confucius about a fine forest on a mountain not far from a large city. The city dwellers repeatedly cut down the trees with their axes, yet new growth continued to sprout. Then goats and cattle were allowed to graze on the young shoots, stripping the mountain to such a degree that the people grew accustomed to seeing it bare. Soon they could no longer even remember there had once been a forest. The parable compares the destruction of the forest to the manner in which our own selfish day-to-day actions are destroying the natural tendency toward goodness and love. The mystics of the world repeatedly remind us of this truth; without cultivation, morality and virtue will cease to be. In the rushed and competitive environment of modern life, it is easy to develop habits that are insensitive, hard-edged, and even callous. Like the once-thriving forest on Ox Mountain, our kinder and more compassionate behaviors can almost be forgotten; we must consciously cultivate them to restore them to their natural place in our lives and realign our actions with our spiritual aspirations.

MOUNTAIN CLIMBING ∼ People who climb high mountains know not only that the skills required to navigate the steeper slopes are more advanced, but that the thin air of the higher altitudes makes the ascent ever more difficult. So climbers who wish to reach the peak jettison all unnecessary weight. Something similar happens as we reach the higher levels of spiritual endeavor. In the beginning of our adventure, our progress can be relatively quick as we gain understanding of the elementary principles and deal with the more obvious aspects of ethical behavior, such as honest business dealings or faithfulness in a relationship. As our climb continues, however, it gets harder to carry the burden of unresolved personal issues and the consequences of unskillful actions. Moral dilemmas of even a subtle nature—an unkind word, an inconsiderate action, unequal sharing of the household duties—largely unnoticed in the beginning of our spiritual ascent seriously hinder advancement at the latter stages of practice.

MUDDY WATER ∼ You cannot see through a glass of muddy water, but if you let it sit for long enough, the dirt will slowly settle to the bottom and the water will regain its original clarity. This is like the way in which the mind gradually clears in the practice of meditation. Our minds are typically filled with torrents of racing thoughts that cloud our judgment. Most of the time these thoughts go unnoticed—until we first attempt to concentrate and the mental chaos to which we have grown accustomed becomes apparent and even overwhelming. Nevertheless, with devoted practice, our minds slowly clear like the glass of muddy water, permitting us to see the truth of what is.

BUNGEE CORD ～ In bungee jumping, you leap from a tall structure—a bridge or a tower—with a thick elastic cord attached to your ankles. One reason people enjoy this thrill sport is because it rivets their attention to the present moment. In this moment, there are no worries regarding the past and no fears regarding the future, only direct, thought-free contact with the magic of the now. This exhilarating experience of freedom lasts until the bungee cord snaps back, ending the free fall and abruptly yanking the jumper back into the world of thought. Most beginning meditators experience something similar as they attempt to concentrate their minds and remain present with what is. If meditators have not yet resolved their issues from the past nor looked directly at the nature of their fears regarding the future, the content of their thoughts, much like the bungee cord, will abruptly snap them out of the present moment and thrust them back into the fabrications of their minds.

FAN BLADES ～ When a ceiling fan is set on high speed, it is impossible to perceive the individual blades in the whirl of motion. At a slightly lower speed, we can begin to distinguish one blade from another, and at the slowest setting, we can follow the individual blades as they turn. Meditation has the same effect on the perception of sensory experiences that arise while sitting. At the beginning of practice, everything runs together in a blur of activity, not unlike the rapidly spinning fan blades. With the attainment of deeper levels of concentration, however, one can discern discrete events with increasing facility. Ultimately, individual thoughts, feelings, and sensations can be observed as they arise and pass away from moment to moment.

The overriding goal of the spiritual journey is to penetrate the illusion of self. With a peaceful heart, faith in the teachings, and a calm mind, we are best prepared to accomplish this. When seekers let go of selfish aims and embark on the path with patience and compassion, they align themselves with the way things are and open themselves to the possibility of direct realization of ultimate reality.

Ironically, the same practices that enable us to gain clarity can, in turn, derail our progress. Instead of eradicating the sense of self, our initial successes can feed the ego and support the very illusion we are trying to see beyond. For example, in trying to cultivate virtue, the good works, fasts, prayers, and sacrifices are not always undertaken out of the *selfless* love of the Divine or devotion to transcendent truth, but rather out of a *selfish* desire for the goods these yield us—social recognition or eternal merit. Meister Eckhart compared such activities of "loving God" to the way one would love a cow for its milk and cheese!

Attaining deep levels of concentration can lead to a different sort of attachment. Some practitioners hone their skills to such a degree that they reach deep states of tranquility and bliss. While such serenity can calm the turbulence of life, give temporary respite from suffering, and greatly heighten powers of perception, it cannot by itself produce insight or lead to enlightenment. Nonetheless, the pleasant feelings can become addictive, so that our efforts tend toward recapturing those alluring and deeply peaceful experiences. Of such detrimental attachment, twentieth-century Indian yogi and philosopher Sri Aurobindo is reported to have said: "The fly that touches honey cannot use its wings; so the soul that clings to spiritual sweetness ruins its freedom and hinders contemplation."

In a similar discussion, Huxley warns against confusing two very different meanings of "experience." The alluring, addictive feelings to which practitioners become attached are what he calls "emotional excitement," not unlike those states induced in revivalist meetings. As he points out, however, these experiences are fundamentally different from the "experience" of direct, intuitive apprehension of nonduality. The latter is possible only for those who are "selflessly pure in heart"; the former is simply the "excitement of an individualized self."[17]

Other traditions also warn against attachment to the peace that intense concentration can produce. In the Zen tradition, the issue is referred to as "quietism" and is considered inherently dualistic: the division of what is into pure and impure, and the idealization of "no-thought" as something to be attained, is believed to pull devotees away from the wholeness of nonduality. The Advaita master Nisargadatta once said that a person can go into deep concentration for ten minutes, ten days, ten years, or a hundred years, but must still come back to where he started. He pointed out that there are forms of yoga that enslave and others that liberate. The motive is supreme. He emphasized that the mind is interested in what happens, but a yogi must be interested in the mind. Deep concentration must be paired with awareness of the mind itself. For this, we need a vehicle to carry us from narrowly focused concentration to an increasingly open and inclusive form of presence in which our true nature can emerge.

13
PRACTICES

It's important to remember that we're not fixing anything. We're not trying to be different from who we are. In fact, practice is simply returning to that which we always are.

—Charlotte Joko Beck

As we move through the initial stages of spiritual development and establish the necessary degree of peace and calm in our lives, we come more into alignment with life and direct our attention to what is happening right now. It is at this point that the real work of self-discovery begins. We must now choose a proven vehicle that can successfully carry us beyond the conceptual boundaries that fragment the wholeness of our true being.

This choice is a critical decision that must be made by each seeker alone—and the challenge is monumental. The task of overthrowing our literally self-centered view of life has been compared to the task Galileo faced when he sought to prove that the earth was not the center of the cosmos. Just as Galileo had first to design a brand-new way of seeing—the telescope—to unravel the old worldview, those embarking on the spiritual journey of self-discovery must find the practice that will allow them to see their place in life with fresh eyes.

As we have seen throughout this book, the separate and independent self is an illusion, a product of the conceptual template that we impose on reality. We have substituted the map for the territory so thoroughly and habitually that few of us question its validity—or even grasp that there is anything to question. Nevertheless, this is exactly what esoteric practice seeks to do. As Meister Eckhart says: "If you would have the kernel, you must break the husk."

The sacred literature of the world's mystical traditions lays out for us a panoply of techniques for awakening as wide-ranging as the capabilities of the human mind and heart. The *Bhagavad Gita*, for instance, divides Hindu mysticism into four classes: *jnana yoga*, the path of knowledge; *bhakti yoga*, the path of devotion; *karma yoga*, the path of action; and *raja yoga*, the path of meditation. This ancient division of spiritual methodology was devised specifically for the Hindu mystical tradition, but its universality is clear: these are the paths to God, no matter what tradition one starts from. Not incidentally, Amit Goswami, nuclear physicist and author of important books on consciousness, points out that these four yogas correspond to Jung's classification of people based on their ways of perceiving reality: thinking, feeling, sensation, and intuition.[1]

The methods that we will explore are more closely related to the paths of knowledge and meditation, or the *jnana* and *raja* branches of yoga. In the former, it is by discrimination and insight that the conceptual screen is penetrated, while in raja yoga, it is through the suspension of the mind process and the resulting stillness that one transcends conditioning. These two modes are especially pertinent to the premise of this book, that we confuse our concepts with what they represent and, thanks to our conditioning, see a dualistic world instead of the wholeness of our true nature.

The remaining two yogas are different in focus, but much in evidence in the mystical traditions as well. The special importance of devotion, for example, is apparent in the writings of many mystics, especially those from the theist traditions of Judaism, Christianity, and Islam. Consider, for example, the words of the anonymous Christian author of *The Cloud of Unknowing*: "By love may He be gotten and holden; but by thought never."[2] We may also think of the bridal imagery so pronounced in the writings of St. Teresa of Avila, in which Christ is the Bridegroom. And love and devotion overflow in the poetry of Rumi and other Sufi mystics, just as they do in the Jewish psalms and prayers. Elements of action are also found in varying degrees within all the mystical traditions, where ethical behavior, selfless service, and generosity are means of expanding one's identification beyond the narrow confines of the ego toward a oneness with an ever-greater part of life. A key Kabbalistic teaching, for example, talks of our deeds as a means of "raising the holy sparks." Based on the same fundamental interconnectivity of life that informs karma yoga, this view sees even our smallest actions as having a potentially profound effect on the universe.

It is beyond the scope of this book to explore more than a few of the diverse disciplines found in the mystical traditions of humanity, or to evaluate the effectiveness of any one approach. What we *can* do is simply offer a different perspective from which to view them: namely, in light of the understanding that the world we know is a product of our perception, and that it is by shifting our focus—from the map to the territory, from the figure to the ground—that we find our way home.

To that end, I'll present here some of the esoteric practices most specifically designed to the lift the veil of duality, organized in three groups according to their emphasis: on *symbolism, concentration,* or *investigation.* Collectively, these represent the methodologies of choice for a majority of the world's spiritual seekers, and all are strategies that help us break through the conceptual barriers that blind us to our birthright. Though it is impossible to produce realization by our own efforts through any particular practice, each of these approaches acts to weaken the grip of conceptualization and render its apparent divisions more permeable to new ways of understanding existence. Those methods that employ symbolism work to soften and *stretch* the divisions and boundaries of life, helping us to *imagine* nonduality. The various forms of concentration meditation generally function to *still* the mind, enabling us to transcend thought and temporarily *be* nondual. The techniques characterized by investigation or inquiry are designed to *probe* the conceptual divisions, making it possible for us to intuitively *see* nonduality. In their own way, each of these three types of practice tills the ground of habituation and conditioning, giving the seeds of insight and transformation their best chance to grow.

Symbolism has been central to religion since humans first began to imagine and worship something greater than themselves. Huston Smith has said that symbolism is to religion what numbers are to science.[3] And in some mystical disciplines, it provides the transcendent link between the all too familiar imperatives of physical existence and an unfathomable Divine. These traditions use the language of analogy to open what is called the third eye of wisdom, an intuitive form of understanding that is uniquely effective in grasping what lies beyond the world of the conditioned mind. In contemporary parlance, we might say that symbols and parables appeal to the right side of the brain, which is known as the source of creativity and intuition and famously adept at seeing the whole instead of the parts. Symbols and parables break through the calcified framework of perceptual habits and expectations and open our minds to previously unimagined modes of understanding, ways to reconcile the contradictions and paradox that abound in esoteric practice. It's not unlike our aim in this book, using metaphors and parables to help us see what prose and logic fail to convey.

The capability of symbolism to convey ideas by way of analogy is fundamental to mythology as well, and Joseph Campbell has explored its role extensively. Writing in *The Masks of God*, he argues: "Such a highly played game of 'as if' frees our mind and spirit, on the one hand, from the presumption of theology, which pretends to know the laws of God, and, on the other, from the bondage of reason, whose laws do not apply beyond the horizon of human experience." In the make-believe sphere of the festival, with the costumes, the masks, and the sometimes rapturous states that the dances produce, Campbell sees a "deepened participation" in which the mundane, secular laws of life dissolve.[4]

There are innumerable examples of this form of practice among mystical paths. Those in the West would likely think first of the parables of Jesus, or the symbolic use of bread and wine to represent his flesh and blood in Holy Communion. For others, the evocative stories of the

Taoist master Chuang Tzu would come to mind, and the artful way he could express the deepest of truths through narratives such as "The Lost Pearl" or "The Empty Boat." Yet again, there is the Sufi poetry of Rumi, with its continuously alternating perspectives of relative and absolute, dual and nondual, reality unfolding in the lyrical flow of his words. In Tantric Yoga we find the same kind of back-and-forth, resonating double nature in the symbolism of its male-female representations. In every case, the technique is the same: using what can be seen and easily understood to convey a parallel relationship at a far more profound level of being.

It is in Jewish mysticism that we find perhaps the most systematic and comprehensive use of symbolization. Though the Torah to some is just a collection of stories, Rabbi David Ariel calls these five books of Moses "the roadmap to God," deeply hidden in the language of symbols and parables, and he describes the mystical quest as a process of peeling back the layers, or "garments," that conceal the essence of the Divine.[5] In Kabbalah, the Torah's depths are mined for hidden significance and analyzed in what oral tradition claims may exceed six hundred thousand different interpretations. Rabbi David Cooper notes that there are no "correct" interpretations, in the same sense that there is no "correct" way to create a painting or any other work of art.[6] Comparing this mystical practice to the creative and sometimes inexplicable relationship between artists and their medium, he sees it as an art that can carry one far beyond the objective, literal realm to secret meanings pregnant with insights into the very structure of the universe.

The second form of practice that we will examine, known variously as serenity concentration, absorption, or *jhana*, builds on the preliminary levels of concentration discussed in the last chapter. These modes typically require years of additional training, with days on end of concentrated attention. The seeker focuses his or her attention one-pointedly on a single object until the mind becomes totally absorbed in the object and whatever else arises to consciousness—thoughts, sensations—falls away unnoticed. Centered in this manner, away from the distractions of the mundane world and the conditioned patterns of thought that define our reality and our place in it, we can merge with what is: being without boundaries.

As we saw in the last chapter, various objects can be used to develop and sustain concentration. One familiar object is the mantra, or ritualized invocation of sacred phrases and holy names. The beginnings of this technique may go back to the earliest forms of human worship, first finding expression in the chants and ceremonies of the shamans, healers, and holy men so important in the life of indigenous peoples. Mantra eventually found its way to the core of many mystical traditions—Hindu, Buddhist, Sufi, and Christian. *Rama, Krishna, Om mani padme hum, Amida Buddha, Allah, Jesus, Love*: these are but a few of the sacred words that acolytes have chanted, sung, or silently repeated for millennia, often filling every hour of every day with their invocations.

The Hindu Upanishads are filled with references to *Om*, which is considered to be the primordial sound, the vibratory essence, from which all other sounds, languages, and the universe itself evolved. *Om* symbolizes the unity and wholeness of what is, and those who concentrate on this sacred syllable are believed to not only perceive the nature of existence, but become one with it. As Alan Watts once put it, they reach a point where "the chant is chanting them."[7] In the Sufi tradition, this discipline is called *dhikr*, and a similar emphasis is placed on the vibratory quality of existence. Hazrat Inayat Khan taught that we are formed of vibrations ourselves, living and moving in them like fish in water. Noting the formless nature of sound, he argued that it is the perfect medium through which to be drawn closer to the formless God we seek.[8]

In any tradition, the potential of mantra practice lies in what Frithjof Schuon calls "the mysterious meeting of the created and the Uncreated, the contingent and the Absolute, the finite and the Infinite." To explain how the divisions collapse to make such a meeting possible, he goes further: "The Divine Name is thus a manifestation of the Supreme Principle, or to speak still more plainly, it is the Supreme Principle manifesting Itself; it is not therefore in the first place a manifestation, but the Principle Itself."[9]

The same inherent dynamic of identification and awareness that Schuon suggests here is clearly reflected in a seminal verse from the Buddhist *Heart Sutra*: "Form is emptiness and emptiness is form." We cannot become something that we are not; we can simply awaken from identification with phenomena to our forever true, but long forgotten, identity with what is. Inner concentration on the names of God so quiets the mind that it allows us for just a moment to experience, or *be*, this oneness that abides no distinctions.

In the Hindu tradition, it is raja yoga, an approach attributed largely to Patanjali, that employs absorption in this manner. The yogi stills and disciplines the mind and senses through concentration and ultimately realizes the unity and wholeness of life. In the *Gita*, the nature of the mind is compared to a flame blown by the winds of desire. Through constant practice, the yogi returns the wandering mind to its home in stillness, steady and unmoving "like the flame of a lamp in a windless place." As Krishna declares, "In the still mind, in the depths of meditation, the Self reveals itself. Beholding the Self by means of the Self, an aspirant knows the joy and peace of complete fulfillment."[10]

For any form of absorption concentration to be effective, and for the nature of reality to become apparent, mindful awareness must be active, allowing one to remain passively alert and attentive in the ever-deepening stillness. Eventually, the primary object used to train and refine concentration fades into sensations, incessant change, and moments of ever-increasing subtlety. The boundaries that define "things" dissolve into a consciousness of unbounded space and energy totally devoid of distinctions. As we passively witness an incomprehensibly rapid flow of tiny moments, the concepts that typically "construct" our dualistic reality and divide us from the rest of life no longer play any role. As with Patanjali's well-known metaphor of the salt figurine dissolving in the ocean, the seeker merges with what is.

The last set of strategies we will consider uses the investigation of phenomena to recognize and transcend the conceptual boundaries that imprison us in the mundane realm of experience. The Buddha taught that there is no self that is part of, at the root of, or in control of experience—no "one" to whom anything is happening. There is only the process of seeing, hearing, smelling, tasting, touching, and thinking. He emphasized that it is our thoughts that create our perceived reality and, as a consequence, give rise to the illusion of a separate self with its own existence. *Vipassana*, insight meditation, is the form of meditation the Buddha gave the world to deconstruct those thoughts and dispel the illusion. With a precision that rivals the controls modern science implements to attain valid results, this ancient science of the mind is so exact that incalculable numbers of practitioners over the centuries have been able to generate the same results through their practice.

Vipassana practice is based on mindful awareness, which means paying bare attention—bare of judgment, decision, or commentary—to what is happening to us and within us during every moment of experience. Progressing through a series of exercises under the guidance of an experienced teacher, we systematically examine every facet of what we believe our "self" to be. Observing how thoughts rise and fall on their own, for example, with no volitional participation helps the seeker to realize that they are not "his." With practice and refined skills, we are able to discern that the self we construct out of form, feelings, perceptions, thoughts, and consciousness has no foundation in reality. One by one, the assumptions that have so long supported our erroneous belief in a permanent, independent self—what we always thought we were—gradually dissolves like a cloud in the rays of the sun. Once we actually *see* this truth about the nature of experience, it becomes apparent that there is no abiding entity to be found.

Since the Buddha gave his teachings, other forms of practice have appeared that share certain characteristics with vipassana. One of the best known is the *vichara*, the method of inquiry described by the ancient Indian philosopher Shankara. Like the Buddha, Shankara aimed to enable his students to discern the true nature of experience and break their identification with their mistaken perceptions. All objects of consciousness, all thoughts or feelings of any kind, were to be recognized as delusion, dismissed with the double negation *neti, neti*—"not this, not this." Shankara explains it this way: "Because the Self cannot be negated, it is that which remains after the practice of saying *neti, neti* to all else. It is directly apprehended through the practice of saying 'I am not this, I am not this.'"[11] As we have seen in chapter after chapter, the ego-notion arises from the idea that we are some "thing," a "this," the entity to which our parents pointed and gave a name. But *neti, neti* points to the fact that your true nature, what Indian sages refer to as the "Self" with a capital S, is not a "thing" that can ever be found. In modern India, Ramana Maharshi used a similar method to draw the attention of his students back to the source of their questions. *Who is it that is seeking the truth?* he would ask them. *Who wants to know?*

Seemingly impossible questioning lies at the heart of another famous insight practice, the Zen koan. Developed in the Zen tradition more than a thousand years after the time of the Buddha, this ingenious form of inquiry consists of a dialogue or enigmatic riddle assigned to the student to solve. According to D. T. Suzuki, the intellect, through which we perceive a world divided into subject and object, is the greatest obstacle to understanding; the koan is used to interrupt its normal operations and "make the calculating mind die."[12]

To the uninitiated, koans make no sense at all. Consider one of the most famous: "A monk asked Chou-chou, 'Does a dog have Buddha-nature?' The Master replied, 'Mu.'" How is one ever to discern meaning in such an inscrutable exchange? As with any problem life presents us, the discriminating intellect immediately takes up the challenge, probing its possible intent with an endless series of questions and comparisons. Is the dog's lack of self-awareness the key to the riddle? Is *mu* pointing to nothingness? What breed of dog is it? The effort continues interminably, but every logical stratagem or creative mental maneuver leads to a dead end. Each time the student approaches the Zen master with such a mentally derived "solution," it is unceremoniously rejected and the student is sent back to further study and meditation.

Our conditioning forces us to see life in fixed, predetermined ways—as Blake would put it, each man seeing "thro' the narrow chinks of his cavern."[13] It limits us to only relative understanding and blinds us to the truth. But when the intractability of the koan has so completely frustrated the mind's attempts to unravel it that the student reaches a psychological impasse, insight begins to ripen. It is from that tense, overwrought state of consciousness, Suzuki explains, that we can make a shift to the deeper, intuitive levels of the mind. When we put down the weight of conditioning and set aside our preconceived notions, mental resistance, and beliefs about how things must be, the third eye opens.

Does this mean that Zen rejects thought and dismisses the mind as irrelevant? The masters have repeatedly assured us that it does not. Rather, it is our *relationship* to our thoughts that we must question. We confuse the means with the end. As Marshall McLuhan would say, the medium has become the message. In our earlier discussions, we have seen repeatedly that words are constructs: arbitrary conventions that divide what cannot actually be divided. They serve a function, like any tool, but can never bridge the divide between duality and the nondual. Parts cannot surmise the whole.

The breakthrough comes when the calculating mind gives up and something deeper takes over. When, as Blake put it, "the doors of our perception [are] cleansed" and we revert to our unconditioned, egoless origins, we can glimpse with fresh eyes behind the veil and see the Absolute. As theologian Ruben Habito explains, it's not that we now *understand* or have *found the answer*. Rather, he says, "the question answers itself." The key lies in direct experience, "the pure and simple fact of being in the here and now."[14] Because the process is not mental, we literally cannot "give" the "answer" here; it doesn't work that way. But in that relaxed natural state, once we let go of all the effort, struggle, and mental turmoil, even a simple sound can open our eyes to what is.

⁓

IMAGES OF PRACTICE

ANTIQUE FURNISHINGS ⁓ A piece of wood furniture is usually coated with some kind of finish to protect it from the elements. As the years pass and the finish begins to wear away, we attempt to maintain the integrity of the furniture by applying fresh coatings over the old. Eventually, however, the layers build up so thickly that we need to strip them all away in order to restore the wood to its natural, pristine state. This process of restoration—painstakingly removing the protective layers of years and decades—can be compared to spiritual practice, in which we peel off the layers of concepts, constructs, and cultural belief systems that conceal the underlying reality of our lives. With untold layers of confusion stripped away, what remains is the uncontaminated truth of who we are.

MICROSCOPE ∼ Looking through the lens of a microscope reveals an entirely new world. We are able to see things we have never seen or even imagined before. Magnified by one of these fascinating tools, even a single drop of creek water contains a whole, strange universe, teeming with activity and life. The same perceptual shift can happen in the practice of meditation. Sitting for even a short time magnifies the inner workings of the mind so that we quickly become aware that it is a disorderly world of thought in ceaseless motion. To commit to such a practice, however, offers us a way to see through the chaos and see reality in an entirely new way.

HOLE IN THE CHEESE ∼ Picture a piece of Swiss cheese. It typically has holes of all sizes and shapes in it. In your mind's eye, pick out one hole. Notice its characteristics. Maybe it is bigger than the others around it; maybe it is deeper. It has existed since the cheese was made. Now imagine eating this piece of cheese, slowly nibbling away at the area surrounding the hole. Watch what happens. The hole slowly disappears. When all the cheese is gone, the hole is gone too. Where did it go? It was there a minute ago. You saw it, and even distinguished it from the others. But as you can see, in the truest sense, there never was a hole. There was only a relationship between the cheese and empty space. By labeling your perception, you created a concept of "hole" and gave it a sense of reality. This is exactly what happens with the self, or ego. The concept of "self" is given substance by the label we affix to a relationship between elements that are not the self—form, feelings, perceptions, thoughts, and consciousness. When we study this relationship carefully in vipassana meditation, we can see that there is only consciousness rising and falling with its objects. The ego is a construct, but not a reality. Now you see it, now you don't.

MIRROR ∼ Nothing ever happens *to* a mirror; everything happens *before* a mirror. A mirror does not react to what it reflects: it does not grasp at pleasant experiences or push away unpleasant ones. It reflects exactly what passes before it—no more and no less. Similarly, when we practice techniques such as mindfulness or choiceless awareness, when we observe without commentary, judgment, or decision making, we can once again see with clarity the simple reality of each new moment. Like a mirror, we don't react to what we see. We only witness the flow of life, without clinging or aversion. This passive, utterly receptive form of awareness is crucial to unraveling the riddle of who we are.

FLAT EARTH ∼ In a world where "seeing is believing," it stands to reason that words alone cannot convince people of spiritual truths that they cannot see with their own eyes. Watts helps us understand this predicament by reminding us that most people once held firmly to the belief that the earth was flat. He explains that you cannot just tell a person that the earth is round when simply looking out the window offers clear evidence to the contrary. Somehow you have to give that person a direct experience of the reality he or she is denying. For example, if a teacher were to lead the "flat earther" all the way around the world in a straight line, when the pair ended up where they started, the disbeliever would "know" that the earth was round after all. In the same way, when someone clings to the belief that he or she has a permanent, independent self, there is no rational argument that will change that belief. It requires, instead, a discipline or technique that leads to the direct *experience* of selflessness. Only by seeing the truth firsthand can we be convinced that there is no fixed self at the center of our experience.

All the approaches we have examined in this chapter direct our attention in ways that shed the light of awareness on the constructs and habitual patterns of thought that imprison us. Paradoxically, though, the techniques are constructs themselves, each including the perception of a doer, prescribed actions for the doer to take, and goals to be achieved with effort and perseverance. By their very existence, these techniques make a distinction between the state from which we begin and the preferred state to which we are directed. In other words, while purporting to open a window to the unconditioned, they themselves are essentially dualistic, the very state we are trying to leave.

Is this a trick? No—such dualistic paradigms are necessary for most of us when we first set out on the mystical journey. There is an ancient saying in the Buddhist tradition that the teacher will appear when the student is ready. More recently, someone added that the student will appear when the teacher is ready! In this same vein, we can say that when the seeker is ready, the practice will appear. Life is the great teacher, and it never fails to present moment by moment exactly what we need for spiritual growth. Though this is a hard fact to accept when serious problems arise, and even when something as insignificant as a flat tire interrupts our day, it is asserted again and again by the sages of esoteric spirituality. Practices of the kind we have surveyed in this chapter play an essential role, and when the seeds of insight begin to germinate and we begin to intuit selflessness, the practices introduced in the next chapter are seen in a new light. Vehicles designed to carry us beyond our conceptual boundaries cannot of themselves carry us all the way back to the state of wholeness we came from. While the shift can occur in the midst of such practices, they do not produce it; they simply point us in the right direction.

Using effort to purify virtue, calm the mind, or attain insights is, according to the Taoists, as useless as "beating a drum in search of a fugitive." "Yogas, prayers, therapies, and spiritual exercises," says Alan

Watts, "are at root only elaborate postponements of the recognition that there is nothing to be grasped and no way to grasp it."[15] Innumerable other teachers have voiced the same truth. The more effort we make, the more we strain to control what happens in our practice, the further away we get from what is. We become so busy *doing* that we forget *being*. Always looking ahead, we overlook where we are. We think we can divide and conquer: increasing the good and eliminating the bad, adding this and subtracting that. But every attempt is futile. Such actions are firmly anchored in the world of time—aspiring to be where we are not, looking to the future for spiritual fulfillment. We are like a cat chasing its tail, not realizing that its own movements are keeping the tail out of reach. Effort to change what is, by itself, reinforces the very delusion that we need to unravel: our existence as a separate self. Ultimately, Matthew Flickstein sums it up: "There is no need to practice becoming what we already are."[16]

NON-DOING

I can, of my own self, do nothing.

—*Jesus*

For most adults, the unselfconscious innocence and wide-eyed wonder of childhood was lost long ago. Once in a while, though, when the circumstances of life temporarily stun us into stillness and our minds grow quiet, we catch a glimpse of life unconditioned, before the fragmentation of concepts—what Eden must have looked like before the Fall. Often unexpected and always unearned, moments such as these bring with them a sense of blessing, well-being, and grace that is unmistakable. And whatever transporting experience gives rise to them—a spectacular sunset, the birth of a child—the grace comes to us not by dint of great effort on our part, but just the opposite: it comes when all our habitual activity ceases and gives way to rapt attention. For most, these openings are fleeting and infrequent, but throughout the ages, those who have devoted their lives to spiritual practice have reported that such moments come more often as they advance on their path.

As a spiritual practice evolves, to see more and more one must do less and less. The one who is practicing moves gradually from active involvement to a more passive, limited, and ultimately nonexistent role in his or her own awakening. Contemporary Zen master Adyashanti compares this level of practice to riding in a car when we don't know where we're going: trusting the driver to get us there, we simply watch the passing sights. It is a process of relaxation, a yielding of our efforts to steer the vehicle ourselves. The transition from the presumption of control to the realization that there is no self to be in control—that there is in truth no "one who is practicing"—may occur in the midst of much more structured practices, but the techniques presented here represent the culmination of this shift. The difference between practice and non-doing is so counterintuitive, so stark a change from our conditioned determination to take charge, to get a handle on whatever task is before us, that it does not take root quickly; even after we see the truth of it, it can take many years to inform our behavior. Practice now is not a matter of doing anything; it is *non-doing*, simply being with what is, allowing life to take the lead in the unfolding of each moment without interference. In this chapter, we will consider some approaches that reflect this level of understanding and represent the various forms of non-doing practice found among the world's wisdom traditions.

In the Christian tradition, numerous mystics have practiced forms of contemplation that are largely devoid of structure. *The Cloud of Unknowing*, an anonymous work produced in the fourteenth century, describes such a formless approach. Given no more specific guidance than to fix one's heart on God and forget all else, we are told to open to a "darkness" or "cloud of unknowing." Two centuries later in Spain, St. Teresa of Avila and St. John of the Cross moved from a more directed form of meditation and prayer to contemplation without an object—simply an open awareness, a passive presence in the here and now. As Gerald May describes it, this form of prayer had no particular goal, but was rather a way of being, an openness infused with reverence. Modern forms, such as Thomas Keating's centering prayer, approach this same state in which one is simply open to God's presence. Wayne Teasdale characterizes this more recent practice as an inner simplification that is "more about what we release than what we acquire on the way."[1]

In the same vein, Thomas Merton affirms that there is no special method or discipline for awakening to one's inner self—his term for what we most truly are, life itself. He explains that we cannot *define* or *deduce* the essential properties of the true self, nor can we produce some methodology by which to control or induce it. It cannot be reached by meditation or any other process; it is "a spontaneity that is nothing if not free."[2] "All that we can do with any spiritual discipline," Merton argues, "is produce within ourselves something of the silence, the humility, the detachment, the purity of heart, and the indifference which are required if the inner self is to make some shy, unpredictable manifestation of *his* presence."[3]

In the Jewish tradition of Kabbalah, devotees move through levels of consciousness ever closer to the Divine Source. One enters *binah* consciousness by simply noticing what is happening in the moment, without ego involvement. The alert, expansive, and calm presence that results is the precursor to far more subtle *chokmah* consciousness. At this point, Rabbi David Cooper explains, all meditation techniques per se fall by the wayside, leaving only "pure awareness" and the sensory input that rises and falls in each moment: "There is 'nobody' here to notice, no identification with self-ness, no one to react; it is simply noticing."[4]

According to D. T. Suzuki, the dominant understanding in Zen Buddhism until sometime in the seventh or eighth century was that our Buddha-nature was something separate, existing in its purity but hidden by the confusion of our individual minds. A famous exchange between competitors desiring to succeed the Fifth Patriarch reflects a pivotal moment in the history of this tradition. The chief monk offered his description of practice: "This body is the Bodhi-tree, the soul is like a mirror bright; take heed to always keep it clean, and let not dust collect on it." Hui-neng, the lowly cook, responded: "There is no Bodhi-tree, nor stand of mirror bright; since all is void, where can the dust alight?" He was arguing that methods of practice designed to eliminate thoughts were inherently dualistic and incompatible with the doctrine of noninterference. The division of *what is* into pure and impure, and the idealization of "no-thought" as a state to be attained, distinct from the state one started from, served to pull devotees away from the wholeness of nonduality.

In Hui-neng's famous utterance "From the first not a thing is" we find the same rejection of concepts (so challenging to our conceptual language and habits of mind) that is characteristic of all practices at this level. There is no mirror, no purity, no inside or outside, no method, nothing to attain, nothing to be done, and no one to do it; there is only what is, not yet obscured by the mind's incessant interpretations, judgments, and comparisons. As Suzuki contends, to say that meditation occurs only when we sit cross-legged, and in that manner we produce wisdom, is to affect a dualism that Zen abhors. He further notes, "If you say you have attained something, this is the surest proof that you have gone astray."[5]

Dzogchen, known as the most direct form of practice in Tibetan Tantric Buddhism (and long kept secret from all but a chosen few), is called the *Great Perfection*. As Keith Dowman, an authority on Tibetan Buddhism, explains it, "The starting point is the path, the path is the goal, and the goal is the starting point."[6] Dzogchen practice is a formless meditation that makes no distinction between subject and object or cause and effect. The conceptual screen that produces our conventional sense of reality, and figures so prominently in the steps on the path that we have examined so far, is effectively transcended in this practice. Through terms like *naked, direct, immediate, natural, simple, pure, uncontrived,* and *unelaborated,* the yogi is pointed in the necessary direction with language "designed to induce transcendence of itself." One is ultimately to be free of all conceptual duality, cultivation of attributes, effort, and even aspiration. "The analysis of consummate Dzogchen meditation," states Dowman, "is a description of the enlightened mind from the standpoint of perfect awareness, total presence, and it remains unutterable."[7]

With desire of all kinds stripped away, only pure sensory perception remains—naked, natural, and uncontrived. "This unsought, spontaneous accomplishment, present from the beginning," Dowman attests, "this is the summit of all attainments."[8] Reading such descriptions, we start to understand why this "practice" was traditionally taught only to a few. To make sense out of such "nonmeditation," one had to intuit that no change or improvement is required in anything. Those selected needed only to live life with total presence until their understanding of nonduality naturally unfolded in the uncontrived expressions of their own being.

The same fundamental sense of detached awareness and selfless participation that we see in these disciplines is physically embodied in many of the Eastern arts. The *sumiye* painting of Japanese Zen offers an excellent example. According to Suzuki, it is more a form of sketching than actual painting, and its traditional materials do not permit corrections, "doctoring," or touch-ups. Working with a brush made to absorb considerable ink, on thin, permeable paper, the artist must use a light touch and move freely and continuously; any hesitation or second-guessing allows ink to pool and splotches to form. The first stroke is often the final one. Sumiye is an art form that requires complete attention and an empty mind, and any attempt to copy or imitate is futile. As Suzuki expresses it, "The brush by itself executes the work quite outside the artist, who just lets it move on without his conscious efforts."[9]

In his own discussions of Eastern art, Alan Watts points out that it is customary for artists to spend years practicing in an effort to produce the desired effect, only to discover that all their techniques fall short. At this point, the artist usually gives up, and this very "giving up" is the key. Watts stresses the selflessness of the process, stating "that 'you' cannot go along with 'things' unless there is the understanding that there is, in truth, no alternative since you and the things are the same process—the now-streaming Tao."[10] He goes on to say that when you fully grasp this, and fully realize that you are the Tao, you manifest its spontaneous magic and grace.

In his classic *Zen in the Art of Archery*, German philosopher and student of mysticism Eugen Herrigel argues the same point. He spent six years learning to shoot a bow and arrow from a Zen master and at first suffered the self-consciousness that most of us experience when we attempt to learn something from someone else. We often feel inept and embarrassed by our obvious lack of skill, but it is that distraction that interferes with our progress. We get in our own way. It became clear to Herrigel that it is when we let go of such preoccupations, finally give up all calculations and effort, and allow *life* to release the arrow, it finds its mark.

∿

IMAGES OF NON-DOING

MUSIC ∿ You sometimes hear musicians talk about "forgetting themselves" during performances or say that the music "plays itself." Music does not use the medium of thought, and in bypassing conceptual activity it allows them to stay in the experience of the moment. Even as listeners, we can have similar experiences. Contemporary master Stephen Levine once said it was with jazz that he gained his first deep connection with the sense of being. When we are listening to good music, it is not unusual to "lose ourselves" and dissolve into the flow of the sounds. According to Watts, when you relax into the sensory experience, "the sound of it becomes your whole mind."[11] There is no longer a sense of being a discrete listener enjoying music coming from somewhere outside you, only the simple flow of what is. This kind of listening closely parallels the essence of non-doing practice. Both processes are devoid of planning or desired results, unfold without contrivance or manipulation, and allow one to simply *be*.

BABY'S PRACTICE ∿ It can be very entertaining to watch a baby playing by himself on the floor. If he is presented with a new toy or an object he hasn't seen before, he will turn it around and upside down and perhaps drop it on the floor to see what happens. He will feel every crack and crevice with his chubby fingers and study each feature intently. Ultimately, he will place it in his mouth, like everything else, to see what the tongue says about it. Having as yet no sense of time, and undistracted by thoughts of past or future, the baby is entirely engrossed in the process of exploration. He has merged completely with what he is doing. There is no idea of self, no thought of who owns the toy, no concern about giving it back. There is just the process of life—pure being. This is the naturalness and spontaneity to which mystics aspire. Listen to Chuang Tzu: "You want the first elements? The infant has them. Free from care, unaware of self, he acts without reflection, stays where he is put, does not know why, does not figure things out, just goes along with them, is part of the current. These are the first elements."[12] Those who progress to the highest levels of practice resemble the baby in very important ways. Like the child, they become so involved with what they are doing that their minds grow silent. Self-consciousness fades; there is no awareness of time; life is left to its own devices. In the absence of ego-based effort and attempts to manipulate what is happening, behavior is adequate in every way. With all the functional skills and knowledge we have gained over the years at its disposal, life takes us to places we have never been.

THE INTERIOR GARDEN ∼ St. Teresa of Avila used the metaphor of watering a garden to describe the stages of her spiritual development. She compared the first stage of practice to hauling water from a well, since both required great effort. The use of a waterwheel, providing more water with less work, illustrated the lessening of exertion in the second stage of practice. The third kind of prayer, which Teresa characterized as helping the "small flowers of virtue" to bloom, left little to be done, and this reminded her of having a nearby stream to provide most of the moisture that the garden required.[13] The last stage of practice was likened to a garden that always received all the water it needed from the rain that naturally fell. In this prayer of perfect union with all that is, the fruit of virtue was borne with no effort at all.

LIGHT AND DARKNESS ∼ The relationship between the seeker and the sought discussed in the mystical teachings can easily be misunderstood. When the different traditions speak of the realization of our true identity, we might mistakenly believe that they mean the ego or persona of the practitioner. An analogy suggested by Ibn Arabi helps to clarify this serious misconception. He compares the mystical experience to the relationship between light and darkness. Darkness may seem to exist; we have all certainly had the experience of getting confused or lost in it. When light shines into the darkness, however, there is nothing there. Light is all that is real. Instead of darkness turning into light in the process, it is proven to be an illusion. Similarly, the seeker does not become divine through mystical practice, as the sages' words might suggest. Rather, it is in seeing through the delusion of self that the boundary between seeker and sought is understood to dissolve. Just as darkness disappears in the presence of light, in proximity to the Absolute, the shadow nature of the individual seeker vanishes, leaving only unity.

Most of us are habitual doers; we want to get somewhere and have something to show for it. We live in a world where self-improvement is a high priority and our accomplishments are the measure of our worth. When we hear that the very concepts of doer and doing lose their relevance on the spiritual path and that practice plays no real role in transformation, it becomes ever more difficult to comprehend. In the modern world we search unceasingly for answers, experiences, insights, and attainment, so claims that there is nowhere to go and nothing to gain can be baffling. And those engulfed in suffering, when told that change and improvement are not only unnecessary but antithetical to enlightenment, often find such paradoxical guidance perplexing, if not outright callous. How are we to do anything without doing? Do we make an effort not to make an effort? Can the aims of freedom and an end to suffering be gained without any attempt to gain them?

As we've seen over and over in this book, the simple truth is that the rational mind cannot make sense of the paradoxical nature of esoteric spirituality. As May explains, our faulty thinking only leads to further contradiction and confusion. Take the following line of reasoning: if the self isn't working the way it should, it needs to be controlled, and a self that can't be found endeavors to accomplish this; moreover, if the self is brought "under control," the same elusive self takes the credit. May concludes that the expression "self-control" embodies in itself "an almost indescribable insanity."[14] Our conceptualization of life establishes boundaries everywhere, even in the very essence of our being.

The principle of non-doing, so strange to the Western mind, permeates much of Eastern thought. In the *Tao Te Ching*, we read: "He who practices [Tao] daily diminishes. . . . Thus he attains to non-doing. He practices non-doing and yet there is nothing undone."[15] Watts introduced this Taoist fundamental to the West forty years ago and stressed the distinction between non-doing and inertia, laziness, laissez-faire, or mere passivity. The key lies in the construct of the doer. In non-doing, no doer is conceived of except life itself, so this issue is moot. In inertia, laziness, and laissez-faire, the "self" considered responsible for the necessary actions fails to act. Nothing is excluded or included when there is only unity, and when this is understood, the extensive efforts made in other traditions to conform to what is true appear irrelevant.

As Watts notes, many of the early Zen teachers dismissed the need for meditative exercises, instead stressing more direct methods designed to trigger intuitive insight. The focus in Buddhism on desire as the cause of suffering was what Watts described as a "preliminary experiment," which allowed the Buddha's followers to see for themselves the impossibility of stopping desire and the vicious cycle of desiring not to desire.[16] Ultimately, when people on any mystical path realize that deviation from the truth, from what is, is impossible, the great search to which they have been so devoted appears in a dramatically different light.

Chuang Tzu tells a story of a man who was afraid of his shadow and footsteps. To get rid of them, he tried running away. Of course, this did not work, and both followed him as closely as before. Concluding that he was running too slowly, he ran faster and faster and, as we might expect, eventually fell dead. The sage then points out how easy it would have been for this man to simply step into the shade, sit down, and be still; both his footsteps and his shadow would have ceased to be an issue! It is this profound simplicity that informs the Taoist path.

In his lucid examination of three of the world's great mystic sages—Shankara, Ibn Arabi, and Eckhart—religion scholar Reza Shah-Kazemi finds that all three are in agreement in regard to the dynamic by which the devoted can "know" the Absolute. As he explains it, "Knowledge of the Absolute in itself is attainable exclusively through *being* the Absolute," and this is possible only when we awaken to the fact that we indeed *are* the Absolute and not the mind-created self we so long believed we were.[17] No one, of his or her own capacity, has ever made the crossing to nonduality, and no one ever will. Rather, it is only as the boundaries fade and the illusion of self is revealed that we discover we are already identified fully with what is. It is then that we see there is nowhere to go and nothing to do. We recognize our true nature by virtue of our true nature, not by the "actions" of a persona that does not in truth exist. As Shankara claimed, "Only the Self knows the Self."[18] In Ibn Arabi's words, "That which is extinguished 'never was,' while that which remains 'never was not.'"[19] In the absence of our conceptual blinders, we once again see only unity. The yearning from within, pulling us back to the Source, is the voice of the immanent Divine in the human breast calling to itself to come home.

Is it by the ocean's grace that the wave finds the shore or the creek winds its way back to its source? The answer lies in the law of existence, the way things are, what Buddhists call the Dharma. The key to the gateless gate is not turned by our actions or efforts. As Watts would say, "It is because we don't know how to make it happen that it can transcend the limits of the will."[20] There is no secret formula, no expedient we need to find, and no "skillful means" that will enable us to cross to the other side of the veil. The entrance is blocked until naked awareness, the beginning and end of the human experience, allows us to see it has never been closed. Nothing needs to be done.

INSIGHT

As one lamp serves to dispel a thousand years of darkness, so one flash of wisdom destroys ten thousand years of ignorance.

—Hui-neng

Mystical intuition and insight are the heart of esoteric spirituality—flashes of illumination beyond any practice or effort that show the way to enlightenment and the realization of our true nature. Without these spontaneous openings, mysticism would be just another philosophy of life, attempting by reason to unravel the riddle of human existence. Only with insight can the conundrums of form and emptiness, truth and appearance, mind and matter, find resolution. Through them we gain, in varying degrees, experiential access to the underlying unseen order that is our true source and being.

These intuitions unveil the long-forgotten world that preceded language, those few years of early childhood untouched by the ceaseless cognitive mapping that has subsequently quantified, qualified, and defined every known aspect of what is. Mystical insight is seeing without boundaries or discrimination, seeing with beginner's mind. It is what the Sufis are pointing to when they speak of discernment through "the eye of the heart." Abrupt and wordless, these fleeting glimpses of what is bypass the conceptual filters of memories, associations, and learning. They are momentary openings into the way things are, providing a sense of the seamless, unified world in which we are intimately, but unconsciously, embedded. Just as a flash of lightning can reveal surprising contours of a countryside concealed in darkness, insights can give us an understanding of things we have never imagined.

Once we learn to relax our efforts to gain realization, even if only temporarily, we open to the possibility of seeing with fresh eyes. If we can shift out of the gear of *becoming*—dropping the expectations, aspirations, and intentions that so often characterize spiritual practice—the push and pull of cultural conditioning is stilled, and we can rest in the neutral stance of *being*. It is our efforts and desire for insight that reinforce the very delusion that insight helps us transcend—that of the doer, the self, that seems to be doing those actions! As long as we keep up our efforts, the opportunity to see directly does not open up. In the wake of relaxation, however, the most tenacious boundary blocking our view to what is begins to fade: the division between self and other. No longer reinforcing the sense of being "in here," and looking for understanding "out there," we simply *are*. As we think, so we see. Accordingly, when the "thinker" steps aside, when there is no sense of one who is meditating, no goal or agenda for the practice, there is a chance to see things uncolored by conditioning.

To understand the nature of insight and its dramatically different vision of reality, many look to the physiology of the human brain, whose division into two hemispheres provides us with distinct and complementary views and experiences of the world. While the left hemisphere is linear, sequential, and analytic, allowing us to scrutinize and investigate our experience of being alive, the right is holistic and concrete, informing us with an all-at-once synthesis of all sensory input, moment to moment. The left brain excels in symbols, language, and logic; the right brain brings facility in processing feelings, recognizing images, and appreciating music. Their equal representation in the brain implies equivalent importance in human activity.

It is common knowledge that creative artists draw heavily on their right-brain skills to produce the marvelous creations we all enjoy, but even the most accomplished critical thinkers recognize the importance of knowing in another, more intuitive way. From Archimedes to Newton, from Plato to Einstein, we find testimony to this effect—instant, unexpected bursts of understanding, the paradigm shifts in art, music, science, and other areas of human enterprise that are so often attributed to "aha" moments, creative insights, or epiphanies. Like the epoch-changing discoveries by the New Physicists or the protean works of Picasso, they yield totally new ways of understanding and doing things.

In 1996, something happened that would open a unique window into the influence the brain's hemispheres have on our sense of reality. Brain scientist Jill Bolte Taylor suffered a massive stroke to the left side of her brain and, over a four-hour period, watched the functions derived from that hemisphere deteriorate with shocking speed. After ten years and a full recovery from that potentially devastating stroke, she shared the bounty of observations gleaned from her experience, all the more cogent and provocative in that the events were seen through scientifically trained eyes.

As one might expect, as the left hemisphere of her brain began to shut down, Taylor witnessed the steady erosion of her ability to talk, read, or even understand speech. More surprisingly, when her mental chatter fell silent, she felt lighter, more peaceful, and no longer burdened by the emotional baggage of thirty-seven years. Another striking observation was her growing inability to define her own boundaries, quite literally: she could no longer determine where she ended and her surroundings began. She sensed her body as being more fluid than solid, no longer separate but "blending in" with the space and energy around her. In a silent prayer, she mused, "I am now at one with the universe. I have blended into the eternal flow and am beyond returning to this plane of life—yet I remain tethered here."[1] While the sensory input remained extremely painful—her head throbbed and any bright light was excruciating—she nevertheless felt "like a genie liberated from its bottle" and wondered how she would ever squeeze "the enormousness of my spirit back inside this tiny cellular matrix."[2]

In bypassing the dominance of the left hemisphere and its conceptual rendition of reality, Taylor's remarkable episode parallels the course of esoteric practices that emphasize quieting the mind and going beyond all concept. Her description suggests the kind of direct experience that enables seekers to break through the thick layers of conditioning that blind us, and it gives us a way to apprehend that experience in a way no amount of talk ever can do. At the same time, Taylor's deeply moving account also lends support to the mystical premise that there are strikingly different ways of seeing the world.

When we view the world from a mystical perspective, the focus is not on particular mind-states or experiences, nor on new and creative ways of thinking. Rather, we shift away from the dimension of conceptual thought and ego consciousness to the domain of pure perception. In sharp contrast to the contention of many in the scientific community that consciousness is no more than an epiphenomenon of matter, a product of the brain, this must be clear: as sages have asserted for millennia, consciousness *precedes* material manifestation. Benedictine monk and Zen master Willigis Jäger explains it this way: "We are not primarily complex biochemical and cellular structures, but spirit—spirit that gives itself one possible form in the mental ego-consciousness. The intellect is one particular manifestation of spirit, and the brain is nothing more than a material condensation or intensification of spiritual energy."[3]

Insight necessitates what spiritual teacher and author A. H. Almaas calls "in-touchness with the beingness itself, with the energy that's there in the moment." From this contact, he asserts that something fresh enters; it is no longer a matter of recollection or reordering of past knowledge, but instead, something new arising.[4] Insight is not mental or intellectual understanding that originates in the brain, nor is it mediated by our conditioned mind. It is life knowing life, catching a glimpse of itself. There is *seeing*, but no one who sees; the subject/object split is transcended and what appears is what we are.

When true insight arises, it is unmistakable. "That kind of intuition," says Joseph Goldstein, "has a certainty about it because it's not the product of some thought or image but rather a sudden clear perception of how things are."[5] Ken McLeod, a teacher of Tibetan Buddhism, makes the same point: "It is experience, experience so direct and vivid that you know and that's that. It is not speculation, inference, or any other form of understanding arrived at through the intellect."[6] According to Thomas Merton, such immediate intuition is no more ambiguous than the experience of our own being. He declares, "One does not have to prove that he exists: he knows it. He may doubt his ability to convince another of the fact. But one does not trouble to prove the obvious.... It is something you either 'see' or don't see. It just bursts upon you, and is there."[7]

In his classic text *The Varieties of Religious Experience*, William James describes such intuition and mystical states at length. He states: "Your whole subconscious life, your impulses, your faiths, your needs, your divinations, have prepared the premises, of which your consciousness now feels the weight of the result; and something in you absolutely *knows* that that result must be truer than any logic-chopping rationalistic talk, however clever, that may contradict it."[8] He concludes in this way: "The unreasoned and immediate assurance is the deep thing in us, the reasoned argument is but a surface exhibition. Instinct leads, intelligence does but follow."[9]

As auspicious as it is for one's practice, though, spiritual insight is not without its perils. It is often accompanied by challenges that can complicate and even derail one's spiritual growth. One such challenge is the very allure of the experiences that insight brings. Though the details of these experiences vary widely according to time, culture, and circumstances, the testimonies of mystics the world over describe them in the same terms: peace, reverence, well-being, rapture, joy, bliss. So it is not surprising that we often become attached to these experiences and direct our energies to recapturing these deeply stirring feelings rather than moving in the direction where they point us. Mariana Caplan describes seekers seduced in this way as "spiritual addicts" and draws a parallel with addiction to any other substance. "They are suffering, they are wounded," she argues, "and they are looking for a way out—instead of through—their suffering."[10] Nisargadatta addresses the same issue, and emphasizes a key point: "Experience, however sublime, is not the real thing. By its very nature it comes and goes. Self-realization is not an acquisition. It is more of the nature of understanding. Once arrived at, it cannot be lost."[11] As one might point directly to the light rather than to the myriad forms that it illuminates, Nisargadatta is pointing to what never changes, the source of all being, life itself. In that alone do we find what we are looking for—our true nature.

Another potential obstacle crops up when we come to believe that we have achieved realization before we actually do. With significant insights under their belts, it is not uncommon for practitioners to presume their own enlightenment. As anyone who has climbed in mountainous terrain knows, it is easy to mistake the next ridge for the summit, only to see new heights come into view when that point is reached. As I have noted before, the ego is ever eager to hijack the spiritual endeavor for its own glorification. Caplan points out that this is not a problem limited to the charlatans and self-ordained gurus crowding the spiritual marketplace whom we sometimes encounter in the beginning of our individual quest for spiritual truth. In a society awash with promises of the quick fix, the first deeply moving experiences of insight can be enough to convince even serious devotees that this one is "it." Such a presumption may well block further spiritual maturation and any chance of true realization.

As problematic as these obstacles can be, perhaps the greatest challenge is the fear and uncertainty that all too often follow on the heels of insight. With each new degree of realization, the delusion of self weakens and our view shifts from figure to ground, part to whole, something to everything, samsara to nirvana. In any age or tradition, when insights begin to penetrate our certainties in this way, shaking the very frame of our reality, it is at best unsettling and at worst terrifying. It is what St. John of the Cross called the dark night of the soul—a process whereby we are challenged to relinquish our most closely held attachments. Those who turn back return once more to an existence where the heart's deepest yearning goes unfulfilled. Only those who have the courage to move forward through this distressing transformation will realize the freedom of truth. "The adventure," Joseph Campbell explains, "is always and everywhere a passage beyond the veil of the known into the unknown; the powers that watch at the boundary are dangerous; to deal with them is risky; yet for anyone with competence and courage the danger fades."[12]

~

IMAGES OF INSIGHT

DOT-TO-DOT ~ When we were children, dot-to-dot drawings were a common pastime and a lot of fun. We would carefully connect one dot to the next, not knowing what the picture would turn out to be. As more dots connected, we could begin to guess, and often, before we even finished, we would suddenly realize we were drawing an elephant or a pony or an airplane. Those who undertake the search for mystical truth, similarly, start by connecting the dots in the dark. Though they may study eagerly, work with a teacher faithfully, and practice daily, for many confusion still reigns. The meaning of such paradoxical teachings is so elusive that few students grasp their intent at the outset. They go on working dot by dot until, without warning, they catch a sudden glimpse of the whole picture—the Promised Land.

SUNRISE ~ We often speak of knowledge "dawning" on us, and in truth, the gradual process by which mystical insight penetrates the ignorance of conditioning is much like the rising of the sun. As its first rays begin to catch the contours of the land, more and more details come to light until the world around us glistens brightly in the morning dew. Similarly, each insight reveals to us with greater clarity the nature of what is, as the light of spiritual realization dispels delusion and unveils the truth of things as they are. For some, this truth may indeed open up in a sudden blaze of understanding like the midday sun, but for many, the moment of true awakening is preceded by the subtle shifts of insight that help to prepare the way. As Emily Dickinson tells us, "The truth dazzles gradually, or else the world would be blind."[13]

COMPUTER PROGRAM ∼ Contemporary Tibetan lama Tarthang Tulku notes how uncritically most of us accept the conceptual portrayal of reality with which we have been inculcated. He compares our habits of thought and our assumptions about what is real to a kind of vast computer program that is operating without our volition or conscious participation, even as we assume we are in control of what we think. He asks, "Are we running the program or is the program running us?"[14] The parallel with the way we reason is striking—and telling: computers are magnificent at analyzing and rearranging old ideas, but they cannot go beyond what they already "know." For this reason the sages of nondual wisdom repeatedly emphasize that we cannot arrive at insight by means of thought.

MULTIPLICATION ∼ Children often memorize their multiplication tables before they understand the mathematical operation that generates them. They can proudly recall the answers to simple problems, but if presented with one for which they have no memorized product, they are stumped. To function beyond the limits of memory requires mastery of the operation. Similarly, devotees may know many of the sayings of the ancients by heart and quote them with ease, but when asked to explain their meaning, they are at a loss if they have not grasped the ideas behind the words. Only with insight can the truth be fully comprehended.

CODES ∼ For thousands of years, people have used codes to prevent others from deciphering what is meant to remain secret. Should an encoded message be intercepted or fall into the wrong hands, its encrypted language would seem meaningless. Only by cracking the code could anyone read the message. In the spiritual quest, the eager practitioner may consume book after book, but find no way to make sense out of the enigmatic teachings they contain. To the uninitiated, these prove as difficult to decipher as the secret documents sent by spies. Only with insight can this mysterious spiritual code be unraveled. Insight is the key, translating impossible enigmas into intelligible ideas and freeing the truth by which all paradoxes are resolved.

~

The understanding we gain by mystical intuition transcends the dualistic mindset and goes straight to the heart of the mystery that characterizes human existence. And those who have true spiritual insights say that they require no proof, no verification. This has been true across millennia: they simply *know*. For the rest of us, though, there is ample reason to question. If knowledge based on others' testimony alone cannot be proved or disproved, how can we distinguish it from dogma or the sort of unsubstantiated claims we sometimes encounter in the popular-spirituality literature?

Some assurance might be found in consensual validation, the confirmation of one person's experience by others who have gone before and attained recognized mastery in the discipline. Just as experts steeped in a subject such as mathematics, literature, medicine, or philosophy can validate others' proffered theories or critiques in that area, experienced masters in the nondual traditions perform a similar function by verifying for the student what is true insight and what is not. In the Hindu tradition, for example, the guru-disciple relationship has played a critical role in ensuring the accurate transmission of the sacred teachings. Similarly, in Buddhism, the master guides the student, combining teaching with testing to discern true insights and discard false assumptions or unfounded convictions. Most of the traditional lineages have procedures by which the maturity of a student's spiritual understanding is assured and decisions made as to which students should be ordained, certified, or given the mantle of the teacher.

For those who as yet have no personal experience with the revelations of spiritual insight, perhaps the most convincing confirmation is the extraordinary consistency with which they have appeared in every culture and epoch. As Huston Smith maintains, these spiritual truths "are not the exclusive possession of any school or individual; were it otherwise they would not be truths, for these cannot be invented, but must necessarily be known in every integral traditional civilization."[15] Campbell recognizes the same universality, drawing the distinction between the historical nature of culture-specific religious belief and the nonhistorical nature of the mystical experience, which is "to such a degree constant for mankind that we may jump from Hudson Bay to Australia, Tierra del Fuego to Lake Baikal, and find ourselves well at home."[16]

James is no less convinced. He notes that throughout all mysticism "we find the same recurring note, so that there is about mystical utterances an eternal unanimity which ought to make a critic stop and think, and which brings it about that the mystical classics have, as has been said, neither birthday nor native land. Perpetually telling of the unity of man with God, their speech antedates languages, and they do not grow old."[17] These three authorities, arguably among the world's most renowned in the area of comparative religion and human spirituality, individually reached the identical conclusion: there is a form of knowing that transcends the bounds of time and cultures and the dictates of sectarian dogma.

In a modern world that is mesmerized by the wonders of modern science and so often looks to its proclamations for guidance, the unchallenged longevity of esoteric wisdom stands in stark contrast to the relatively brief shelf life of scientific "truth." Repeatedly over the last five centuries, the models of reality proffered by science's leading experts as absolute, and widely accepted by the rest of us as such, have been discarded in favor of new constructs. One needs only a superficial grasp of the revolutions precipitated by Copernicus, Descartes, Newton, Darwin, Freud, and Einstein to realize that in the frame of human history the laws of science have held for no more than a few generations before being turned upside down. All the while, one and only one truth has reigned supreme in the esoteric realm.

The reason for such stunning consistency lies in the very essence of this truth, the wholeness hidden behind the veil of phenomena. Science investigates the workings of multiplicity and the ceaseless play of name and form, time and space. Nondual practice delves into the unconditioned, the Source. In the conventional domain, we learn to see the figure, the foreground of reality. It is only through insight that we are given glimpses of the ground that is our being. There is nothing we can do to produce the breakthrough, though all esoteric practice is designed to open us to that possibility. Like a forgotten name that we can't recall until we stop trying, insight happens on its own schedule despite our every effort. It is a function of life as a whole, more akin to an organic process than a mechanical one. The sought is sending clues to the seeker, as a young child might call out to a playmate blindly seeking him or her in the timeless swimming-pool game of "Marco Polo." All we can do is wait in silence and listen for the next call.

AWAKENING

All agree the first opening is just the start.

—*Jack Kornfield*

Throughout this book, we have been following the steps that lead to an understanding of our true nature—the mystical truth of what is. There are countless names for this awakening, and perhaps as many ways to describe it as there are seekers in the world, but at the heart of the transformation lies something inherent in humanity itself. All our mythologies underscore this fact, that to awaken is to remember what we have known all along. On the archetypal hero's journey of exile and return, "the godly powers sought and dangerously won," says Joseph Campbell, "are revealed to have been within the heart of the hero all the time."[1] Even so, the sudden breakthrough that yields the coveted prize is irrevocably transforming. The moment when we cross the threshold of return is the moment when we transcend our rational understanding and encounter the Absolute.

The place where the Buddha sat on the night of his enlightenment is described in the early Pali sutras as the "immovable spot." According to Karen Armstrong, this is the mythological axis of the universe, the "still point of calm," that enables the individual to see life in perfect balance. When greed, hatred, and delusion no longer blind us, and the conceptual framework of conventional reality falls away, the duality of our self-oriented world is replaced by the vision of unity at the heart of all mystical transformation. "It is the 'place,'" Armstrong tells us, "where things that seem diametrically opposed in the profane world come together in that *coincidentia oppositorum* that constitutes an experience of the Sacred. Life and death, emptiness and plenitude, physical and spiritual merge and conjoin, like the spokes of a wheel at its hub, in a way that is unimaginable to normal consciousness."[2]

Perhaps the simplest way to describe the moment of liberation is to think of the universal experience of waking up in the morning, an analogy that has been used for thousands of years. Coming out of the unconsciousness of sleep and leaving behind the dream world that seemed so engrossing and so real, we recall who we are and what happened the day before. In mystical realization, the seeker awakens from the conceptual "dream" of life as it seems to be, and awareness of the truth floods back in. There is no secret understanding that is gained, no esoteric knowledge we suddenly uncover, but rather our eyes open to the indisputable, manifest nature of what is—a world we knew as very young children and find self-evident when we see it again. Nevertheless, following a lifetime of conditioning, it is a stunning reversal that turns one's world upside down. And just as a sleeper emerging from a nightmare breathes a sigh of relief, those who become enlightened are flooded with exaltation, gratitude, and wonder.

Listen to Kabir, the mystic Sufi poet of the Middle Ages: "Joy for ever, no sorrow, no struggle! There I have seen joy filled to the brim, perfection of joy; no place for error is there."[3] Gendun Gyatso Palzangpo, the Second Dalai Lama, describes it this way: "The highest bliss and wisdom then shine like a sun at the center of the heart, halting all activity of attachment, aversion, and ignorance. This is the unmistaken state of mahamudra, the Great Seal."[4] In a similar vein, the nineteenth-century Indian sage Ramakrishna writes: "The one thing which I was internally conscious of was that through my soul was rolling an ocean of ineffable joy, the like of which I had no experience before."[5] Upon realization, eighteenth-century Zen master Hakuin recalls, "I began clapping my hands and whooping with glee, frightening the people who had gathered around me."[6]

Around the same time, Rabbi Israel ben Eliezer writes of his awakening: "Thus all worlds become united and they ascend so that immeasurable rapture and the greatest delight is experienced. You can understand this on the analogy of the raptures of bride and bridegroom in miniature in the physical world."[7] An Eskimo shaman, recounting his own breakthrough experience, exclaims: "Then for no reason, all would suddenly be changed, and I felt a great, inexplicable joy, a joy so powerful that I could not restrain it, but had to break into song, a mighty sound, with only room for the one word: joy, joy!"[8]

In this moment of realization, we transcend the boundaries we have always believed to be real and consciously reconnect with the Source. By whatever name we call it—the Ground, the Absolute, God, Tao, Pure Mind, the Unborn—this is the reality we inhabited before we identified with ego or took on the concepts of time and space and language; in other words, before we became self-conscious. Contemporary Christian mystic Bede Griffiths declares: "Suddenly we know we belong to another world, that there is another dimension to existence.... We are freed from the flux of time and see something of the eternal order that underlies it."[9] Like effervescent bubbles rising to the surface of a soda, we burst into the freedom of Being.

Accounts of spiritual awakening vary widely, but across all traditions certain essentials are unchanged—including the challenging truth that we cannot make the crossing from duality to wholeness in the vessel of our own ego: the self cannot transcend the self. While there are, unfortunately, some forms of "liberation" offered in the spiritual marketplace that actually serve to aggrandize the self or promise it eternal survival, true enlightenment shatters the ego shell so that the light of the Absolute can dispel the darkness. It is as much a wake as an awakening. "Authentic transformation," attests Ken Wilber, "is not a matter of belief, but of the death of the believer."[10] When one sees, *really sees*, that he or she is not the doer, not the thinker, the body/mind is dropped, as Dogen used to say, and in its place is left only wholeness. Spiritual liberation does not free the self from suffering; to the contrary, it is we who are freed from the self's tragic reign, allowing us to realize our oneness with what is.

And to "really see" requires that profound shift in perspective by which we see the ground instead of the figure, the whole instead of the part. As with the classic face/vase illusion in chapter 1, when we focus on one image, the other disappears. To see both simultaneously is impossible. It is in this context that we must understand the words of Angelus Silesius, the seventeenth-century German priest: "God, whose love and joy are present everywhere, can't come to visit you unless you aren't there."[11]

Just as the self is transcended in the transformation, all our concrete and historically specific beliefs about the Divine must likewise fall away in that boundaryless realm. This is what Meister Eckhart means when he says: "Man's last and highest parting is when, for God's sake, he takes leave of God."[12] God is a concept, and thus, like the self, incompatible with transcendence. There is no identification with name or form in the Absolute. As Reza Shah-Kazemi notes, the sages Eckhart, Shankara, and Ibn Arabi all drop the traditional names and designations used in referring to the Divine. Shankara points to the abstract truth of *advaita*, or nondual, preferring the double negation of *neti, neti*—"not this, not this"—to any inference of name or form. Ibn Arabi prefers the name "the One" in lieu of Allah, and Eckhart uses "the solitary One" instead of the three persons of the Trinity to identify the Divine.[13] They all desire to give God a name that minimizes any inference of an object or an entity distinguishable or separate in itself—a name that includes all that is.

The truth of oneness cannot be contained in a name or a concept any more than the ocean can be held in a spoon: in the absence of the divisions and polarities that define the human experience, what remains is ineffable. So accustomed are we to expressing ourselves conceptually and describing the events of life so that others can understand them, a world undefined, untouched by thought, defies the grasp of language. It is the experience Rudolf Otto calls *mysterium tremendum*, something "wholly other," overpowering, and completely beyond the bounds of normal experience. It brings to mind the awe, fascination, and dread with which the prophets of the Old Testament drew near to Yahweh. It was surely what Rumi is describing when he exclaims, "My amazement was amazed,"[14] or what Wu-men is referring to when he declares, "You're like a mute person who has had a dream—you know it for yourself alone."[15]

Gregory of Nyssa, an early father of the Eastern Orthodox Church, sums it up like this: "The divine nature, as it is in itself, according to its essence, transcends every act of comprehensive knowledge, and it cannot be approached or attained by our speculation. Men have never discovered a faculty to comprehend the incomprehensible, nor have we ever been able to devise an intellectual technique for grasping the inconceivable."[16] Indeed, the *Tao Te Ching* begins with the admonition that "the Tao that can be spoken is not the eternal Tao / The name that can be named is not the eternal name."[17]

In this absence of all dualistic distinction, even the ideas of awakening lose their relevance. Ramesh Balsekar relates a story of a woman who came to Nisargadatta to tell him of her exciting mystical experiences, which other teachers had verified as enlightenment. After listening to her account, the sage asked the woman who exactly had had these experiences. Whom did they please? He then explained to her that true transformation was something in which no individual could be involved. "Personal entity and enlightenment cannot go together," he told her.[18] This is yet another parallel Shah-Kazemi finds in the writings of the three sages he has studied: they all recognize that the very process of realization is an illusion. From the Zen tradition, we find Dogen making the same point: "When all things exist, there are enlightenment and delusion, practice, life and death, Buddhas and ordinary people. When all things are without self, there is no delusion, no enlightenment, no Buddhas, no ordinary people, no life and no death."[19]

To awaken spiritually is to enter the Gateless Gate and, paradoxically, return to the Eden one never left. The hero's journey is a virtual one, unfolding in the mind of each individual and played out with the same engrossing effort we see in people playing today's video games. From the transcendent perspective of nonduality, the tragedies and triumphs we experience in life are no more significant than those of players lost in that make-believe. In either case, our racing thoughts concerning past and future events so preoccupy us that we are oblivious to the only thing that is real, the magical unfolding of now. We are surrounded by a rich tapestry of sights, sounds, and other sensations that require only our attention to dazzle us with their suchness. As Jesus tells us: "The kingdom of the Father is already spread out on the earth, but people don't see it."[20] Huang-po points to the same inconceivable fact: "It is what you see in front of you. Start to think about it and immediately you are mistaken."[21] Thich Nhat Hanh says this: "The mind seal of the Buddhas is reality itself. Nothing can be added to it, nothing can exist outside of it. One does not get it, one does not lose it."[22]

Over and over we find the same assertion in the teachings of the world's sages. Our exile is a mental one, a delusion of the ego. We are like the fish searching for the great ocean, the metaphor we examined in the chapter on suffering. Like the fish unable to perceive the water all around it, we are blind to the extraordinary wonder of life that surrounds us. Often it's not until we know we are dying that we actually notice the uncanny presence of the clouds that drift above us, with their astonishing play of light and form, or our kitten sleeping peacefully in the afternoon sun. Our vision is simply obstructed by our conceptualized reality. We learn our lines so well and so fully identify with the parts we play that we forget our beginnings and the splendor of the Absolute that still surrounds us.

Enlightenment is simply what is. As the distinction between subject and object fades away, one does not see the truth, one becomes it. What is left is unity that abides no divisions. All opposites are reconciled—the lamb and the lion lie down together. This is the goal of all who accept the Perennial Philosophy: to be delivered out of separate selfhood into what Aldous Huxley calls the "unitive knowledge of the divine Ground."[23] As Rumi declares: "I am all orders of being, the circling galaxy, the evolutionary intelligence, the lift and the falling away."[24]

In light of this assertion, it is not difficult to see why those from deistic traditions who break through to nonduality have met such fierce and fear-driven resistance to their claims. Most of us are familiar with the story of Jesus's crucifixion; it came in the wake of his misunderstood claims and teachings, as when he said, "I am the way and the truth and the life. No one comes to the Father except through me."[25] But consider also this line from the tenth-century Sufi mystic Mansur al-Hallaj: "I am He whom I love, and He whom I love is I: We are two spirits dwelling in one body. If thou seest me, thou seest Him, and if thou seest Him, thou seest us both."[26] Refusing to recant, al-Hallaj too died on a cross for his blasphemy. Meister Eckhart narrowly avoided the same fate after he proclaimed, "In this breaking-through I find that God and I are both the same."[27] In the nondeistic cultures, where more abstract ideas of the Absolute were woven throughout the traditional scriptures, seekers faced no such danger, but found the very same insight. As Deng Ming-Dao claims: "True enlightenment is the realization not that there is a Tao to follow, but that we ourselves are Tao."[28]

∾

IMAGES OF AWAKENING

PEARL ∾ Chinese sage Huang-po tells a story about a warrior wearing a precious pearl on his forehead who thought it lost and traveled the world to find it. Once informed of his mistake, he realized that the pearl had been there all along. Huang-po compares this to the experience of seekers who look everywhere for their true nature, pursuing many practices and undergoing strenuous spiritual exercises to attain realization, all to no avail. When the moment of awakening at last reveals the truth of what is, one feels like the warrior discovering his pearl and immediately understands that all effort is useless. What we almost always seek elsewhere is always right where we are.

CLOCK ∾ The suddenness of spiritual awakening is like the way in which a grandfather clock strikes the hours. The apparatus is designed to mechanically measure the passage of time, and the arrival of each hour triggers its resonant series of chimes. Until that point, there is only the steady ticking of the clock, even when only seconds remain before the chimes sound. As many who have experienced awakening know, right up to the climactic moment there may be no inkling that it is close at hand. But when the aspirant is "ripe," transformation may be triggered by something as simple as the snapping of a twig or the call of a bird.

MOVIES ∼ When we are really engrossed in a movie, we forget about everything but what is on the screen. We may identify so thoroughly with the actors that we lose our sense of the life that waits for us outside the theater. When the protagonist is happy, so are we. When he or she is afraid, we feel the same fear. We are lost in the action of the film until it ends and we reorient ourselves to our "real" lives. Those who have awakened spiritually describe a strikingly similar dynamic, though on a much more profound level. For them, instead of stepping from the theater back into the world, there is the recognition that the phenomenal world itself is a projection of the mind. Just as moviegoers know that the drama played out on screen is not real, one who is awakened discerns the difference between the movie of the mind and the true nature of reality.

PUPPET ∼ Everyone knows that the actions of a puppet are not of its own agency, but of the hand inside that moves it. The same is, in a sense, true of human seekers. Those who are fortunate enough to break through to nonduality realize that the breakthrough is not their own doing. While they may have been purified by the flames of misfortune, by years of self-denial or solitude, by giving away all they have, or by faithfully serving as disciples under demanding masters, the credit for their accomplishments is no more "theirs" than are the "accomplishments" of the puppet. When our identification with the self is undone, so is our identification with the actions of that self. It is from a deeper reality that both are moved and draw their being. As Jesus told his disciples, "You did not choose me, but I chose you and appointed you so that you might go and bear fruit—fruit that will last—

and so that whatever you ask in my name the Father will give you."[29] When we understand that life is the only doer, the strain and angst that characterize so much of what we do drops away, allowing the wonder of what is to unfold in the natural actions of our being. This must not translate into a lazy, apathetic attitude toward our responsibilities, but rather allow us to intuit the workings of something far greater than ourselves pulling the strings.

SWITCHED AT BIRTH ~ Think of an infant born to parents of considerable wealth and influence, but mistakenly switched with another in the nursery. Rather than living a life of affluence and privilege, the child is raised in poverty. She dresses in tatters, receives little education, and is unaware that she is, in truth, heir to vast wealth. If by chance she were to encounter a member of her biological family, she might quickly recognize familiar traits and dispositions that would point her to the truth. Like her, we too are victims of mistaken identity and rarely guess our true heritage. Everyone treats us like someone else, and there are few hints of our origin. We, too, find ourselves engrossed in our surroundings and distracted from the deeper things that might give some intimation of the truth. But if we are exposed to individuals with whom we find deep connection—those whose words, ideas, or actions resonate in our innermost being—we may discover our real lineage and claim our inheritance.

It's easy to imagine that awakening is the perfect culmination of the spiritual journey. But in fact, the path does not end there; though the dramatic shift in orientation that we experience is profound and irrevocable, most of us do not assimilate such a reordering of reality all at once. Like the numerous aftershocks that often follow an earthquake, many further openings and refinements occur as the impact of realization continues to deepen over time. Awakening is a threshold we must cross, but in truth it is only that: a doorway to new stages of spiritual maturation. Looking back at the Ten Oxherding Pictures of the Zen tradition, we see this very clearly. Even though the seeker gets a glimpse of his ox in the third picture, and catches it, in the metaphorical depiction of enlightenment, in the fourth, six more stages are shown before the highest levels of spiritual maturity are attained. In the next several pictures, taming the ox, riding the ox, and leading the ox homeward represent the deconditioning of deeply ingrained patterns of thought that continue to manifest in our lives. In the eighth level, an empty circle depicts a point where neither concepts nor self have meaning.

The empty circle represents the realization of oneness, and the two stages that complete the cycle show the man, freed from delusion and reentering the mundane world to share the fruits of his understanding with others. In reality, though, those who are awakened continue to find themselves encumbered with the same karmic patterns of conditioned behavior that they knew before their transformation. "Do not expect perfection." says Nisargadatta. "There is no perfection in manifestation."[30] This is not to say that enlightened individuals do not reflect wisdom and compassion, but simply that they are human and subject to the law of impermanence. Jack Kornfield emphasizes this point: "There is no state of enlightened retirement, no experience of awakening that places us outside the truth of change. Everything breathes and turns in its cycles. The moon, the stock market, our hearts, the wheeling galaxies all expand and contract with the rhythm of life. All spiritual life exists in an alteration of gain and loss, pleasure and pain."[31]

The crucial difference is that with realization, one's identification with the ego falls away. Our body/mind continues to display its conditioned habits, some good and some not, but they are no longer seen as what we are. Ram Dass was speaking in this same spirit when he told people that, while he hadn't gotten rid of a single one of his neuroses, they no longer had the power to define him. Whatever the moment brings is the truth of what is. To try to conform to an ideal of how an awakened individual might act or look is a sure sign that one has not yet awakened.

Life unfolds as it will, and realization will play out on its own schedule and in its own way. There is an equanimity, however, that comes with the wisdom of seeing things as they are: there is only life and we are That. As Matthew Flickstein tells his students, prior to awakening, practice is seen as a *prescription* for what is to be done. In its wake, practice is understood to be only a *description* of what is.[32] As clinging and aversion, the habits of the past, gradually fade, they are replaced with compassion and an understanding that all is well. Rediscovering the Now, already and forever what is, the body/mind contracted and distorted by identification begins to loosen its white-knuckled grip on life. Freed from the imposition of purpose and objectives, pride and guilt, anticipation and regret, this body/mind process blends seamlessly back into the flow of existence. There is only what is, timeless and undivided. There is neither one who follows the path nor any path to follow. What has always been continues to be, but we struggle less and less against it.

SELFLESSNESS

It is in dying to self that we are born to eternal life.

—St. Francis of Assisi

Joseph Campbell's classic *The Masks of God* opens with an eloquent discussion of the festivals and ceremonies of early man.[1] Unable to grasp the deepest and most profound themes of life in the prosaic expressions of everyday communication, and not wanting to presume identity with the pantheon of spirits that animated their world, participants wore masks in ways that call to mind the dress-up games of children. In such games, there are moments in which the bounds of reason and ordinary understanding are eclipsed and, in the alchemy of imagination, the player becomes the portrayed. Donning the garb of demons and gods and dancing around the fires of so long ago, in a serious kind of make-believe the masked performers were "experienced" as the supernatural itself. As Campbell says of the dancer, "He does not merely represent the god; he *is* the god."[2] Through such experiences, Campbell asserts, both dancer and onlooker take the first step toward the intuitive wisdom of wholeness buried deeply within them, yielding glimpses of the ultimate reality: their true nature, beyond the masks of self.

Self is, ultimately, a mask, as we have seen throughout this book—no more than the mental concept we have of who and what we believe ourselves to be. *Selflessness*, in its mystical sense, is the label we give to the experience that arises when we no longer take the concept at face value. Once we recognize that we are not what we think we are—that we do not, in any conventional sense, exist—the world is transformed. The walls of separation come down, and the elaborate stratagems we once needed for self-defense are no longer necessary: there is no longer a self to defend. In the faces of others we see a reflection of our own being, and we begin to recognize a profound oneness with the rest of life. As this truth takes root in our awareness, the fear of death itself begins to fade, and nothing in our world remains the same. We see with new eyes.

The theme of selflessness has been threaded through the world's sacred teachings for millennia and confirmed over and over in the explorations of countless seekers on the mystical path, but for many of those new to the idea, it is too unimaginable even to register. Our worldly lives seem to center around building, improving, and embellishing our self-identities, and we believe that these identities are synonymous with who we are. Mesmerized by our personal stories and thoroughly convinced by our dualistic perceptions of self and other, we can hardly entertain the notion that our true nature is something so profoundly different from what we believe. What is more, the idea has little or no currency in Western cultures, and you will rarely hear selflessness discussed on a TV talk show or see it depicted in film or art. It follows that when we are first exposed to the idea of selflessness, we often see it as little more than an abstract idea, a kind of novel philosophical premise without much connection to our personal experience—something we can discuss or ponder in general terms with minimal impact.

If we enter into mystical practice and engage in a more serious investigation of selflessness, our relationship with this provocative subject deepens, and so does our response. When we seriously contemplate our own existence, and read the many writings of teachers who point to the self's unreality, it can be unnerving. And when we relate this idea to our personal lives, our loved ones, and all we hold most dear, it can cause us apprehension, uneasiness, and real fear. If I am unreal, are my wife and children unreal? The times I play with my grandson, the games, the laughter—am I imagining them? Will I cease to enjoy such things if I follow this path? And what of the values I hold dear, the attitudes and beliefs that have always distinguished me from others? Are they meaningless? If the accomplishments that I am most proud of are not "mine," whose are they? Who did them? If you are reading this now, questions like these and many more surely will arise. And if, in your spiritual practice, you have insights that start to seriously undermine your sense of reality—even the visceral certainty that you are here right now reading this page—it can become so threatening that you turn away from practice altogether.

If this is the case, why are people drawn to such a practice in the first place? Who would ever willingly plunge into something so mysterious and disconcerting? The answer is within, the inner yearning I described in chapter 10 and the still latent truth toward which it draws you. That truth is that you *do* exist, you *do* have a life, but not in the way you think you do. Another way to put it is that you exist in a relative sense, in our dualistic world, but from an absolute perspective you do not. There is more than one way to view your life, to understand your experience of being alive. Conventionally, everything you have, value, and do is real. If you weren't real, you'd never get a bite of your mother's chocolate cake, or hear your children laughing outside, or reminisce with your lifelong friend about the good old days! It's not that these experiences have no reality; it's just that there is more, much, much more, to understanding what you truly are.

Perhaps surprisingly, since most of the industrialized world gives little credence to nondual spirituality, the sciences have helped opened the door to this understanding. A major article in *Time* magazine in 1995 assessed the current state of research on the nature of consciousness, the very foundation of our concept of self. Until the last few decades, consciousness was the purview of philosophy alone, but that has changed with new technology, such as magnetic resonance imaging (MRI) and positron-emission tomography (PET), which together produce images of internal structures as well as of the functional processes in the body. Scientists in the disciplines of neurology, biology, and psychology now report being able to locate specific areas of the brain that change when a thought is taking place, when fear is experienced, or when memories are recalled. Yet even with such remarkable techniques, nothing has been identified that looks like the locus of a self or the source of consciousness.

The author in *Time* sums up the current scientific opinion with this statement: "Despite our every instinct to the contrary, there is one thing that consciousness is not: some entity deep inside the brain that corresponds to the 'self,' some kernel of awareness that runs the show, as the 'man behind the curtain' manipulated the illusion of a powerful magician in *The Wizard of Oz*." The article goes on: "After more than a century of looking for it, brain researchers have long since concluded that there is no conceivable place for such a self to be located in the physical brain and that it simply doesn't exist."[3] This is the same position that behavioral scientist B. F. Skinner took twenty-five years earlier in *Beyond Freedom and Dignity*. In that provocative book, he dismisses the existence of any "indwelling agents," that is, the intentions, wills, feelings, or purposes that we commonly consider intrinsic to what we view as the self.

With its stark portrayal of the human condition, *Beyond Freedom and Dignity* was not well received by the general population. It appeared to contradict the most sacrosanct aspects of humanity: Without intention or will, how could we have responsibility for our behavior? What would be the basis for morality? Would no one attain the salvation promised by spiritual traditions? Nevertheless, Skinner's premise remains widely accepted in the scientific disciplines concerned with this issue. Consciousness is generally believed to be an artifact of the nervous system, arising when a critical level of complexity is attained, and not something that lies beyond the province of the physical sciences. Human beings are seen as biological machines, with remarkable abilities to think and act but devoid of those characteristics generally considered essential to being fully human.

One thing is clear. From both the mystical and scientific perspectives, there is no self to be found. As we have seen in the last several chapters, the esoteric quest for wholeness has consistently ended with this assertion. The Buddhist practice of vipassana, discussed in chapter 13, offers a striking parallel to the method employed by today's scientists. As different as modern neurology appears to be from that ancient form of meditation, both forms of investigation study the nature of experience and observe the components we associate with self, and neither finds any self-existing entity to grasp. Thoughts are observed but no thinker who thinks them, intentions observed but no one who has them. Under the careful scrutiny of the practitioner or scientist, the sense of self, so apparent in our everyday experience, seems to disappear when we try to pin it down.

Nondual practitioners and modern scientists do not agree as closely when it comes to consciousness, however. As we discussed above, science has long given primacy to the physical realm, and most scientists see consciousness as emerging from matter. Mysticism asserts a very different view, one in which consciousness is primary. It is inherent in the nature of life itself and arises simultaneously, moment by moment, with each and every manifestation of life. Without consciousness there would be nothing. It is what is. Without consciousness we would, indeed, find the kind of nihilistic abyss the existentialists describe.

And despite the continuing belief among many scientists that consciousness is no more than a side effect of brain function, this understanding has never been scientifically proven. No plausible theory has been produced to explain how matter creates sentience, nor have there been any findings to support the hypothesis that the brain is the cause of consciousness and not simply its instrument. In the absence of any convincing empirical evidence, and in recognition of a substantial body of research that supports a very different position, calls for change have been steadily growing in the scientific community. This shift in thinking actually began nearly a century ago when New Physics was unveiling a revolutionary vision of reality. Those who conducted that pivotal research gave long overdue attention to the role of consciousness: Sir Arthur Eddington used the term "mind-stuff" to describe the nature of reality, and Erwin Schrödinger portrayed the universe itself as a living mind. Niels Bohr compared the wave aspect of matter to "cosmic mind." None of the pioneering physicists of this new movement were able to satisfactorily explain what they were seeing in their research without taking consciousness into account in some elemental way.

Since then, others have taken the same position. Roger Sperry, the 1981 Nobel Laureate in Physiology or Medicine, advocated recognition of the causal role of inner conscious awareness in experimental setups where the observed results could not be explained solely on the basis of biological, chemical, and physical properties. Consciousness, he argued, was not simply the medium of observation, but somehow a player in what was observed. Sperry anticipated that this breakthrough in our understanding of human consciousness would usher in what he referred to as a "second Copernican Revolution." Philosopher David Chalmers, in his 1995 *Scientific American* article entitled "The Puzzle of Conscious Experience," rejected reductive explanations, concluding that it was time for science to recognize that consciousness is on a par with matter and energy and fundamental to the understanding of our reality.[4] More and more we are seeing experts from various fields come together to explore and better understand the experience of being alive. As we delve into the idea of self, and question its very reality, please hang on and remember it is only in the absence of the self that our eyes open to the breathtaking truth we so keenly yearn for.

~

IMAGES OF SELFLESSNESS

WAVICLE ~ New Physicists coined the term *wavicle* to convey the fact that subatomic objects exhibit two very different properties, that of a "wave" and that of a "particle." Since it was impossible to observe both properties at the same time, the off-and-on existence of an object proved to be dependent on the apparatus chosen for the experiment. In other words, it was the way the observer chose to measure it that determined what he or she saw. If the observer used one instrument to determine its location, the object appeared as a particle; if the observer chose a different instrument to calculate its speed, it behaved like a wave. This wave/particle phenomenon offers an interesting analogy for the nature of selflessness: the particle is like the self that exists in duality, while the wave represents nonduality, where no separate entity is "seen." Just as the apparatus of observation determined whether an observer saw the wave or the particle, it is our apparatus of perception—our use of concepts to package what we experience—that reveals a world filled with "particles," or separate entities, and most importantly the self. When we use intuition and insight to replace our dependence on thought, we can see the wave: we can awaken to an extraordinarily different reality, a world without boundaries. And in both cases, consciousness is key in determining what we experience. There is no preexisting reality "out there," independent of the participant observer.

TICKING WATCH ⟿ Listen to your watch tick for a moment. Now imagine trying to isolate the tick that you hear. If you took the watch apart one piece at a time, you would never find it, because the tick by itself does not exist. It is created by the interaction between the different elements of the watch. When the mechanism is disassembled, the tick disappears. Something similar happens when scientists look for the illusory self in the body or mind. Neuroscientists, biologists, physiologists, and psychologists have systematically examined and dissected the psychophysical organism for over a hundred years and have never been able to locate a self or a quantifiable source of consciousness. There is no scientific evidence to refute the mystical realization that the body and mind operate without any apparent direction. As the tick in the watch disappears when the timepiece is disassembled, the self cannot be found when the non-self parts are scrutinized one by one.

HURRICANES ⟿ At certain times of the year, the hurricane and typhoon seasons begin in the oceans of the world. Weather forecasters watch for disturbances in water and air; when a storm system gains enough size and strength and definition, the forecasters give it a name, chart its progress, predict its path, and issue warnings. Then, just as quickly, the storm fades from the radar. Like the self, storms are processes devoid of any fixed or inherent entity. When the elements necessary for their arising coalesce, they appear to exist, and as those same causes and conditions drop away, the appearance dissolves.

BOAT ∼ Think of yourself as a boat without a motor, adrift in a strong current. In this image, the boat is a fixed entity floating on a river of rapid change. The river is different every second, but the boat stays the same. You fear where the river might take you and feel powerless to control your direction. What if there are rocks or waterfalls downstream? The idea of the self as a fixed and stable entity gives rise to a similar kind of fear. We see life rapidly passing by, and seeing others dashed on the rocks reminds us of the ever-present danger posed by an uncertain fate. In the rapids of life, we sense that our "boats" are out of control. But if we try, we can view this situation from a dramatically different perspective. With the insights of impermanence and selflessness, we can begin to identify not with the boat, but with the very flow of life. The sense of separation evaporates, and, no longer floating precariously on top of the rushing torrent, we become the river itself. When rocks appear, we can flow around or over them as the river does. No longer trapped in a fixed and static self, we see there is nothing to fear. We can relax and enjoy the ride.

∼

Our daily experience as individuals is so concrete and seemingly undeniable in its reality that the idea of selflessness is very difficult to grasp or hold. It can seem unfathomable, even absurd, from the perspective of the everyday. If I have no self, who is writing these words? If you have no self, who is reading them? Even when we see the truth about ourselves firsthand, the habit of thinking and acting as if we were separate beings remains deeply ingrained.

Alan Watts said it is similar to looking at the night sky. If you have been taught from an early age to recognize the constellation known as the Big Dipper, your eyes will automatically be drawn to the pattern formed by those seven stars. Once you realize that the stars have no intrinsic connection, and that there is no actual dipper up there, only your conditioned perception, you still find it nearly impossible to glance up at the sky on a clear night and not pick it out. The same is true of the self. We are so deeply inculcated with the concept that it is extremely difficult to keep from "seeing it" and to truly go beyond the suffering that this mistaken identity causes us throughout our lives.

Accustomed as we are to seeing life from the perspective of the separate self, we may think that life without it will be robbed of all its richness. Nonetheless, when the truth of selflessness is seen and experienced, the meaning and beauty of life do not vanish into some nihilistic abyss. It is a matter of transcendence rather than disappearance, and it generates the ability to see the same reality in a profoundly different way. Instead of identifying with the figure, we see that in truth we are the ground as well!

Remember from our figure/ground discussions how it was impossible to see from both perspectives at the same time? You could see the vase or the face, but not both. It is in this sense that you must understand selflessness. From the conventional perspective, every aspect of your social existence reinforces the relative, dualistic side of your existence—in other words, the *figure*. Everywhere you go—home, school, or work; parties with friends, family reunions, or shopping at the mall—the emphasis is on you, constantly reinforcing who *you* are, what *you* need to learn, where *you* live, what *you* do, what *you* think, what *you* want, when *you* will retire, and on and on. It is the way we all understand our lives in this thought-created world. And we stake out our small corner of it with the words *I*, *me*, and *mine*.

Now you are reading about esoteric spirituality and being told that there is something that promises to turn your very world upside down. These mystical teachings are, in effect, directing your attention to the *ground* and away from the figure. It is a hard sell, given the fact that it is so foreign, so strange, so *esoteric*, in Western culture. But that reorientation is what is needed for you to realize that your true nature is something unimaginably greater than your conventional self.

Until you recognize and understand this, fear and dread dominate your experience, but when you truly awaken to the nature of what is, you see that you are *that*, the *whole* of life, and your awareness of it is none other than the awareness of life itself. The fears, apprehension, and torment so often accompanying the self evaporate, and in their place you find joy, peace, exaltation, wonder, and the wisdom that comes from knowing the truth of what you really are. You can see life with a kind of double vision, experiencing both the triumphs and the tragedies of your everyday existence, while at the same time understanding them from a higher perspective that takes the sting out of loss, pain, and death. Neither figure nor ground makes sense in the absence of the other—it takes the presence of *both* to see either. You are, in truth, both of these fundamental expressions of life.

It is as if a leaf realizes its oneness with the tree and in this knowledge "returns" home. The leaf's shape and its pattern of veins are, no doubt, particular and unique in countless ways, but such differentiation does not imply separation. The circumstances of our lives are similar. We are one of a kind, with a full constellation of strengths and skills, habits and hang-ups, that give us our unique character, but at the same time we are all one; we only appear to be separate. When we see the illusion of the "self" construct, there is a resurrection of sorts in the rediscovered vision of the whole. We are released from the constriction of the ego; we recognize our oneness with the unimaginable expanse of life and the full wonders of creation.

As human beings, we lost our sense of belonging to that whole with the first emergence of self-consciousness. During the Axial Period, generally thought of as extending from the sixth century to the second century BCE, there were tremendous changes in social organization as the nomadic wanderings of our forebears gave way to more sedentary ways of life. With refinement of farming techniques came stratification of society, accumulation of wealth, and leisure time, and consequently the opportunity for reflection and a deepening of self-consciousness.

It was at this point in history that the angst and alienation that we ourselves know so well became widespread. With the emergence of self-consciousness and individuality, human beings found themselves alone and isolated from everything else—separated from the Divine and exiled from paradise. There was a clear need for more effective spiritual answers to make sense out of this new human predicament, and major religions arose in response. The Buddha, Jesus, Lao Tzu, Krishna, Socrates, Plato, Confucius, and the mystics of the Upanishads all appeared around the same time to, in effect, address the suffering that was growing ever more pronounced in the human world. The Buddha taught that identifying with the idea of self is the single cause of suffering. The selflessness that he espoused, and to which all the nondual traditions point, was founded on the recognition of the wholeness that precedes belief in our separation. When we see through the delusion of self and transcend the limitations it imposes, we realize that life without ego identification is one of peace, equanimity, and freedom.

Across several millennia and great variations in cultural context, there have naturally been differences in how the idea of selflessness is explained in the sacred writings and mystical teachings of the nondual traditions. Nevertheless, the overall theme remains the same. It is a movement from the very small to the very large, from figure to ground—an escape from the limits and restrictions of selfhood to freedom from all conceptual bonds. There is no suggestion anywhere in the nondual doctrines that selflessness is a dead end or the termination of consciousness.

Listen to how mystics across the ages have described this paradoxical truth: in the words of Abu Yazid al-Bistami, the ninth-century Sufi mystic, "What I was I no longer am, for 'I' and 'God' are a denial of God's unity. Since I no longer am, God is his own mirror. He speaks with my tongue, and I have vanished."[5] A very different description, but one with a similar understanding, is found in the words of the anonymous fourteenth-century Christian mystical work *The Cloud of Unknowing*: "Because nowhere bodily is everywhere spiritually."[6] Ken Wilber, a modern sage, offers a contemporary version, explaining selflessness as a change from content to context, in which we are no longer defined in the relative terms of body and mind. "I am no longer on this side of my face looking at the world out there; I simply am the world. I am not in here. I have lost face—and discovered my Original Face, the Kosmos itself."[7] Across times and cultures, it is the conventional and conceptual understanding of existence that is called into question and ultimately transcended, not the magic and wonder of life itself.

When we recognize that the self is only a convention, with no absolute existence, and we realize our oneness with the rest of life, we are in truth the seamless intersection of the immanent and the transcendent. Our oft-noted insignificance in the scheme of things is now replaced by a vast, all-inclusive oneness with life. Freed from the cramped confines of your ego, you now know your identity with everything—absolutely everything! Whether you look into the eyes of a homeless man, a socialite in a glittering gown, a starving child on TV, an esteemed world figure, your kindly next-door neighbor, or someone arrested for a terrible crime, you are looking into your own eyes—and you *know* it.

A line attributed to the Sufi poet Kabir expresses it this way: "All know that the drop merges into the ocean, but few know that the ocean merges into the drop." This becomes a living truth for you, informing your most prosaic activities with a sense of the transcendent. You now realize your identity with all of life in an extraordinarily mysterious, astounding, and wonderful way, something humbling, incomprehensible, and breathtaking. That doesn't change the fact that you have to pick up some milk at the grocery store on your way home! Life goes on as it always has, but you watch it unfold with new eyes.

FREEDOM

The mind of no clinging is open and vast.
It is receptive to everything, but holds on to nothing.

—Joseph Goldstein

From the beginnings of civilization, the pages of history chronicle the human struggle for freedom—for release from physical and emotional realities that ravage the lives of so many. No matter what we have struggled against, the objective has always been to improve the lives of the oppressed. These are stories of victory or tragedy in which people attempt to free themselves from conditions that make their lives unbearable. It is a struggle without end.

The truth is that this struggle never makes us free. As long as we resist what is, pitting self against other and part versus whole, we will never find the true freedom we yearn for. In duality, the gains we make in the ceaselessly shifting circumstances of life are as vulnerable to change as everything else in our everyday world. The life, liberty, and happiness so hard won are inseparable from the ever-present fear of their loss, and we are always moving away from perceived threats and toward some supposed relief. As A. H. Almaas explains, our minds are split between some aspect of what is and something else that we want. "How are you going to arrive at harmony, integration, happiness, and freedom," he asks, "when there is a war inside you, when you are acting according to division and conflict?"[1] Identification with the finite puts us in opposition with the infinite, and our endless efforts to gain the upper hand fall forever short. Ultimately, the existentialist ideal of the individual bravely standing alone against the universe portrays a hollow victory. As Sartre expressed it in his acclaimed *Being and Nothingness*, with nothing to rely upon but our self, we are "condemned" to be free.

So is the dream of "doing it my way," memorialized in Sinatra's song, no longer viable? Must we jettison the heroes and heroines of individuality whom we have glorified from the Renaissance to the present pop-culture day? Can we not break the bonds of conventional expectations and "go it alone," riding into the sunset, or sailing into the unknown, to "become someone"? We can, of course, but these appealing constructs of our imagination won't set us free. They are the dreams of the ego, expressions of a free will as illusive as the self that presumes to enjoy it.

Yet mystical seekers who have broken through the boundaries of conventional understanding universally talk about their realization as a liberation. What kind of freedom are they finding in nonduality? Eckhart Tolle explains it this way: "The ego believes that in your resistance lies your strength; whereas in truth, resistance cuts you off from Being, the only place of true power."[2] Our futile attempts to control life play out in the fiction of a dualistic worldview; they bear no relevance to the freedom that comes from spiritual awakening. The former is based on the liberty of the individual person; the latter hinges on the realization that the individual person does not exist. The joy and exaltation we experience upon enlightenment is a result of our release from the delusion of self, not from constraints we perceive our "self" to be under.

As we have seen in examining the latter stages of esoteric practice, when we no longer believe in a self, separate and alone, that has a past and a future, the walls of our prison come tumbling down. We are liberated from our life stories and all the conditioning and habituation that have blinded us to what is. In the absence of an ego to experience and give meaning to the ongoing events of life, the beliefs, worldviews, possessions, accomplishments, and countless other attachments that used to define our being lose their point of reference. Without these, we don't form agendas or objectives or expectations, so the egocentric determination that once drove us is relaxed. And when we no longer project on the world our preconceived idiosyncratic view of what is, or cloud our vision with fears of the unexpected, our actions simply respond intuitively to the dictates of each new moment. Ramana Maharshi argued repeatedly that since the supreme power of God makes all things happen, we need not worry ourselves constantly with thoughts of what must be done. He compared such behavior to a passenger on a train who carries his load on his head, even though it will reach the destination just the same!

Though we in the West live in a society where individual choice is considered the essence of freedom, and we agonize continually over many of the decisions that confront us, it is *life* that makes the choices, not the individual self. Until we realize this, we are driven by the compulsion to "get it right" every time. Whether we're comparison-shopping for the best deal on a big-ticket item such as a car, or facing the sometimes excruciating dilemma of whom to date or marry, we can find ourselves paralyzed by our inability to decide. But those who realize that life makes the choices for us are released from the ceaseless shoulds and oughts by which we drive ourselves, as well as the what-ifs and if-onlys that are sure to follow. Then our struggles give way to trust. When there is nothing we can do, nothing to gain or lose, we are able for the first time to truly relax, to let go of our frenetic efforts and melt into the ecstasy and transience of being. It is this feeling of lightness and release that we find in this line from the *Tao Te Ching*: "Such tranquility, like the ocean / Such high wind, as if without limits."[3]

Many would argue that this is sheer fatalism, a submission to the whims of a heartless universe. But this argument, reasonable enough in the conventional dualistic context, loses all relevance in nonduality, where there is no one to submit to fate or to fight against it. In the absence of boundaries and divisions, neither self nor other exists. There is only what is, and we are That.

Freedom, destiny, fatalism—they are all just words we use to make sense of our struggles while we are still embedded in duality. As we have seen throughout this book, they are conventions with no intrinsic reality: the map, not the territory. What we do in the course of life cannot be distinguished from the flow of life itself. When we realize our true nature, and understand our oneness with what is happening, our relationship to what unfolds is transformed. After spiritual awakening, we no longer perceive ourselves as separate, bystanders watching the pageant of life unfold. Rather, we *become* the pageant and consciously participate in the unfolding. Accepting what is, knowing life from a higher perspective, produces the kind of equanimity that grandparents might feel as they watch their grandchildren play. While the children's wins and losses, their ups and downs, shift their moods from laughter to tears, their elders look on calmly, seeing these as the natural rhythms of life. In the same way, when the fantasy of separation and exile is found out and the dramas of our lives are put into context, the worry and anxiety, once so pronounced in our lives, fade away.

"Letting go of the futile battle to control," Sharon Salzberg explains, "we can find ourselves rewoven into the pattern of wholeness, into the immensity of life."[4] We can lay our burdens down. The difference between this stance and our customary, conventional struggles is profound. As Tzu-ssu, a Chinese philosopher of the fifth century BCE, explains, "the mature person lives in perfect serenity, awaiting the decrees of heaven, while the unworthy person walks on the edge of danger, always trying to keep one step ahead of his fate."[5]

When we pass beyond the last vestiges of dualistic thinking, we become the Unknowable. When identification with the body/mind falls away, the only thing left is the ephemeral play of energy—the rising and falling of sensations. Listen to the words of the Buddha: "In what is seen, there must just be the seen, in what is heard, there must just be the heard, in what is sensed, there must just be the sensed, in what is thought, there must just be the thought."[6] To what is he pointing? Amaro Bhikkhu interprets it this way: "There are forms, shapes, colors, and so forth, but there is no *thing* there. There is no real substance, no solidity, and no self-existent reality. All there is, is the quality of experience itself. No more, no less."[7] We have no more substance than the notes of a sonata played on a flute, coming out of nowhere and just as quickly disappearing. Mystical freedom is radical and absolute: our boundaries disappear and our oneness with the All floods in. We become freedom itself, the fleeting, evanescent flow of what is.

~

IMAGES OF FREEDOM

CAGED LION ~ Think of lions born in captivity. They spend their lives within the confines of a caged existence, completely unaware of the freedom that is their birthright. Domesticated and their senses dulled, they have eyes but can no longer see the promise with which they were born. If they were returned to the wild and the free life that is rightfully theirs, they would be frightened, bewildered, and lost. They have within them the potential to adapt to, and ultimately flourish in, this new reality, but the transition would be daunting. We are not so different. We too live in captivity—the captivity of ignorance. The bars of our cage are made of concepts and beliefs that keep us from seeing our true nature. Habits of thought and the untold divisions they impose have become so ingrained in us, so embedded in our way of life, that we are totally unaware of our potential for living in freedom. We don't see that the cage door has always been open.

BICYCLE ~ How is a bicycle like an ego? That may sound more like the setup for a punch line than a significant analogy, but there is one clear similarity: it is impossible to pinpoint the moment when either comes into existence. Could it be said that a bicycle is born in the mind of the inventor? Does it come into being when the iron ore is mined? Does it exist when the necessary parts are all gathered together, or is it real only when the last part is attached? And when a bicycle is disassembled, at what point can we say that it has ceased to exist? Is a two-wheel bike still a bike when one of the wheels is missing? What about both wheels? As you can see, it is impossible to determine objectively when a bike exists, since it consists of a complex interrelationship between various non-bike parts. The same is true of our sense of self. When does *it* actually come into existence? We have a genetic makeup that is derived from millions of years of life. So did our self begin millions of years ago? Would it be more accurate to say that it began when our parents fell in love, or is its birth linked to our physical birth in the hospital? At the end of life, does our sense of self die when our memory fades or when we no longer look like we used to? Does it die when we go into a coma, when we take our last breath, or when our lives are no longer fresh in the memories of others? The "birth" and "death" of our sense of self are just as arbitrary as the bicycle's: conceptual cutoffs imposed on the seamless process of energy known as life. When we realize this truth, and see there is no entity—bicycle or self—separate from the flow of life, we realize that we *are* that freedom. There is no place for a self to put down roots or hang its hat!

MUSICAL SCORE ∼ For people with no musical training, the score followed by a conductor would be all but impossible to decipher. The unique "alphabet" of notes and the complicated system of musical notation would be meaningless. Yet the master conductor perceives this array of visual symbols as an elegant auditory experience, "hearing" with his or her inner ear the creation as it sounds in its entirety. In the same way that the conductor can make sense out of a complicated musical score, seekers who have achieved mastery in the nondual tradition are able to make sense out of the seeming chaos and discord in their world of experience. Like the master conductor, those who have reached a deep level of spiritual understanding can see from the perspective of the absolute as well as the relative and find the harmony of the competing themes in the extraordinary symphony of life. Freedom is in the *seeing*, in the way we package our moment-to-moment experience. When life is seen dualistically, the maze of divisions and dissonant relationships, and the suffering they produce, often defy our ability to comprehend. Life seen as nondual, in contrast, is devoid of conceptual partitions and the fragmentation and the futility they engender, and it reflects a rhythm and harmony unmatched in the calculated efforts of even our greatest composers.

EMPTY BOAT ∼ If you were an experienced boater, you would know that when navigating through dense fog you must proceed with caution to avoid any mishaps. If, in spite of your efforts, another vessel collided with yours, it would be very upsetting. In anger, you might yell at the other boater, "Why don't you watch where you're going? Because of your carelessness, my boat is ruined!" But what if you realized that the other craft was empty and drifting by itself? Once you acknowledged that reality, your anger would quickly dissipate. There would be no one to blame, no one asleep at the helm. This is the attitude that an enlightened individual can take toward all the bumps and knocks of life. With the clarity that comes with higher understanding, we realize that there is no one to blame; life is the doer, the source of all the circumstances we encounter. With this wisdom, we are liberated from all judgment, bitterness, and anger.

HANDS ∼ When we are working with our hands, it becomes apparent that the left hand *does* know what the right hand is doing. For example, if our right hand gets pinched, hammered, or burned, the left hand comes to its assistance immediately. It holds it, rubs it, puts a soothing compress on it, and does anything else it can to ease the pain. It doesn't think about it first or consider its own interests. It simply acts to help the other. This is a beautiful illustration of how individuals no longer blinded by the conceptual boundaries between self and other can support those who are suffering. Help is offered before it is even asked, with nothing expected in return. It is giving for the sake of giving, and it comes naturally to those who know that, in truth, there is no difference between themselves and others. Just as the left and right hands are one with the body, all humanity is part of the one great whole. Mystical freedom does not mean that we don't have to do anything at all, or that important things don't get done. It simply relieves us of the erroneous belief that we must accomplish important objectives and overcome daunting challenges alone. When we see this, and we stop fouling up the works with anxiety and second-guessing, our tasks are completed as naturally as the left hand helps the right.

EYE OF THE STORM ∼ When a hurricane is at its strongest, satellite photos show a small, clearly defined inner area surrounded by thick, swirling walls of clouds and rain. The central region of the storm is known as the eye, and within its small enclosure there is peace and calm, in stark contrast to the frenetic activity that swirls wildly around its edges. This peace in the midst of chaos is like the serenity known by those who have dedicated their lives to spiritual practice. Living as if in the eye of a hurricane, they observe the travails of life from a place of inner peace and stillness. Unaffected by the vicissitudes of everyday existence, they weather life's storm with calm, confidence, and clarity.

In chapter 1, we saw that our journey into exile begins with the most fundamental dualistic division—that between subject and object. As our language develops and we are taught to identify and label "things" in our environment, the first and foremost entity is the self with which we learn to identify. From that pivotal moment when our delusion of self begins, the world we observe is dualistic, replete with the untold divisions and diversity of multiplicity. And we find ourselves separate and vulnerable. You know the story from there and the eventual yearning we experience to return to the wholeness of our true nature.

Now we are approaching the end of that cycle of exile and return, with the promise of once again realizing our oneness with life itself. However, one hurdle remains—the last vestige of the subject/object polarity that our journey began with and the subtle dualism it still produces. And it is not an easy task. We have seen what happens when we first begin to feel the illusion of self fade. When its boundaries grow transparent and we intuit its unreality, apprehension and fear follow. Some seekers turn away from practice altogether, while those who choose to continue look for a safety net elsewhere. If we were hanging over a precipice and losing our grip, we would naturally grasp at something else to hold on to, and this is what happens in esoteric practice. Practitioners find refuge in the way they interpret the sense of presence that seems to "watch" everything; they project a kind of spiritual self that looks on with detachment. This Witness, as it is commonly called, is what people cling to at this critical point in practice.

In truth, consciousness is indivisible from the organic flow of life, rising and falling with each and every object we perceive. It is not separate from what is, but a fundamental element of life, without which nothing would exist. The Witness is just another construct, another product of our mind. And our sense of its reality is maintained by thoughts we have of it while something is being observed—in the exact same way we experience our sense of self. In truth, when you think about the Witness, that thought is the *only* experience there is. When you are aware of something else, that is the *only* experience there is. There is always and only *one* object of consciousness at a time. Only the rapidity with which they rise and fall yields the impression that both the subject and the object are present at the same time.

If we persevere in our mystical quest for wholeness and remain unwavering in our desire to discover our true nature, there comes a time when we enter a nondual state. This usually happens in deep meditation, when the mind grows so still that the conceptual maps no longer appear and words lose their power to describe what we find there. The guideposts that used to orient us are nowhere to be seen. In this pure void, there is no time or space, no here or there, no cause or effect, no beginning or end. This is the moment when the seeker merges with what is, self-consciousness evaporates, and no one remains to make sense of it all—not even the Witness! It is only after the fact, when we reemerge from the nondual state and can once again employ concepts, that we can make any attempt to describe or interpret what took place—much as we may surmise that we had a good night's sleep even though we were not conscious of it.

In this state, the Witness suffers the fate of all other constructs, and with it go all the remaining vestiges of duality. Even such prominent polarities as form and emptiness, relative and absolute, or multiplicity and unity, by any name, are no more than conventions to one who has attained realization. There is no boundary, no division, no separate entity that exists in what is—not even the one who realizes it!

How are you to make sense out of all this, especially if this is your first exposure to such ideas? In this chapter, as in the last, we are in uncharted waters. In the last chapter, we looked at life without a self. Now you are being asked to envision the nature of a world without *anything* that exists as you have always assumed it did. What is left? If there are no entities, no subject or object, what does freedom even mean? Such notions run counter to everything we have learned throughout our lives and everything we know to be true about the world. We may still have misgivings even when we grasp that the mystics who teach the truth of nothingness are not speaking of a bleak, nihilistic abyss like the vision of twentieth-century existentialists. Our doubts are natural, as our beliefs and assumptions about what is real are borne out in the most immediate and tangible ways. When you hit your thumb with a hammer, how can you doubt the pain that stands in such vibrant witness to the existence of both hammer and thumb?

The answer is simple and essential. Nonduality does not suggest a vacuum devoid of any characteristics whatsoever, but rather the absence of any *entities* that exist and continue to exist in and of themselves over time. It is not that there is no hammer, but that we see it from the perspective of wholeness, just as William Blake saw the universe in a grain of sand. We see everything coming into being as causes and conditions in the flow of life create it, and disappearing when they disperse. As with the bicycle metaphor, we realize that it is impossible to determine where anything begins or where it will end. When we understand the conventional role of concepts and are no longer misled by them, we open to the truth that the hammer contains virtually all of life.

The same is true of every other "thing" in our reality, for that matter. They are all temporary manifestations of oneness. Everything is created by everything—*unity* is the doer, the doing, and the thing done, all seamlessly fused into the ephemeral display of sensations upon which we impose our conceptual maps. In the absence of conceptuality and the arbitrary divisions it creates, there are no things, no entities, no objects to be found. The "no-thing-ness" that remains might be best described as the ceaseless flow or process of what is. When we intuit that, in truth, there are no partitions whatsoever, we come to see that we are not observers standing apart from the observed; rather, the awareness that makes this display accessible is, itself, the very nature of suchness, and our true nature. Life is a reality that must be realized by Life, and that only happens when the delusion of separation—either as self or as Witness—dissolves. As Ken Wilber puts it, "There will soon enough come the great catastrophe of final Freedom and Fullness: the Witness itself will disappear entirely, and instead of witnessing the sky, you are the sky; instead of touching the earth, you are the earth; instead of hearing the thunder, you are the thunder."[8]

There is only what is, but now life has remembered itself and consciously *embodies* the paradox of its own creation. Life lives life, and *knows* it. When you awaken to your true nature, your oneness with life, you watch all the activities of your body/mind occur spontaneously, knowing them to be the manifestations of life. You are something incomprehensively vast in something very, very small, and seeing this unfathomable truth play out in each and every thing you do is something that cannot be explained.

The freedom inherent in this understanding is likewise beyond our ability to articulate. Deng Ming-Dao expresses it this way: "Be still to know the absolute. / Be active to know the outer. / The two spring from the same source, / All of life is one whole."[9] We hear the same wisdom from Gregory of Nyssa: "Do not be surprised that we should speak of the Godhead as being at the same time both unified and differentiated. Using riddles, as it were, we envisage a strange and paradoxical diversity-in-unity and unity-in-diversity."[10] In the often-quoted teaching of the ancient sage Nagarjuna, this fundamental principle comes up yet again: "The words 'There is,' means clinging to eternal substance, 'There is not' connotes the view of nihilism. Thus in neither 'is' nor 'is not' is the dwelling place of those who know."[11]

This is why the archetypal figures of mythology are so often androgynous, and why it is in the union of figures like Shiva and Shakti that the truth is found. The traditional carvings and sculptures that have appeared in different times and cultures, blending aspects of both male and female anatomy or intertwining them in some symbolic way, are pointing to the unity of opposites. As I have noted before, the abundant characteristics and features that describe our world never disappear or lose their beauty and appeal. We simply learn to see them as they are and not assume that they imply the existence of separate entities.

When the veil of phenomena drops, our own boundaries vanish along with all the others. We are whole, no longer one-dimensional. We have gone backstage and seen behind the masks of reality. We are, and we are not. We exist and we do not exist. Our dualistic perspective envisions samsara, form, self, karma, Witness, birth and death, exile and return, while our nondual being sees nirvana, emptiness, selflessness, and freedom. As with the waves of the ocean, there are perceivable features and characteristics, but in truth there is only constant motion and change. The waves don't disappear, and the gentle play of the surf on the sand or the awesome power with which it sometimes pounds the shore never ceases. We simply recognize their underlying truth. Seeing separate waves, some large and some small, some gentle and some with a majestic white crest, yields one interpretation, while knowing the vast oneness and depth of the ocean gives us another.

Ultimately, we come to understand that all descriptions are arbitrary; the incessant, miraculous flow of life is all that is. As Matthew Flickstein says, "It is not that everything is impermanent but that impermanence is the only 'thing' that there is."[12] It was this same understanding to which Rabbi David Cooper was pointing when he declared God to be a verb, and it is in this same light that we find resolution for the most profound enigmas of life.

There is an ancient riddle that teachers have used to express three stages in which practice and realization unfold. Mountains are mountains; mountains are not mountains; mountains are mountains. As we look back on the journey of self-discovery outlined in these pages, we can see that the first statement represents the dualistic, conventional paradigm of subject and object—the "one-storied," objective world full of hard facts and firm boundaries. This is the realm of the Exile, where samsara is mistakenly taken as real, and words and labels are believed to accurately describe what we find before us: mountains are mountains, anyone can see that. The second statement captures the intermediate intuition, arrived at on the inward journey of practice, that our conceptual maps merely conceal the ultimate emptiness of all appearances. Here, the division of subject and object continues in the subtle guise of the Witness and we subjectively view the world as having two levels, duality and nonduality, form and emptiness, samsara and nirvana: mountains are not mountains, because the concept of "mountain" is a delusion of duality.

We understand from the third sentence, at last, that concepts are precious and essential tools with which to communicate, while we remain simultaneously aware of the interdependent, unbounded, indivisible nature of all existence. It is with this more complete realization that we can employ words as naturally as birds sing or dogs bark, without becoming lost in the conceptual dream that entrances most of humanity. Duality *is* nonduality, form *is* emptiness, samsara *is* nirvana, and the Witness merges with what is. The subject/object split is no more. As nothing, we are everything—suchness self-aware. *What is* arises in awareness, as awareness—the incomprehensible mystery of life. Mountains are mountains, and in the truest sense, our very being. At last we are free to be what we are.

Those who plumb the mystery of nonduality, and realize its inherent freedom, manifest both the relative and the absolute aspects of life with the same harmony in which the mind and the heart coexist in each of us. The wisdom of the whole stays in balance with compassion for the parts in a rhythm as natural as the expansion and contraction of the lungs or the alternating movement of our legs as they carry us to and fro. While the realization of emptiness lightens our sense of being and gives our identity a transparency and grace, the heart is filled with compassion for those still caught in the delusion. We no longer see them through the materialistic mindset as *others*—things, objects, competitors—but as self. Transformed in this manner, the sages, mystics, and Bodhisattvas across the ages have returned to the marketplace to serve all in need. None are excluded from receiving the blessings of those who know themselves, for in the eyes of the awakened, all are one, and they share their gifts of wisdom and love as freely as the tree spreads its shade or the spring blossoms offer their fragrance.

HOMECOMING

We shall not cease from exploration
And the end of all our exploring
Will be to arrive where we started
And know the place for the first time.

—T. S. Eliot

When we venture forth on the mystical journey, we may imagine our destination as a place far away from where we are, in every sense—someplace profoundly, essentially other. But at the end of the path, there is no final ascent to a transcendent, otherworldly realm. Rather, the quest leads seekers back to the suchness of the present moment, to "just this." Setting down the burdens of identification, the attachments of the ego, and the weight of self-consciousness, we find ourselves back where we started—the same place, but appareled in newness and unimagined splendor. Indeed, the fragmented terrain we left, the "lesser world" in which we have spent most of our lives, turns out to be the Promised Land to which all wisdom traditions have pointed. The world has not changed—it is still replete with all the characteristic suffering and dilemmas of existence—but we have changed, and we see it with new eyes: the eyes of life itself.

In the wake of illumination, when conditioning no longer obscures our vision, the world is transfigured, and the sages of every lineage sing its joyful praises. In the midst of earthly turmoil and distress, they see overflowing wonders. As medieval mystic St. Catherine of Siena declares, "All the way to heaven is heaven."[1] From Hakuin, we hear this: "This earth where we stand is the pure lotus land, and this very body, the body of Buddha."[2] With virtually the same idea, the poet Mirza Ghalib tells us, "The world is no more than the Beloved's single face."[3] Shankara declares, "This universe is nothing but Brahman. See Brahman everywhere, under all circumstances, with the eye of the spirit and a tranquil heart."[4] Yet again, in the Pirkei Avot of the Talmud we read: "To attend to creation is to attend to God. To attend to the moment is to attend to eternity."[5] In every tradition we find the same theme: those who have come home to their true nature see no reason to go elsewhere. They recognize no boundaries between the sacred and the profane, and they find perfection in imperfection.

When you realize what you are, you see what is. The commentary of the mind no longer obscures the intuitive wisdom of the heart. There is seeing, knowing, and being, but it is not from the finite perspective of your self, your ego. In awakened awareness, life beholds the wonder of its own being—and you are That. Released from the imprisonment of the conditioned mind and the countless boundaries that previously fragmented our vision, we see that the radiant majesty of the world is everywhere. A mountain meadow, for example, retains the detail and definition of the trees, flowers, birds, and rippling creek that meadows so often boast, and it abounds with the unique and particular traits that reveal its beauty, but one with the discernment of realization can enjoy the play of color and form while recognizing the unity of all things. The focus broadens, so that instead of naming and recognizing separate elements, we see things in the context of the seamless harmony of the meadow's organic oneness. As Catherine Ingram puts it, we find "no two alike, yet no two at all."[6] The relative and absolute perspectives are fused, and the sage beholds a world where such constructs have lost their relevance.

When mystics attend to even the smallest and most simple of things, they see the full greatness of Being unbounded by conventional dimensions; life is no longer frozen in the measure of a name. This is what Blake meant by the famous dictum I alluded to in the last chapter: "To see a World in a grain of sand and a Heaven in a wild flower, hold infinity in the palm of your hand and eternity in an hour."[7] From Huang-po we hear the same thing: "When you see a grain of sand, you see all possible worlds, with all their vast rivers and mountains. When you see a drop of water, you see the nature of all the waters of the universe."[8] This wholeness appears when our habits of discrimination are broken and we refrain from imposing the constraints and comparisons that have so long divided life in our minds—the judgments that say, "This is a drop and that is an ocean." When we drop the numberless designations with which we define and distinguish this from that, here from there, big from small, self from other, we see what we saw when our eyes were new. Everything is interconnected, nothing exists on its own—and nothing is insignificant.

While some travel to distant lands to find the answers they yearn for, the masters of esoteric spirituality have always known that Paradise is close at hand. "If you wish to know the Divine," the Buddha told his students, "feel the wind on your face and the warm sun on your hand."[9] Over and over we are directed back to what is right in front of us—back to this very moment.

The Gates of Eden were never shut for those with eyes to see. Once we no longer peer through the thick lens of conditioning, we find ourselves surrounded by the astounding, improbable wonder of things *as they are*. Looking at the ordinary trappings of our lives—our daily conversations, our food, our children's grades, and even our loved ones' passing—without the distortions of desire or aversion, uncolored by opinions or preferences of the past, we see them for what they are: wondrous creations of life. Realizing that the moment is all there is, and freed from the compulsion to be somewhere else, we appreciate *here* and *now* for the first time.

This is the message of Zen master Layman P'ang in his famous declaration: "Even the poorest thing shines. My miraculous power and spiritual activity: drawing water and carrying wood."[10] Catholic mystic

Angelus Silesius says in seventeenth-century Europe: "Nothing is imperfect, the pebble equals the ruby, a frog is as beautiful as any seraphim."[11] Two centuries later, the same thread runs through the words of Whitman: "And the narrowest hinge in my hand puts to scorn all machinery, and the cow crunching with depress'd head surpasses any statue, and a mouse is miracle enough to stagger sextillions of infidels."[12] They understand that it is in being present with what is, and not in our ideas and notions about what is, that we find what we have been looking for. We don't need to witness supernatural phenomena. As Thich Nhat Hanh tells us, it is miracle enough to walk on this earth.

With eyes opened to the truth, we are released from the bondage of the ego, and the rigid forms of thought that imprison it. Our attempts to figure things out or to adjust them according to our personal preference cease, and we become intimate with what is. This is what Kabir means when he says: "Something inside of me has reached to the place where the world is breathing."[13]

Whether in a city teeming with activity or in the peaceful stillness of a forest, there are miracles waiting for all who take off their shoes and enter with the deference of unknowing. The epiphany of the tiny insect navigating across the page we are reading manifests an intelligence that belies its size, and, counterintuitive as it may be, it can seem to say more to us than libraries of knowledge. A daffodil blooming in the middle of a litter-strewn ditch, and the discarded empty cans and wrappers themselves, share equally the oneness of what is. The children's gleeful laughter rising from the ruins of the tenement, and the youth flashing gang signs on the corner, point to a deeper truth.

The timeless enchantment of a rainy day, with its syncopated rhythms of falling water, speaks to something unfathomable within, even while you wait by your broken-down car for the tow truck. A chattering mockingbird, the whisper of the flowing stream, or the primal voice of a crackling fire bypass the rules of our conventional idiom and play their unfiltered magic directly on the organ of our senses. November's leaves falling in their gentle spirals or the flight of the eagle in communion with the wind produce a visual music that confounds the discipline of words. The elegant design of the dandelion seed gently floating on the breeze, and the seductive aroma of baking bread, bear markings of the Absolute—as does the peeling paint on the side of your house. Even the ebb and flow of our own bodies and the seasons of our being are remarkable reflections of the seamless unity of what is.

When the guidebook for living that we have so studiously followed for decades is put aside, we can revel once again in the unbounded fullness of our very own being. In a world so thoroughly conceptual, such living is hard to even imagine, but perfect examples are close at hand—wherever you find one-year-olds exploring the magic of being alive. Their world has not yet been split into subject and object, self and other. Playing with their toes is no different from fingering a rattle or kissing their teddy bear. As easily fascinated by a muddy twig or stone they find on the ground as they are with a shiny new toy, toddlers see what we ourselves saw before society taught us what was "real," "good," "valuable," "beautiful," "important," and what was not. The world they explore is not yet translated into concepts; it is the timeless, undivided, nonideational wholeness of what is, and of what they are.

Just as sound rises from and falls back into silence, awakened seekers know that their own being unfolds out of the formless and returns to it, again and again. Of course the lessons of experience and the skills and knowledge we have gained are essential for dealing with the practical matters of daily life, but their conventional nature cannot be forgotten. As you discovered in chapter 3, memories create time, and time is the enemy of presence, of being right where you are. When each day is lived with the understanding that one is simply the experience as it is happening, we can see that there is *only* the journey, no "one" who sets out or arrives.

This is it, the Holy Land of the timeless moment. "This radiant insubstantiality, total presence of the here and now," says Keith Dowman, "this is the *summum bonum* of all vision."[14] Alan Watts expresses a similar idea: "Eternal life is realized when the last trace of difference between 'I' and 'now' has vanished—when there is just 'now' and nothing else."[15] There is only the manifestation of the moment, rising and falling without leaving a trace. As nothing lasts, there is nothing to lose or hang on to. Rumi conveys the sense of it when he asks us to imagine "the delight of walking on a noisy street and *being* the noise."[16] The play of phenomena appearing in the light of awareness—that is what is and what we are. The dance and the dancer disappear together into the dancing.

Seeing their oneness with all, masters know that even the gesture of a hand is an action of the whole, powered by the energy and intelligence of the entire universe. In this total fusion with the rhythms of life, even the simplest actions of one so engaged have a distinctive grace and beauty. When one is relaxed and open to what is, each instant arises without contrivance or expectation. Actions and circumstances blend harmoniously in expressions of life undivided. When masters sit, they sit. When they eat, they eat. There is just the current activity. What does this mean? You may well wonder how it differs from when *you* sit. After all, isn't that what you do when you "just sit"? The key to all this is what *else* you are doing when you sit. Are you worrying about what you just heard on the news? Are you trying to decide what business decision you are going to make tomorrow—and concerned for the reaction that may come from it? Are you texting on your phone while you are sitting, or looking over your son's homework?

Does this mean that the mind of a master never wanders, never thinks of past or future? Of course not. It is simply that there is no attachment, no engagement with such ideas that divides your attention from sitting. Perhaps this is easier to grasp when you think of your experience when you "just eat." Have you ever eaten a delicious meal without tasting the food at all? Of course. We all have when engaged in an argument or serious conversation. And remember the last bag of chips you ate while watching a suspenseful movie on TV? How many of them did you "just eat"? In esoteric spirituality, one finds less and less need to look beyond the blessing contained in each moment. All desire to do something different or be somewhere else fades. This may seem very strange to you, when society in general puts such stock in multitasking, but life undivided depends on attention undivided.

In silent simplicity, and with the innocence of a child, you can find abundance in the least things and savor the miracle of being alive in this very moment.

~

IMAGES OF HOMECOMING

DREAMER ~ Though our dreams are often surreal in their shifting scenery and sequencing of events, they are generally furnished with the customary objects and people we find in our waking lives. Most things appear to be separate, as in life, and unfold in the same general context of space and time. We talk to other people, do many of the things we do in waking life, such as eat or walk or drive a car, and experience the full spectrum of common emotions in the encounters we have. When we awaken from the dream, however, we realize that we are the authors of it all: it is a reality of our own creation. We are the dreamer, the dream, and the dreaming at once—a single, undivided process. Homecoming is the realization of this truth, and it brings our release from cause and effect, from the cold, hard facts of life as we have known it. Our *waking* lives are now seen as a play of the mind, with no more real substance than the dreams we have at night. We are in it, participating in the drama and living through the shifting fortunes—and yet we aren't. Consequently, we return to our daily affairs with a lightness, grace, and playful spirit, for we know that *both* the relative and absolute, the figure and the ground, are equal sides of our true nature. *We* are the ineffable oneness of what is.

DAYLIGHT ~ Mystical insight reveals that the basis of life is consciousness and that it is our true nature. We, of course, know what it is to be aware, but beyond that we have no notion of what or where consciousness is. We cannot see our nature any more than an eyeball can see itself; we can only identify things that we are not—our name, body/mind, thoughts, knowledge, life stories, possessions, accomplishments, strengths and weaknesses, and so on. Think of the qualities of daylight, however, and you may glimpse some semblance of what your own true nature is. First of all, daylight, like consciousness, is everywhere and pervades everything. Second, the world as we know it would not exist in the absence of either. Light is a prerequisite for anything to be *seen*; consciousness is a prerequisite for anything to be *known*. We cannot see daylight except when it falls on an object (such as the shuttle in space or dust in afternoon sun), and we are conscious only when there is something to be conscious of. At the same time, daylight does not judge, discriminate, or interfere with the objects it illuminates, and consciousness does not judge, discriminate, or interfere with the objects to which it brings awareness. Finally, all daylight is inseparable from its source, the sun—there is no such thing as a discrete body of daylight or a separate sunbeam that exists unto itself—just as ultimately, inseparably, all forms of consciousness are one.

PROPRIOCEPTION ~ In physiology, *proprioception* is a term used to refer to the sensory modality that provides feedback on the internal status of the body. Stimuli produced and perceived within the body inform us as to the location and movement of the various parts in relation to each other. When you have proprioception of the arm, you don't represent the arm to yourself in any way; you're not thinking about the arm and how it is moving, but nevertheless you are aware of it. It is a stream of consciousness that coordinates the movements of the body, but there is no subject/object division. There is just simple, direct knowing without a knower, perceiving without a perceiver. This is analogous to awareness in which there is no self-consciousness—those times when we forget the conventional self that we use to function in the practical affairs of society. When we come home to our true being, the oneness of life, there is seeing, knowing, and being, but none require a subject—no "one" to see or know or be. Life is basking in the miracle of its own being, through the sense organs of all its numberless forms.

This book began with an inscription written by Gauguin on the bottom of one of his Tahiti paintings: *Where do we come from? What are we? Where are we going?* As we draw to a close after tracing the mystic's journey of exile and return, coming full circle, can we answer Gauguin's timeless question? Do we know now what we are? Perhaps, from all the ideas we have explored and the metaphors we have examined, you have a glimmer of an answer, but the truth is we cannot say, at least not in any common language. Our being, by definition, lies beyond all concepts and defies all descriptions. We stretch from the quark to the quasar. We embody life and death, samsara and nirvana, yin and yang, and all the other polarities of life. There is vastly more to our being than our physical dimensions suggest. Our true nature—our absolute identity with what is—verges on the incomprehensible.

How are we ultimately to express the miracle of it all? To brush our teeth is the labor of ages, and when thoughts arise in our minds, they are life's thoughts. The same force that makes the planets spin in their orbits causes our hearts to beat, coordinates the minutest movements of our eyes, brings the wave to the shore, and lifts the doe over the fence. We participate in every moment of creation and watch firsthand as wonders unfold in our presence. How can we put into words the extraordinary fact that, within our finite frames of flesh and blood, we envelop the measureless spaces of the universe? And how could we ever express the blessings contained in the evanescence of our being? How make sense of a heart overflowing with gratitude amid the suffering and distress of life? Language cannot snare our being in a net of words or plumb the contents of our hearts. The measures of science cannot capture the splendor of the setting sun, nor gauge the reach and power of our love. However we try—as I have tried throughout this book and am trying still in this very line—there is no way to articulate such a mystery. We simply yield to its unfolding with deep reverence, grati-tude, and profound joy. Mystics do not unravel the mystery so much as live it. As you come full circle, turning exile into return again, you don't find the answer you have been looking for—you *are* the answer.

Think about that for a minute. *You are the answer.* When you read such a statement, it's natural to interpret "you" as the same familiar body/mind you identified with when you started this book—and for that "you," nothing has changed. *You* need a new computer and the air conditioner needs repairs. *You* got the promotion you were hoping for, but face a steep learning curve to assume your responsibilities. Tonight is open house at *your* children's school, and the yard needs mowing. Maybe *you* have struggled with a lot of what you have read here. But it's my hope that the seeds of insight have been planted. If you yield to the yearning within you, find a mystical path that resonates with you, begin to practice, continue to explore the teachings of esoteric spirituality, and perhaps find a group of fellow seekers to join, you will be preparing a fertile soil in which those seeds will grow and blossom. And when insights begin to penetrate your conditioned view of life, it will gradually become clear that, indeed, you *are* the answer. With dedication and devotion, the possibility of opening to that truth will grow.

The real reader of this book is life itself, hidden only by the mask of who you *think* you are. You are both seeker and sought, playing the eternal cosmic game of hide-and-seek with yourself. And, just as paradoxical, this book has been written by the very same consciousness—that of life itself, hidden by *my* mask. We are one and the same. The only doer of *anything and everything* is this unnamable, immeasurable, inexplicable, wondrous nature of what is. There is no name or concept that can circumscribe our true nature or define our being—but we truly are what is.

When you started reading this book, your conception of who you are was likely defined by hard facts. We all know them—race, nationality, age, height, weight, level of education, profession, religion, and so on. Yet, as for so many of us today, there was something missing. If you are like most people drawn to this subject, even if blessed with a wonderful family, a well-paying and meaningful job, and plenty of rewarding friendships, you felt somehow incomplete and yearned for a sense of wholeness. This is the impetus that propels us all to become seekers. It is life calling us back home.

In the course of this book we have traced a movement from the very small to the very large. We have moved from names to the unnamable, from society's hand-me-down version of reality to the unmediated wonder of what is. In our quest for meaning and understanding, we have shifted from part to whole, from figure to ground, from individual human being to the whole of life itself. Yet we must remember that our quest does not end there. As we saw in the last chapter, the journey does not end until we realize that it is in the *union* of both part and whole, figure and ground, that we find what is. The two halves of our being are truly one. Samsara *is* nirvana, relative *is* absolute, form *is* emptiness, the part *is* the whole.

Ultimately, you will remember what you are and realize your extraordinary birthright. As life aware of itself, you will be able to shift effortlessly back and forth from figure to ground—from the details and duties of the name and role you play to the big picture, the ground of all being. No longer identifying with the finite body and mind of your conventional self, you will have a front-row seat for the greatest show of all—a kind of magical mystery tour of creation, life unexplained, undefined, and unimagined. The everyday problems and everyday pleasures don't cease; you simply see them in the context of the whole, with deep reverence and gratitude, in a new and wonderful light of wisdom, compassion, and peace. Seeing, knowing, and being the wonders of your true nature, you have come home.

NOTES

Introduction

1. Mariana Caplan, *The Way of Failure: Winning through Losing* (Prescott, AZ: Hohm Press, 2001), 518.
2. Joseph Campbell, *The Hero with a Thousand Faces* (Princeton, NJ: Princeton University Press, 1973), 259.
3. Ibid., 39.
4. Leonard Shlain, *The Alphabet Versus the Goddess: The Conflict Between Word and Image* (New York: Penguin, 1998), 20.
5. Marvin W. Meyer, trans., *The Secret Teachings of Jesus: Four Gnostic Gospels* (New York: Vintage, 1986), p. 33, saying 75.

Chapter 1 ~ Duality

1. Matthieu Ricard and Trinh Xuan Thuan, *The Quantum and the Lotus: A Journey to the Borders Where Science and Buddhism Meet* (New York: Three Rivers Press, 2001), 106.
2. Alan Watts, *The Wisdom of Insecurity: A Message for an Age of Anxiety* (New York: Pantheon, 1951), 86.
3. Campbell, *The Hero with a Thousand Faces*, 153.
4. Isaiah 45:7 (New International Version).
5. Laotzu's *Tao and Wu Wei*, trans. Dwight Goddard and Henri Borel (New York: Brentano's, 1919), 5.
6. Walt Whitman, "Song of Myself," in *Walt Whitman Reader: Selections from Leaves of Grass* (Philadelphia: Running Press, 1993), 49, 55–56.
7. Thich Nhat Hanh, "Please Call Me by My True Names," in *Being Peace* (Berkeley, CA: Parallax Press, 1987), 63–64.

Chapter 2 ~ Thought

1. Huston Smith, *The Forgotten Truth: The Common Vision of the World's Religions* (San Francisco: Harper, 1976), 6.

2. Daniel C. Matt, ed., *The Essential Kabbalah: The Heart of Jewish Mysticism* (Edison, NJ: Castle Books, 1997),113.

3. Stephen Mitchell, ed., *The Enlightened Mind: An Anthology of Sacred Prose* (New York: HarperPerennial, 1993), 47.

4. Albert Einstein and Leopold Infeld, *The Evolution of Physics: From Early Concepts to Relativity and Quanta* (New York: Simon and Schuster, 1966), 31.

5. Jerome S. Bruner, *On Knowing: Essays for the Left Hand* (Cambridge, MA: Belknap Press, 1962).

6. Mitchell, *The Enlightened Mind*, 165.

Chapter 3 ～ Time

1. Ken Wilber, *No Boundary: Eastern and Western Approaches to Personal Growth* (Boston, MA: Shambhala, 2001), 65.

2. Mitchell, *The Enlightened Mind*, 169.

Chapter 4 ～ Knowledge

1. Luke 9:62 (NIV).

Chapter 5 ～ Self

1. Eckhart Tolle, *A New Earth: Awakening to Your Life's Purpose* (New York: Plume, 2006), 28.

2. Ken Wilber, *The Atman Project: A Transpersonal View of Human Development* (Wheaton, IL: Quest Books, 1996), 120.

Chapter 6 ～ Attachment

1. Thich Nhat Hanh, *The Heart of the Buddha's Teaching: Transforming Suffering into Peace, Joy, and Liberation* (New York: Broadway Books, 1998), 56.

Chapter 7 ～ Karma

1. Ralph Waldo Emerson, *Essays and Lectures* (Lawrence, KS: Digireads.com Publishing, 2009), 150.

2. *Tao Te Ching: Annotated & Explained*, trans. Derek Lin (Woodstock, VT: SkyLight Paths, 2006), 77, http://taoism.net.

3. Aldous Huxley, *The Perennial Philosophy* (New York: Harper and Row, 1999), 239.

4. Matthew Flickstein, *The Meditator's Atlas: A Roadmap of the Inner World* (Boston: Wisdom Publications, 2007), 114.

5. Ramana Maharshi, *Talks with Ramana Maharshi: On Realizing Abiding Peace and Happiness* (Carlsbad, CA: Inner Directions Publishing, 2001), 387.
6. *The Bhagavad Gita*, trans. Eknath Easwaran (Tomales, CA: Nilgiri Press, 1985), p. 89, 4:37–38.
7. Joel S. Goldsmith, *The Thunder of Silence* (New York: Harper, 1961), 29.
8. Geddes MacGregor, "The Christening of Karma," in *Karma: Rhythmic Return to Harmony*, ed. V. Hanson, R. Stewart, and S. Nicholson (Wheaton, IL: Quest Books, 1990), 88.
9. *The Essential Rumi*, trans. Coleman Barks (San Francisco: Harper, 1996), 36.
10. Goddard, *Laotzu's Tao and Wu Wei*, 38.
11. Quoted in Huxley, *The Perennial Philosophy*, 83.

Chapter 8 ∾ Suffering

1. *Zen Buddhism: Selected Writings of D. T. Suzuki*, ed. William Barrett (New York: Doubleday, 1996), 6.
2. Barks, *The Essential Rumi*, 20.
3. Job 38:4–39:26 (NIV).

Chapter 9 ∾ Meaning

1. Smith, *The Forgotten Truth*, 149.
2. Karen Armstrong, *A History of God: The 4,000-Year Quest of Judaism, Christianity and Islam* (New York: Ballantine Books, 1993), 390–399.
3. See Philip Kapleau, *The Three Pillars of Zen: Teaching, Practice, and Enlightenment* (New York: Anchor Books, 1989), 313–323.
4. Lin, *Tao Te Ching*, 29.
5. Alan Watts, *The Tao of Philosophy: The Edited Transcripts*, ed. Mark Watts (Boston: Charles E. Tuttle, 1995), 66.
6. Wayne Teasdale, *The Mystic Heart: Discovering a Universal Spirituality in the World's Religions* (Novato, CA: New World Library, 1999), 208.

Chapter 10 ∾ Yearning

1. Andrew Harvey, ed., *The Essential Mystics: The Soul's Journey into Truth* (Edison, NJ: Castle Books, 1996), 143.
2. Easwaran, *The Bhagavad Gita*, p. 143, 10:20.
3. *The Soul of Rumi: A New Collection of Ecstatic Poems,* trans. Coleman Barks (San Francisco: HarperSanFrancisco, 2001), 16.
4. Mitchell, *The Enlightened Mind*, 99.
5. Harvey, *The Essential Mystics*, 8.
6. Ibid., 32.
7. Ibid., 114.

8. Eckhart Tolle, *The Power of Now: A Guide to Spiritual Enlightenment* (Novato, CA: New World Library, 1999), 1.

9. Sharon Salzberg, *Faith: Trusting Your Own Deepest Experience* (New York: Riverhead Books, 2002), 155.

10. Mitchell, *The Enlightened Mind*, 80.

11. Ibid., 76.

12. Jack Kornfield, *A Path with Heart: A Guide through the Perils and Promises of Spiritual Life* (New York: Bantam Books, 1993), 161.

13. Deng Ming-Dao, *Everyday Tao: Living with Balance and Harmony* (San Francisco: HarperSanFrancisco, 1996), 95.

14. Harvey, *The Essential Mystics*, 190.

15. Deepak Chopra, *The Way of the Wizard: Twenty Spiritual Lessons for Creating the Life You Want* (New York: Harmony Books, 1995), 116.

16. Quoted in T. Byram Karasu, *The Art of Serenity: The Path to a Joyful Life in the Best and Worst of Times* (New York: Simon & Schuster, 2003), 224.

Chapter 11 ∼ Paths

1. Wilber, *The Atman Project*, 46–49.

2. *The Note-Books of Samuel Butler*, ed. Henry Festing Jones (New York: E. P. Dutton, 1917), 326.

3. Caplan, *The Way of Failure*, 134.

4. Matt, *The Essential Kabbalah*, 7.

5. *Paul Tillich: Theologian of the Boundaries*, ed. Mark Kline Taylor (Minneapolis, MN: Fortress Press, 1987), 164.

6. Smith, *The Forgotten Truth*, 52.

7. Barrett, *Zen Buddhism: Selected Writings of D. T. Suzuki*, 183–184.

8. Meyer, *The Secret Teachings of Jesus*, p. 28, saying 51.

9. Lin, *Tao Te Ching*, 41.

Chapter 12 ∼ Alignment

1. Quoted in Reza Shah-Kazemi, *Paths to Transcendence: According to Shankara, Ibn Arabi, and Meister Eckhart* (Bloomington, IN: World Wisdom, 2006), 99.

2. Amaro Bhikkhu, *Small Boat, Great Mountain: Theravadan Reflections on the Natural Great Perfection* (Redwood, CA: Abhayagiri Monastery, 2003), 93.

3. Frithjof Schuon, *The Transcendent Unity of Religions* (Wheaton, IL: Quest, 2005), 151–152.

4. Flickstein, *The Meditator's Atlas*, 10–14.

5. Shah-Kazemi, *Paths to Transcendence*, 20.

6. Hazrat Inayat Khan, *The Mysticism of Sound and Music* (Boston: Shambhala, 1996), 116.

7. Thomas Merton, *The Inner Experience: Notes on Contemplation*, ed. William H. Shannon (New York: HarperCollins, 2003), 15.

8. Quoted in Merton, *The Inner Experience*, 17.

9. Salzberg, *Faith*, 67.

10. Quoted in Shah-Kazemi, *Paths to Transcendence*, 23.

11. Huxley, *The Perennial Philosophy*, 235.

12. Ibid., 236–237.

13. Salzberg, *Faith*, 67.

14. Merton, *The Inner Experience*, 18.

15. Easwaran, *The Bhagavad Gita*, p. 196, 17:3.

16. Easwaran, introduction to *The Bhagavad Gita*, p. 43.

17. Huxley, *The Perennial Philosophy*, 255.

Chapter 13 ⁓ Practices

1. Amit Goswami, *The Visionary Window: A Quantum Physicist's Guide to Enlightenment* (Wheaton, IL: Quest Books, 2000), 186.

2. Evelyn Underhill, ed., *The Cloud of Unknowing* (New York: Cosimo, 2007), 14.

3. Huston Smith, *The World's Religions* (New York: HarperCollins, 1991), 262.

4. Joseph Campbell, *The Masks of God: Primitive Mythology* (New York: Penguin Books, 1969), 28.

5. David S. Ariel, *The Mystic Quest: An Introduction to Jewish Mysticism* (New York: Schocken Books, 1988), 121.

6. David A. Cooper, *God Is a Verb: Kabbalah and the Practice of Mystical Judaism* (New York: Riverhead Books, 1997), 46–58.

7. Alan Watts, *Buddhism: The Religion of No-Religion*, ed. Mark Watts (Boston: Charles E. Tuttle, 1996), 75.

8. Khan, *The Mysticism of Sound and Music*, 81.

9. Schuon, *The Transcendent Unity of Religions*, 145.

10. Easwaran, *The Bhagavad Gita*, p. 106, 6:19–20.

11. Quoted in Shah-Kazemi, *Paths to Transcendence*, 27.

12. Barrett, *Zen Buddhism: Selected Writings of D. T. Suzuki*, 138.

13. Mitchell, *The Enlightened Mind*, 169.

14. Ruben L. F. Habito, *Healing Breath: Zen for Christians and Buddhists in a Wounded World* (Somerville, MA: Wisdom Publications, 2006), 63.

15. Alan Watts, *Nature, Man, and Woman* (New York: Vintage Books, 1970), 116.

16. Flickstein, *The Meditator's Atlas*, 155.

Chapter 14 ~ Non-Doing

1. Teasdale, *The Mystic Heart*, 133.
2. Merton, *The Inner Experience*, 6.
3. Ibid., 7.
4. Cooper, *God Is a Verb*, 215.
5. Barrett, *Zen Buddhism: Selected Writings of D. T. Suzuki*, 184.
6. Keith Dowman, trans., *The Flight of the Garuda: The Dzogchen Tradition of Tibetan Buddhism* (Somerville, MA: Wisdom Publications, 2003), 9.
7. Ibid., 20.
8. Ibid., 95.
9. Barrett, *Zen Buddhism: Selected Writings of D. T. Suzuki*, 280.
10. Alan Watts, with the collaboration of Al Chung-liang Huang, *Tao: The Watercourse Way* (New York: Pantheon Books, 1975), 98.
11. Alan Watts, *Taoism: Way Beyond Seeking*, ed. Mark Watts (Boston: Charles E. Tuttle, 1998), 49.
12. Thomas Merton, *The Way of Chuang Tzu* (New York: New Directions, 1965), 132.
13. St. Teresa of Avila, *Life of Prayer*, ed. James M. Houston (Colorado Springs, CO: David C. Cook, 2005), 125.
14. Gerald G. May, *Simply Sane: The Spirituality of Mental Health* (New York: Crossroad Publishing, 1977), 15.
15. Goddard, *Laotzu's Tao and Wu Wei*, 48.
16. Watts, *Tao: The Watercourse Way*, 96n.
17. Shah-Kazemi, *Paths to Transcendence*, 207.
18. Ibid.
19. Ibid., 209.
20. Watts, *Buddhism: The Religion of No-Religion*, 70.

Chapter 15 ~ Insight

1. Jill Bolte Taylor, *My Stroke of Insight: A Brain Scientist's Personal Journey* (New York: Plume, 2009), 68.
2. Ibid., 69.
3. *Mysticism for Modern Times: Conversations with Willigis Jäger*, ed. Christoph Quarch (Liguori, MO: Liguori Publications, 2006), 8.
4. A. H. Almaas, *Diamond Heart, Book Four: Indestructible Innocence* (Boston: Shambhala, 2001), 294–95.
5. Joseph Goldstein, *The Experience of Insight: A Simple and Direct Guide to Buddhist Meditation* (Boston: Shambhala, 1987), 68.
6. Ken McLeod, *Wake Up to Your Life: Discovering the Buddhist Path of Attention* (San Francisco: HarperSanFrancisco, 2002), 354.
7. Merton, *The Inner Experience*, 81.

8. William James, *The Varieties of Religious Experience: A Study in Human Nature* (New York: Collier Books, 1961), 74.

9. Ibid., 75.

10. Mariana Caplan, *Halfway Up the Mountain: The Error of Premature Claims to Enlightenment* (Prescott, AZ: Hohm Press, 1999), 134.

11. Nisargadatta Maharaj, *I Am That: Talks with Sri Nisargadatta Maharaj*, ed. Sudhaker S. Dikshit and Maurice Frydman (Durham, NC: Acorn Press, 1999), 323.

12. Campbell, *The Hero with a Thousand Faces*, 82.

13. Helen Vendler, *Dickinson: Selected Poems and Commentaries* (Cambridge, MA: Harvard University Press, 2010), 431.

14. Quoted in Almaas, *Diamond Heart, Book Four: Indestructible Innocence*, 287.

15. Huston Smith, foreword to Schuon, *The Transcendent Unity of Religions*, xxxiii.

16. Campbell, *The Masks of God*, 263.

17. James, *The Varieties of Religious Experience*, 329.

Chapter 16 ∾ Awakening

1. Campbell, *The Hero with a Thousand Faces*, 39.

2. Karen Armstrong, *Buddha* (New York: Penguin Books, 2004), 90.

3. Robert Ullman and Judyth Reichenberg-Ullman, eds., *Moments of Enlightenment: Stories from Ancient and Modern Masters* (New York: MJF Books, 2001), 51.

4. Ibid., 59.

5. Ibid., 93.

6. Ibid., 73.

7. Ibid., 81.

8. Philip Novak, *The World's Wisdom: Sacred Texts of the World's Religions* (New York: HarperCollins, 1995), 355.

9. Harvey, *The Essential Mystics*, xi.

10. Ken Wilber, *One Taste: Daily Reflections on Integral Spirituality* (Boston: Shambhala. 2000), 27.

11. Stephen Mitchell, *The Enlightened Heart: An Anthology of Sacred Poetry* (New York: HarperPerennial, 1993), 87.

12. Quoted in Armstrong, *A History of God*, 253.

13. Shah-Kazemi, *Paths to Transcendence*, 194.

14. Barks, *The Essential Rumi*, 263.

15. Mitchell, *The Enlightened Mind*, 95.

16. Ibid., 36.

17. Lin, *Tao Te Ching*, 1.

18. Ramesh S. Balsekar, *Pointers from Nisargadatta Maharaj* (Durham, NC: Acorn Press, 1998), 92.
19. Mitchell, *The Enlightened Mind*, 96.
20. Meyer, *The Secret Teachings of Jesus*, p. 51, saying 112.
21. Mitchell, *The Enlightened Mind*, 65.
22. Thich Nhat Hanh, *Zen Keys: A Guide to Zen Practice* (New York: Doubleday, 1995), 77.
23. Huxley, *The Perennial Philosophy*, 21.
24. Barks, *The Essential Rumi*, 25.
25. John 14:6 (NIV).
26. Quoted in Armstrong, *A History of God*, 228.
27. Quoted in Thomas Merton, *Zen and the Birds of Appetite* (New York: New Directions, 1968), 114.
28. Deng Ming-Dao, *365 Tao: Daily Meditations* (San Francisco: HarperSanFrancisco, 1992), 301.
29. John 15:16 (NIV).
30. Nisargadatta Maharaj, *I Am That*, 527.
31. Jack Kornfield, *After the Ecstasy, the Laundry: How the Heart Grows Wise on the Spiritual Path* (New York: Bantam, 2000), 124.
32. Flickstein, *The Meditator's Atlas*, 255.

Chapter 17 ~ Selflessness

1. Campbell, *The Masks of God*, 21–24.
2. Ibid., 21.
3. Michael Lemonick, "Glimpses of the Mind," *Time*, July 17, 1995.
4. David J. Chalmers, "The Puzzle of Conscious Experience," *Scientific American* 273 (1995): 80–86.
5. Mitchell, *The Enlightened Mind*, 76.
6. Ibid., 122.
7. Ken Wilber, *The Simple Feeling of Being: Embracing Your True Nature* (Boston: Shambhala, 2004), 252.

Chapter 18 ~ Freedom

1. A. H. Almaas, *Diamond Heart, Book Two: The Freedom to Be* (Boston: Shambhala, 1989), 65.
2. Tolle, *The Power of Now*, 180.
3. Lin, *Tao Te Ching*, 3.
4. Salzberg, *Faith*, 96.
5. Mitchell, *The Enlightened Mind*, 13.
6. Kapleau, *The Three Pillars of Zen*, 10.
7. Amaro Bhikkhu, *Small Boat, Great Mountain*, 42.

8. Wilber, *The Simple Feeling of Being*, 8.
9. Deng Ming-Dao, *365 Tao*, 87.
10. Harvey, *The Essential Mystics*, 187.
11. Quoted in Ricard and Trinh Xuan Thuan, *The Quantum and the Lotus*, 76.
12. Flickstein, *The Meditator's Atlas*, 49.

Chapter 19 ∽ Homecoming

1. Quoted in Bruce Brander, *Love That Works: The Art and Science of Giving* (Peabody, MA: Templeton Foundation Press, 2004), 144.
2. Quoted in Catherine Ingram, *Passionate Presence: Experiencing the Seven Qualities of Awakened Awareness* (New York: Gotham Books, 1994), 82.
3. Mitchell, *The Enlightened Heart*, 103.
4. Mitchell, *The Enlightened Mind*, 51.
5. Pirkei Avot 6.2, in Harvey, *The Essential Mystics*, 100.
6. Ingram, *Passionate Presence*, 90.
7. Ricard and Trinh Xuan Thuan, *The Quantum and the Lotus*, 74.
8. Mitchell, *The Enlightened Mind*, 68.
9. Quoted in Frederic Brussat and Mary Ann Brussat, *Spiritual Literacy: Reading the Sacred in Everyday Life* (New York: Scribner, 1996), 121.
10. Mitchell, *The Enlightened Heart*, 35.
11. Harvey, *The Essential Mystics*, 207.
12. *Walt Whitman Reader: Selections from the Leaves of Grass*, 67.
13. *Kabir: Ecstatic Poems*, ed. Robert Bly (Boston: Beacon Press, 2004), 72.
14. Dowman, *The Flight of the Garuda*, 95.
15. Watts, *The Wisdom of Insecurity*, 145.
16. Barks, *The Essential Rumi*, 3.

Photo by Christopher Greer

John Greer has spent nearly twenty years inquiring deeply into the sacred texts and teachings of the world's traditions, spurred by his own spiritual search. He is a dedicated practitioner of meditation and has taught insight meditation for over a decade. John Greer holds a Ph.D. in education from Pennsylvania State University, and in three decades as a professor at the University of Memphis published numerous articles, coauthored several books on education and special education, and was a recipient of the university's highest award for distinguished teaching. He also served for two years in Nepal with the Peace Corps and has traveled extensively on six continents. He lives with his wife in Memphis. To learn more about John Greer and his work, visit www.SeeingKnowingBeing.com.